Arthur Carr

The Church and the Roman Empire

Arthur Carr

The Church and the Roman Empire

ISBN/EAN: 9783743308039

Manufactured in Europe, USA, Canada, Australia, Japa

Cover: Foto ©ninafisch / pixelio.de

Manufactured and distributed by brebook publishing software (www.brebook.com)

Arthur Carr

The Church and the Roman Empire

Epochs of Church History

EDITED BY THE

REV. MANDELL CREIGHTON, M.A.

THE CHURCH AND THE ROMAN EMPIRE

PRINTED BY
SPOTTISWOODE AND CO., NEW-STREET SQUARE
LONDON

THE CHURCH

AND

THE ROMAN EMPIRE

BY THE

REV. ARTHUR CARR, M.A.

LATE FELLOW OF ORIEL COLLEGE, OXFORD

LONDON

LONGMANS, GREEN, AND CO.

1887

All rights reserved

PREFACE.

This little volume does not profess to be a Church History of the momentous period with which it deals. Its scope is limited to a particular aspect of the Ecclesiastical movement in that period. The internal questions which agitated the Church, and the great Councils in which those disputes were arranged—in other words, the dogmatic and conciliar history of the Church—must be looked for elsewhere. Here it is intended to trace in outline the relations between Christianity and the Roman Empire, and the external growth of the Church, during the fourth and fifth centuries. It was an era of change and revolution more complete and far-reaching in consequences than any which had yet befallen the civilised world. The disruption of the Roman Empire, the invasion and settlements of the Teutonic races, the reception of the Church into the political system, and its growth into a force strong enough to remould the shattered world, form a subject of supreme interest and of great complexity.

It is clear, therefore, that in a work of this kind the leading events and personages alone can be touched upon. Its aim is to describe especially those acts which seem to have had a decisive and determining effect on the external growth of the Church. And if sometimes an undue proportion appear to be given to what are termed secular affairs, if sometimes a great statesman or a great general rather than a great bishop or theologian be the prominent figure in these pages, none the less will the subject still be ecclesiastical history. The advance of the Church in its external aspect is sometimes visibly and appropriately the work of a priest or statesman-bishop; another crisis requires the sword of a conqueror; sometimes even the tyranny of a barbarian leader remotely ends in good. The march of Constantine from Gaul to Rome, and the alliance of Theodoric and Aetius against the pagan Hun, were in a real sense ecclesiastical events; though in a different way, they bore upon the future of the Church as definitely as the decisions of the Œcumenical Councils.

The thoughts which give the impulse to acts are the key to history. And whether emperor or general or ecclesiastic seemed for the moment to have the leading influence in affairs, all the while Christianity was the spirit which breathed into every movement and in reality shaped results.

It is with results alone that we propose to deal. But even thus limited the subject is a vast one, far surpassing the possibility of adequate treatment in a work like this. But the object will be achieved if a wider interest be awakened in this period of Church History, and fresh attention be directed to these earlier attempts to work out problems in Church and State which are still unsolved.

The chief original authorities for this period are: Eusebius, 'Ecclesiastical History' and the 'Life of Constantine'; Lactantius, 'Deaths of the Persecutors'; the ecclesiastical histories of Socrates, Sozomen, Theodoret and Evagrius; the 'Misopogon' and Letters of the Emperor Julian; the histories of Zosimus, Ammianus Marcellinus, Procopius, and Priscus; the historical poems of Claudian; the works of St. Athanasius, St. Basil, St. Gregory Nazianzen, St. Chrysostom, St. Jerome, St. Augustine, St. Ambrose, and other Fathers of the fourth and fifth centuries.

Modern works which may be consulted to fill in the details of the sketch in this volume are: Gibbon,

'Decline and Fall of the Roman Empire'; De Broglie, 'L'Eglise et l'Empire Romain au IV⁵ Siècle'; Professor Bright's 'History of the Church, A.D. 313-451'; Milman, 'History of Christianity'; Gieseler, 'Ecclesiastical History'; Neander, 'General History of the Christian Religion and Church'; Mason's 'Diocletian'; and the different articles relating to this period in the 'Dictionary of Christian Biography,' edited by Dr. William Smith and Professor Wace.

ARTHUR CARR.

St. Sebastian's Vicarage, Wokingham:
March 24, 1887.

CONTENTS.

CHAPTER I.
INTRODUCTORY.

        PAGE

Importance of the term *Basileia* or Kingdom of God—It implies attributes of imperial power—Therefore rivalry with Rome—This sense of rivalry felt—The strength of the Church in this contest 1

CHAPTER II.
DIOCLETIAN. A.D. 286–305.

Death of the emperor Carus—Diocletian elected emperor—The imperial system of Diocletian—Consequences to the Church of this system—The Cæsar Galerius—The Cæsar Constantius—The division of empire—Diocletian's attitude to the Church—The numbers and resources of the Christian body—Persecution begins—The first edict—Mysterious fires in the palace—The persecution becomes more fierce—The second edict—The persecution not equally severe in different parts of the empire—The third edict—Diocletian leaves Rome in disgust—His abdication—The fourth edict 6

CHAPTER III.
FROM DIOCLETIAN TO CONSTANTINE.

Constantine escapes from Nicomedia—Elected emperor by the troops—Maxentius in Rome—A great conflict imminent—The end of Maximian—Death of Galerius—The meaning of the favourable decree of Galerius—The plan of Maximin—Death of Diocletian—Christianity misrepresented in schools 21

CHAPTER IV.
CONSTANTINE.

The great resolve of Constantine—The sign of the Cross—The march of Constantine—Constantine is victorious—The battle of Ponte Molle—Constantine professes Christianity in Rome—The edict of Milan—Defeat and death of Maximin—Church controversy in Africa—The fanaticism of the Donatists—Effect of Christianity on the laws—Slavery and Christianity—Paganism still a force in the empire—Struggle between Licinius and Constantine—Licinius defeated—The changes in the empire favourable to Christianity—The new Rome 27

CHAPTER V.
THE COUNCIL OF NICÆA—ATHANASIUS.

Arianism—The Council of Nicæa—Eusebius—Athanasius—Charges brought against Athanasius—Death of Arius—Death of Constantine—His influence on the Church . . . 40

CHAPTER VI.
THE SONS OF CONSTANTINE.

Accession of the three emperors—Athanasius returns to Alexandria—Again in exile—The growth of the Roman see—Influence of Athanasius in Rome—The Council of Sardica—Athanasius again returns to his see—Constantius sole emperor—Athanasius driven from Alexandria—George of Cappadocia—Council of Ariminum—The sequel of Athanasius' career. 47

CHAPTER VII.
THE EMPEROR JULIAN CALLED THE APOSTATE.

The interest of Julian's career—Gallus—Julian at Milan—He studies at Athens—Julian's education—The title of Apostate—Basil and Gregory fellow-students of Julian—Julian despatched to Gaul—St. Martin of Tours—The jealousy of Constantius—The march of Julian against Constantius—Constantius dies—Julian succeeds to the empire—The paganism of Julian—Julian's attempt to rebuild the temple at Jerusalem—Julian abstains from persecution—Persecution becomes inevitable—Christians debarred from reading the classics—Julian at Antioch—Julian's last campaign and death 56

CHAPTER VIII.
ST. BASIL AND ST. GREGORY.

Early life of Gregory and Basil—Student life at Athens—Basil adopts a monastic life—Gregory assists his father at Nazianzus—Basil Bishop of Cæsarea—The teaching of these two lives 71

CHAPTER IX.
JOVIAN—VALENTINIAN—VALENS.

Jovian elected emperor—The change from paganism—Jovian's Church policy—The death of Jovian—Choice of a new emperor—Valens—Valentinian's Church policy—Non-intervention impossible—An ecclesiastical dispute in Rome—Growth of the episcopal power in Rome—The Church a refuge from despotism 76

CHAPTER X.
VALENS—INVASION OF THE GOTHS.

Valens conquers Procopius—An Arian persecution—The Gothic invasion—Gothic version of the Scriptures—The Goths cross the Danube—The Goths occupy the imperial provinces—The battle of Hadrianople—Death of Valens . . 85

CHAPTER XI.
GRATIAN—ST. AMBROSE.

The childhood of Ambrose—Ambrose goes to Milan—Elected Bishop—St. Ambrose and Gratian—Gratian's policy in Church matters—Theodosius—St. Ambrose and Theodosius—The massacre at Thessalonica—Repentance of Theodosius—The empress Justina—St. Ambrose and Valentinian II.—Death of St. Ambrose—The work and policy of St. Ambrose—Heresy made a capital offence 92

CHAPTER XII.
THEODOSIUS. A.D. 379–395.

Theodosius avenges the death of Valentinian II.—The defeat of Eugenius—The death of Theodosius—The decline of the empire—Stilicho—The sieges of Rome by Alaric . . . 103

CHAPTER XIII.

THE FALL OF PAGANISM.

Tolerance of paganism in a Christian state—Tolerance enjoined by Constantine—The inutility of Christian persecution—The effects of Julian's policy—Important action of Gratian—The meeting of St. Ambrose and Symmachus—Theodosius brings the question of religion before the senate—Decisive measures of Theodosius—Pagan apologies—Pagan temples destroyed—Theophilus of Alexandria—The destruction of the Serapeum—Evils of prosperity—Hypatia—The weakness of Honorius—The year 365—Paganism still powerful in places—evidence of Salvianus 107

CHAPTER XIV.

ST. JEROME.   A.D. 346–420.

Theories of the Christian life—Monasticism in Egypt—Different phases of the monastic life—Early life of St. Jerome—St. Jerome at Bethlehem—The Vulgate—St. Jerome's literary labours 121

CHAPTER XV.

ST. AUGUSTINE.   A.D. 354–430.

St. Augustine's early life—St. Augustine at Milan—Meets St. Ambrose—Is made Bishop of Hippo—The influence of St. Augustine—The 'De Civitate Dei'—Death of St. Augustine 127

CHAPTER XVI.

ST. CHRYSOSTOM.   A.D. 347–407.

Early life of St. Chrysostom—His asceticism—Seditious outbreak at Antioch—St. Chrysostom calms the people—The emperor's sentence—Announcement of pardon—Chrysostom Bishop of Constantinople—Attacks abuses among the clergy—He raises enemies by his faithfulness—Antipathy of the empress—Chrysostom is driven into exile—Review of his life . . 131

CHAPTER XVII.

HONORIUS. A.D. 395–423—RUFINUS, STILICHO.

Accession of Honorius—Early life of Rufinus—His rise—The crimes of Rufinus—Rufinus foiled in his ambition—His fall and death—The early life of Stilicho—His rapid rise to power—Defeats Gildo—Assassination of Rufinus—Marriage of Stilicho's daughter 139

CHAPTER XVIII.

ALARIC AND THE GOTHS.

Invasion of Greece by Alaric—Stilicho repels the invasion—Alaric's first invasion of Italy—General confidence in Stilicho—His measures—Defeat of Alaric—The victory too late to save Rome from ruin—The real force in the world—Gladiatorial shows stopped by Christianity—The transference of the capital—Ravenna—The artistic and historical interest of Ravenna—The invasion of Radagaisus—St. Augustine's view of the defeat of Radagaisus—Alaric allies himself with the Western empire—Stilicho's policy unpopular—Intrigues against Stilicho—His death—Stilicho's wisdom proved by events—Olympius—Disqualification of pagans—First siege of Rome by Alaric—Generidus—Second siege of Rome—Attalus proclaimed emperor—Capture of Rome by the Goths—Results for Christianity—Death and burial of Alaric 146

CHAPTER XIX.

THE WEST UNDER HONORIUS.

The hold on the West by the two empires—The usurper Constantine—He is slain—The end of Ataulf—Galla Placidia—Britain—The effects of the Saxon invasion . . . 164

CHAPTER XX.

THE EAST.

Characteristics of Church and State in East and West—Eutropius—Gainas and the Goths 170

CHAPTER XXI.

THEODOSIUS II. AND PULCHERIA.

Pulcheria virtually regent—The education of Arcadius—The empress Eudocia—Persecution of Christians in Persia—Christianity a *casus belli*—Christian charity—The character of Theodosius II.—Intimate union of Church and State . 173

CHAPTER XXII.

THE WEST FROM THE DEATH OF HONORIUS.

Galla Placidia—The rebellion of John—Valentinian III.—Boniface and Aetius—The Vandals under Genseric invade Africa—The capture of Carthage 180

CHAPTER XXIII.

THE HUNS AND ATTILA.

The barbarians gradually civilised—The Huns—Attila—The invasion begins—Theodoric—Attila's pretexts for war—Attila marches across the Rhine—The battle of Chalons—Attila invades the north of Italy 185

CHAPTER XXIV.

POPE LEO I. AND THE CHURCH OF ROME.

Prestige of the Roman see—This prestige due to growth of jurisdiction—The increase in wealth—Growth of episcopal power—Checks on the power of the Church—Rome becomes the arbiter of disputes—The apostolical origin of the see—The authority of Leo—His rise to the Papacy—His claims for the see of Rome—The idea of the unity of Christendom—Italy not wholly subservient to Rome—Disputes with Leo—Spain—Africa—Mistakes of the Roman see—The influence of Leo in the East—Leo's attitude towards heresy—Leo and the barbarian invasion—Leo intercedes for Rome with Genseric—Leo the greatest statesman as well as the greatest Churchman of his day 193

INDEX 207

MAP

THE ROMAN EMPIRE, A.D. 292–305 . . . . *To face Title*

PRINCIPAL EVENTS OF THIS EPOCH.

A.D.
- 284 Diocletian emperor
- 286 Maximian chosen as his colleague
- 292 Constantius and Galerius, *Cæsars*
- 303 Persecution of Christians
- 305 Diocletian and Maximian abdicate
  Constantius and Galerius *Augusti*
  Severus and Maximin *Cæsars*
- 306 Maxentius proclaimed emperor by the Prætorian guard
  Constantine begins to reign
- 307 Severus slain
  Licinius declared *Augustus*
- 311 Death of Galerius
- 312 Maxentius defeated and slain at Ponte Molle
- 313 Edict of Milan
  Maximin defeated by Licinius
- 314 Battle of Hadrianople
- 323 Licinius defeated
- 324 Death of Licinius
- 325 Council of Nicæa
- 331 Birth of Julian
- 335 First exile of St. Athanasius

A.D.
- 336 Death of Arius
- 337 Death of Constantine
  The three sons succeed as *Augusti* — Constantine II., Constantius, and Constans
- 340 Constantine II. defeated and slain
- 341 Second exile of St. Athanasius
- 346 Birth of St. Jerome
- 350 Death of Constans
  Usurpation of Magnentius
- 351 Battle of Mursa — Magnentius defeated
- 354 Birth of St. Augustine
- 356 Third exile of St. Athanasius
- 359 Council of Ariminum
- 360 Julian proclaimed *Augustus* by his army at Lutetia (Paris)
- 361 Death of Constantius
  Julian emperor
- 362 Julian at Antioch
  Fourth exile of St. Athanasius
- 363 Julian's disastrous campaign and death
  Jovian succeeds

A.D.	
364	Death of Jovian
	Valentinian I. Emperor of the West
	Valens of the East
370	St. Basil Bishop of Cæsarea
373	Death of St. Athanasius
374	St. Ambrose Bishop of Milan
375	Valentinian I. dies
	Valentinian II. and Gratian succeed
378	Battle of Hadrianople
	Death of Valens
379	Theodosius proclaimed *Augustus* by Gratian
	Death of St. Basil
381	Council of Constantinople
383	Gratian murdered
386	Conversion of St. Augustine
390	Penance of Theodosius
392	Murder of Valentinian II.
394	Defeat of Eugenius and Arbogastes
395	St. Augustine Bishop of Hippo
	Death of Theodosius I.
	Arcadius Emperor of the East
	Honorius of the West
	Alaric invades Greece
397	Death of St. Ambrose
398	St. Chrysostom Bishop of Constantinople

A.D.	
403	Battle of Pollentia—Retreat of Alaric
405	Radagaisus defeated by Stilicho
407	Death of St. Chrysostom
408	Theodosius II. succeeds Arcadius in the East
	Stilicho slain at Ravenna
410	Capture of Rome by Alaric
420	Death of St. Jerome
	Persecution of Christians in Persia
424	Valentinian III. succeeds Honorius
429	Invasion of Africa by the Vandals under Genseric
430	Siege of Hippo—Death of St. Augustine
431	Council of Ephesus
440	Leo the Great, Bishop of Rome
441	The Huns under Attila cross the Danube
450	Marcian succeeds Theodosius II., whose sister Pulcheria he marries
451	Council of Chalcedon
	Battle of Chalons—Attila defeated by Aetius and Theodoric
452	Attila ravages the north of Italy
453	Death of Attila and of Pulcheria
461	Death of Pope Leo the Great

THE CHURCH
AND
THE ROMAN EMPIRE.

CHAPTER I.

INTRODUCTORY.

THE first leading idea implanted by Christ in the minds of His followers was the idea of a kingdom. 'Seek ye first His Kingdom [βασιλεία] and His righteousness; and all these things shall be added unto you'[1] were words which bore fruit. It was a command with a promise, and the promise was fulfilled in time. The Church did seek the Kingdom of God and His righteousness. And for three centuries those things which the Gentiles sought after seemed to be denied to her. The Gentiles still sought after the power and riches of the world, and the Church grew on without them in her quest for righteousness, in organised strength, in patience, love, faith, clearness of view, wisdom of judgment and interpretation. At length the centuries of oppression and persecution ended, and the Church

[1] St. Matt. vi. 33.

became allied with kings. Riches poured in upon her: political power came in too abundant measure. She had sought first the Kingdom of God and all things were added to her. For if by ruling the world is meant to dictate the principles of government, to control legislation, to repeal or to change one class of laws, to pass and carry into effect another, to regulate the pursuits and amusements of the people, to define the limits of right and wrong, then Christianity ruled the world, and the Empire of Christ—the Kingdom of Heaven—was constituted. The Twelve sat on thrones, ruling and judging the earth. Their words and thoughts and rules have inspired the code of modern civilisation.

These results are historical facts. It may be added that the direction given to the advance of Christianity *Importance of this term basileia* was clearly ruled by the term which describes it—the *basileia*, the Kingdom, *the imperium*, of God. For although the spiritual aspect of the Kingdom was carefully defined and pressed, yet this term adopted by the Master and always prominent in the teaching of His Apostles could not be used without a sense of comparison with the Roman Empire. In inscriptions and in all contemporary historians such as Zosimus, Socrates, or Sozomen, the Roman emperor was known as *basileus* (βασιλεύς) and the Greek for the empire was *basileia* (βασιλεία).[1] *It implies some attributes of imperial power* In some sense the Kingdom of which Christ spoke would be mightier and more enduring than the empire of the Cæsars. And in some sense

---

[1] In 1 Tim. ii. 2, and 1 Peter ii. 17, the Apostles are of course speaking of Claudius or of Nero.

that cruel and hated despotism was a symbol and image of the Kingdom of God. History disproved the earthly conception of the *basileia* at first present to the Apostles' minds. But certain elements of empire— and that meant of the Roman Empire—organised rule, unity of headship, universality of extension, resistless success, power of growth, discipline and law, were characteristic of the divinely organised society which Jesus Christ founded.

Another result of this word *basileia* or *imperium* was to suggest a rival and therefore a hostile power. <small>Therefore rivalry with Rome</small> For the modern notion of great and powerful kingdoms existing side by side at peace, and respecting one another, was foreign to the political sentiment of the ancient world.

This thought is a key to many incidents in the course of Church history. It explains the attitude of the civil power towards the Church—there was a point where persecution became a necessity—and it explains the magnificent courage of the Christian martyrs, and the far-reaching hopes and exalted confidence of great Churchmen in every age.

The very words of the Lord's Prayer carried in them the seeds of a revolution. No Roman magistrate could hear with perfect complacency that the words ἐλθάτω ἡ βασιλεία σου (Thy Kingdom come) were uttered in a most sacred, and to some extent a secret, form of prayer every day by hundreds of thousands who formed part of what seemed to him to be an organised and dangerous conspiracy.

The instinctive sense of this danger soon came to the front. It had already appeared in the trial of

Christ before Pilate: 'If thou let this man go thou art not Cæsar's friend;' and it appears in the trial of St. Paul before the politarchs of Thessalonica.[1] It is, however, a remarkable point in Church history that the Christians never did organise themselves against the empire, as the Jews, for instance, organised themselves, with far less chance of success, against the earlier emperors. But it is no wonder that the danger of such disaffection was felt. Expressions which would sound like open sedition were frequently on the lips of Christians. In the Diocletian persecution Alphæus and Zacchæus, two clergymen, suffered death for declaring that they acknowledged but one God, and Jesus as the anointed emperor, χριστὸν βασιλέα Ἰησοῦν. And when Procopius, the first martyr whose death Eusebius saw with his own eyes, was told to sacrifice to the gods, he answered there was only one God to whom it was right to offer sacrifices in the way he wished, and then being urged at least to pour a health to the four emperors, he replied with Homer's well-known verses:

marginal note: The sense of a rival power felt

Οὐκ ἀγαθὸν πολυκοιρανίη, εἷς κοίρανος ἔστω,
Εἷς βασιλεύς

('it is not good to have lords many, let there be one lord, one king' [or emperor]). To the presiding magistrate the meaning would be treason, an utterance against Diocletian's system, to say nothing of the suggestion of another emperor. Procopius was ordered to instant execution.[2] In this way Cæsarism and Christianity clashed. In this way the idea of the

---

[1] Acts xvii 7.   [2] Mason's *Diocletian*, p. 187.

βασιλεία worked itself out to the supremacy of the Church in the world. All that vast development which we lightly trace in these pages sprang from the thoughts which Jesus Christ infused into this conception of a *basileia*. The possession of this imperial idea has made Church history what it was. The Church was to absorb all the forces of the world. Its history was to be the history of a conquest. All the proud expressions in which the Augustan poets describe the greatness of Rome and the empire were capable of being transferred in a figure to the Church of Christ. 'Tu regere imperio populos, Romane, memento,' might serve as a watchword for Christian missions.

In this contest of rival powers, the two βασιλείαι or *imperia* of Rome and the Church, which began their great careers almost simultaneously, the Church won the victory. In a true sense 'the kingdoms of the world became the Kingdom of Christ.' But, in truth, against all seeming the advantages all along had been on the side of the Church. How fully this was realised in Christian thought we may learn from the pictures and parables of the Apocalypse, which are the real sequel to the Acts of the Apostles.

The strength of the Church in this contest

Glance at the history of the Roman Empire. At any moment the career of an emperor might be closed by assassination. This became so serious an evil, and the succession so swift and changeable, that the system of Diocletian, by which the government was shared by four princes, associated in rule and by family ties, became a necessity. But this change, though a gain in one direction, involved the loss of unity, and introduced the weakness of rivalry. Again, the empire was exposed to dissolution by the plague-spots of luxury and moral corruption, and by the attacks of the vigorous hordes of barbarians pressing on the Danube and the Rhine.

But the Kingdom of Christ could suffer from none of these things. No blow could strike it down. Christ the King could not be slain, or deposed, or influenced. There could be no partition of the $\beta\alpha\sigma\iota\lambda\epsilon\iota\alpha$, no loss of unity. It did not rest on the passions or fears of men, or on corrupting influences, but on an appeal to the spirit of liberty, and on all that is finest and noblest in the nature of man. It was invincible, because there was not only no fear of death, but its subjects were, as their persecutors said, 'only too ready to die.' A history with such principles underlying it could not fail to be glorious. And no epoch in that history has been more fruitful in great men and great events than the fourth and fifth centuries.

CHAPTER II.

DIOCLETIAN. A.D. 284–305.

IN the year 283 the hopes of the Roman world were raised to the highest pitch by the successes of the emperor Carus in the East. It seemed that at length the most formidable danger which had menaced the empire from Augustus to Aurelian was to disappear before the advance of an emperor whose simplicity of life and severity of discipline recalled the

Death of the emperor Carus

old and virtuous days of the Republic. His victorious armies had crossed the Euphrates and the Tigris, and were encamped a few miles from the latter river, when a terrific storm broke over the plain. After one of the loudest peals of thunder, a cry arose that the emperor was dead, and his tent was observed to be in flames. His death was variously ascribed to the stroke of lightning, to the natural course of a malady from which he suffered, or to assassination. In any case the visions of conquest vanished, and the 'patient' East once more witnessed the retreat of a Roman army.

The death of Numerian, the young and virtuous son of Carus, soon followed. Aper, the Prefect of the Prætorian guard, aspiring to the empire, for some time concealed the death, of which he was probably the cause. When this intrigue was discovered, Aper was loaded with chains and dragged before a council of officers.

In the hasty trial which followed, Diocletian, commander of the late emperor's bodyguard, was at once *Diocletian elected emperor* the chief witness, the judge, and the executioner. He had probably also been the accomplice of Aper. At any rate, the precipitate action by which he plunged his dagger into the prisoner's heart before he had time to reply, has left a dark and merited suspicion in history.

Such was the sinister beginning of a reign which makes an epoch in the constitutional annals of Rome, and is ever memorable in the history of the Christian Church.

Diocles (such was the earlier form of the name) was of servile origin. His father, however, obtained his freedom, and exercised the office of a scribe—a calling which implies some amount of culture, and certainly left its mark on Diocletian. The campaigns of Aurelian—restorer of the Roman Empire [1]—and those of Probus and of Carus had produced and trained in a severe school of discipline a number of able and illustrious officers. Among these Diocletian had been highly distinguished, and on the death of Numerian was pronounced to be the most worthy to assume the purple. There was, indeed, one rival for the possession of empire—the despicable Carinus, son of the late emperor. But the decisive battle of Margus, in which Carinus was slain, left Diocletian sole master of the Roman world. From that moment the qualities which distinguished Diocletian were rather those of the great statesman than of the brilliant soldier.

He conceived a system of government which entitled him to be called the second founder of the empire, and which certainly had momentous consequences for the future of the world's history.

The imperial system of Diocletian

A monarchy holding sway over a vast and varied empire like that of Rome was a terribly insecure and unsettling form of government. It placed the peace of the world and the tenure of power at the mercy of the assassin's knife, or the caprice of a military conspiracy, at any moment in any distant corner of the earth. As a matter of fact the despotism had been transferred from the emperor to the soldiers of the Prætorian guard.

Diocletian's plan was to create four rulers in place of one. Two, holding a higher rank with the supreme title of Augustus, were to govern the prefectures of

---

[1] Vopiscus, *Div. Aurel.* § 1.

Italy and the East; two others of lower but still imperial rank, bearing the name of Cæsar, were to hold their respective courts, and to keep the enemies of Rome at bay on the banks of the Rhine and the Danube. The members of this quadruple autocracy were to be so closely associated by the bonds of common interest and of family alliance as to combine the strength and solidity of a monarchy with the advantage of an extended and ubiquitous defence.

Combined with this system, and an integral part of it, was the deliberate and final abandonment of Rome as the capital of the world. Hereafter, as there were to be four rulers, there were to be four capitals of the empire. Hence the names of Nicomedia, of Milan, of Sirmium, and of Augusta Trevirorum—the modern Trier or Trèves—rise into importance.

It was a masterly scheme and had many consequences. It made assassination useless, it crushed the influence of the Prætorian guard, and reduced the Roman senate to the status of a municipal council. Its consequences to the Church, which was still latent as a political force, will be developed as this history proceeds. Two results were obvious, and, when persecution arose, immediate. Differences of rule must produce differences of administration, however carefully a compact is sealed. Consequently, if persecution raged in one quarter, toleration if not immunity prevailed in another. Again, division of power however carefully guarded, and the creation of separate courts and armies, could only result in rivalries and a contest for supremacy. In such a contest Christianity as a political force must sooner or later be

Consequences to the Church of this system

recognised, used and suitably rewarded. In carrying his plan into effect, Diocletian chose as his immediate colleague and brother Augustus Maximian, a rude uncultivated soldier, son of a Dalmatian peasant, a compatriot therefore of Diocletian, and one who had like him risen to distinction in the wars of Aurelian and Probus. This was in the year 286. It was not till the year 292 that Diocletian's system was completed by the choice of the two Cæsars—Galerius and Constantius—both names of grave import to the Christian Church.

Galerius like the two Augusti had risen entirely by his military talents. These he possessed in an eminent degree. He deserves the name of a great general. In other respects the historian has no good thing to tell of Galerius. 'In this evil beast,' says Lactantius, 'there dwelt a native barbarity and a savageness foreign to Roman blood.' Even if we do not accept to the full the hideous and repulsive portrait which the Christian historian has drawn of the persecutor of the Church, it is difficult to credit Galerius with the redeeming features possessed by such pagans as the humane and statesmanlike Diocletian.

The Cæsar Galerius

Constantius, surnamed Chlorus or *pale*, claims a nobler birth and was certainly endowed with a finer culture and more generous qualities than his compeers. By his mother he was connected with the emperor Claudius Gothicus, and by his father with a noble house in Mœsia.

The Cæsar Constantius

In accordance with that part of Diocletian's plan which was to connect the Augusti and the Cæsars in marriage, Galerius married Valeria, daughter of Diocletian, and Constantius was compelled to divorce his first wife Helena the mother of Constantine, and to become the son-in-law of Maximian by marriage with his stepdaughter Theodora.

In the distribution of power, Diocletian, fixing on Nicomedia in Bithynia as the seat of empire, retained under his immediate authority Thrace, Egypt and Asia. Maximian ruled from Milan, Italy and Africa. Galerius, in his arduous post on the Danube, was answerable for Illyricum and the adjoining provinces. To Constantius were assigned the care and defence of Gaul, Spain and Britain.

The division of empire

The new experiment in governing the world at first succeeded admirably. Peace, indeed, there was not in any of the imperial provinces; but in each the empire prevailed. While Constantius and Galerius were fighting on the line of the Danube and the Rhine, Maximian and Diocletian crushed a dangerous rising which extended from Mauritania to Egypt. Persia, too, after a momentary triumph suffered a decisive defeat by the Roman forces under the command of Galerius.

These great successes were celebrated by what had now become an unusual and remarkable event—a Roman triumph. For the first time in his reign, which was now drawing to its close, Diocletian determined to visit the ancient capital of his empire, and in company with Maximian to celebrate a triumph destined to be the last, though certainly not the least magnificent or the least sumptuous with the spoils of conquered nations, that had proudly moved along the Sacred Way.[1]

---

[1] According to Gibbon, ch. xiii., this triumph was coincident with the celebration of the Vicennalia at Rome (p. 18), but the latest authorities distinguish the two events.

The beginning of the end had come. To Diocletian's friends this great and politic career was almost concluded. The interest of it had gone. But to the Christian historian the enduring interest is centred in its concluding years. Here begins its direct and dire relation to Christianity. What up to this time had been Diocletian's attitude to the Christian Church? The only possible answer is that it had been most favourable. Diocletian had surrounded himself with Christians. The most influential, the most confidential offices in his household, those which were most nearly concerned with his own person, were filled by Christians. His wife and daughter had roused the suspicion of the pagan society by their absence from sacrifices to the gods, and by their leaning to Christianity. There were some who asserted that Diocletian himself was almost a Christian. It is certain that he admired Christianity, and it is probable that as a statesman he saw the folly and the danger of stirring the hostility of an organisation, which had spread quickly and mysteriously, but firmly and increasingly, throughout the Empire.

Diocletian's attitude to the Church

It is difficult to gather statistics now, but various indications had shown that the Christian body was numerous. There was a large contingent in the army. Another proof of the numbers, the wealth, and the energy of this strange people, lay in the frequency and growing magnificence of Christian churches, which now appeared in all large centres of population. At Nicomedia the Christian Church dominated the whole city. Persecution of Christians, indeed, had never quite ceased; but it was

The numbers and resources of the Christian body

not officially authorised, and each particular instance, if investigated, would show that there were secondary causes at work, such for instance as military insubordination.

Now there were signs of a change. In the autumn of the year 302, Galerius, 'the evil beast,' as Lactantius calls him, came to Nicomedia to confer with Diocletian. No third person was present at these interviews. But events soon disclosed the nature and meaning of them.

Persecution begins

Symptoms of reviving hostility against Christianity had shown themselves in various quarters. The sense of danger arising from an organised secret confederacy within the empire grew as the evidence of its strength became more manifest. On one occasion Diocletian himself had given the signal for persecution. He had asked the advice of his soothsayers, who examined the entrails of victims in the emperor's presence. When no signs or tokens appeared which should give indications of the future, the trembling soothsayers repeated the sacrifices, but still no response came. 'At length Tages, the chief of the soothsayers, either from guess or his own observation, said: "There are profane persons here who obstruct the rites." Then Diocletian in furious passion ordered not only all who were assisting at the holy ceremonies, but also all who resided within the palace, to sacrifice, and in case of their refusal to be scourged. And further, by letters to the commanding officers, he enjoined that all soldiers should be forced to the like impiety under pain of being dismissed the service. Thus far his rage proceeded, but at that season he did nothing more against the law and religion of

God.'[1] Such a thunderbolt might have fallen harmless. But the fierce and impolitic nature of Galerius had also been stirred to passionate hatred against the Christians. His mother, a devoted worshipper of the gods, invited to her frequent sacrificial feasts the officers of the army and her own household. But when the Christians among them refused to partake of those meats offered to idols, she was deeply incensed, and stimulated her son in his designs against the Church. Diocletian was too great a statesman to approve of a general persecution of Christians. He had recognised the strength and powerful organisation of the Church, and saw the desirability of winning her as an ally. He knew that Christians, so far from fearing death, were only too eager to die. Nevertheless, he was overcome by the violence of Galerius. Diocletian agreed to two steps which showed a faltering resolution. He convened a council, and he consulted the oracle of Apollo at Branchidæ near Miletus. It was easy to forecast the result; council and oracle joined in persuading the evil course, and Diocletian consented to persecute. But he made one reservation; he insisted that there should be no bloodshed.

Diocletian yields to Galerius and consents to persecution

The festival of the god Terminus, the god of limits and boundaries, was fixed upon for the beginning of the persecution, as if that day was to mark the limit of the Christian religion and influence. In the dim light of a winter's morning—it was on February 23, A.D. 303—the imperial officers forced open the doors

---

[1] Lactantius, *Deaths of the Persecutors*, ch. x.

of the church in Nicomedia, searched, it is said, for an image of the deity—so great was still the ignorance of Christian ritual—then proceeded to burn the sacred books and to pillage the furniture of the Church. The building itself was levelled to the ground by the axes and iron implements of the Prætorian guard.

Next day the imperial edict was published—1. All churches were to be demolished. 2. All sacred books committed to the flames. 3. All who per-
<small>The First Edict</small> sisted in Christianity to be deprived of any office or dignity they might possess; if free, to lose their freedom.

The third clause was by far the most serious in its effects. It was a sentence of outlawry against all free men who professed Christianity; it subjected Roman citizens to torture, and prevented all redress of grievances or possibility of pleading in the courts of law. It was a deliberate return to the persecuting *régime* of Valerian. The first act on the side of the Christians showed the spirit with which the persecutors had to deal. A certain man, whom Eusebius describes as of no mean origin and esteemed for his temporal dignities, tore down the decree and cut it in pieces 'improperly, indeed, but with high spirit,' says Lactantius with true sobriety of judgment. This man suffered a cruel death of torture and slow burning, not, strictly speaking, because of his Christianity, but, in form of law, for contempt of the emperor's authority.

But it was precisely in this way that Diocletian's humane reservation against bloodshed was certain to become a dead letter. It was not difficult for pagan judges to put a fatal construction on the acts of outlawed Christians. It was impossible for them not to punish obstinacy or acts of open treason.

Diocletian was now compelled to plunge more deeply into persecution. A fire broke out in the palace at Nicomedia, which is ascribed not without good reason to the crafty policy of Galerius. Diocletian instantly commanded his household slaves to be put to the torture to force some confession of guilt. No discovery was made; and it was significant that the servants of Galerius were not put to the question. Shortly afterwards for a second time the palace was set on fire. Galerius did not cease to ply the aged Augustus with suspicions, and before long hurried out of the city to escape, he said, being burnt alive.

<small>Mysterious fires in the palace</small>

The poison of suspicion did its work. Diocletian now allowed the persecution to rage without let or hindrance. His own daughter Valeria and his wife Prisca were compelled to sacrifice. He had the pain of handing over to torture and death the officers of his household, whom he had loved and trusted as his own children. The annals of the historians are filled with horrors only relieved and enlightened by the testimony of patience, devotion, and courage which the persecution of Christians has elicited in every age. In the secure times, which followed the era of persecution, the maimed confessors, who triumphed over Diocletian's torturers, had tales of wonderful endurance to tell to the Christian annalists. 'Having been nine times exposed to racks and diversified torments,' says Lactantius, writing to Donatus, 'nine times, by a glorious profession of your faith, you

<small>The persecution becomes more fierce</small>

foiled the adversary; in nine combats you subdued the devil and his chosen soldiers . . . after this sort to lord it over the lords of the earth is triumph indeed!'

A second persecuting edict was directed against the clergy. It was ruled that the clergy everywhere from the Bishops to the humblest ministers of the Church should be arrested and cast into prison without the option of sacrifice.

The Second Edict

The shafts of the persecutor had been discharged with cruel skill. They were aimed not so much to slay the Christian as to ruin and break up the Church. How could this hated confederacy continue to exist without temples for worship, without the right of assembly, without bishop or priest to rule the Church and officiate at her altars? Rigorously, remorselessly, and consistently carried out, the decrees were calculated to exterminate Christianity. It has been said that it is impossible to bring an indictment against a whole people, and the Christian community had become a people whom it was impossible to slay by legislation. The new constitution, too, prevented the systematic and even enforcement of the edicts without which they could not be effectual.

The records of Christian suffering have not been preserved with sufficient accuracy of time and place to draw a certain inference; but it is clear the persecution was keen and cruel in the countries which fell under Diocletian's special government. Galerius might safely be trusted with the execution of the edicts in his division of the world. We find the zeal of the enemies of the faith quickened, and fires of martyrdom blazing more fiercely in the

The persecution not equally severe in different parts of the empire

places visited by the Cæsar in his progresses. Maximian, too, was well pleased to indulge his coarse and cruel nature by carrying out the edicts which were now construed to authorise, without any limitation whatever, the infliction of death in forms of the most exquisite and protracted agony. But one imperial province enjoyed a comparative immunity. 'All the world was afflicted,' says Lactantius; 'and with the exception of the Gallic provinces alone, from east to west three rancorous wild beasts continued to rage.'

The decrees could not, indeed, become completely a dead letter even with Constantius. One famous instance—the story of a martyrdom dear to the English Church—the passion of St. Alban, is enough to prove that the edicts were published in the provinces ruled by Constantius. But, allowing for some rhetorical license in the reign of Constantine, we may believe that the historian's words are substantially true: 'Constantius permitted the demolition of churches—mere walls, and capable of being built up again—but he preserved entire that true temple of God which is the human body.'

From the November of the year 303, in which the edicts were issued, dated the commencement of the twentieth year of Diocletian's reign. He arranged to celebrate the occasion, technically called the *Vicennalia*, in Rome.

At such a time it was usual to grant a general amnesty. It was an act of clemency which largely affected the imprisoned Christians. But a note added to the edicts made release conditional on doing sacrifice to the gods. The Christian

<small>The Third Edict</small>

historian frankly admits that many even thus availed themselves of the amnesty. Others, and the acts of some of these are recorded, endured torture and a lengthened imprisonment rather than yield.

Diocletian had intended after the ceremony of the *Vicennalia* to remain in Rome until the Calends of January, when he was to be invested with the consulship. But Rome became distasteful to him. Vexed, it is said, with the freedom of the imperial city, he burst impatiently away from it. The Roman emperor had in fact with the dress and adornments and the titles assumed also the proud exclusiveness of an Oriental monarch. This is, indeed, to be ascribed to the policy rather than to the pride or ostentation of the Dalmatian freedman's son. Still, custom infects the nature of a man, and the spirit of freedom in speech and act which still breathed in the streets of the city of the Gracchi was displeasing to the monarch of Nicomedia. Diocletian entered on his consulship at Ravenna. The journey thither having been made through intense cold and incessant rain, he contracted a slight but lingering disease, which obliged him to be carried in a litter. He left Ravenna in the summer, and travelled first to the Danube and thence to Nicomedia. His malady now assumed a dangerous form—a report of his death, and even of his burial, was spread through the palace. He recovered, however, sufficiently to show himself in public, but probably never wholly regained his mental vigour and power of judgment.

<small>Diocletian leaves Rome in disgust</small>

Shortly afterwards Diocletian abdicated the government—a step long contemplated, indeed, but hastened in the end by the vehement pressure of Galerius. His colleague Maximian was compelled to follow his example. Galerius and Constantius now became the Augusti. The title of Cæsar was bestowed upon Severus, a man of the lowest reputation, and Daia, afterwards named Maximin, whose only claim was relationship to Galerius.

<small>Diocletian's abdication</small>

With this change a fresh and still more cruel era of persecution set in. While Diocletian was still battling with disease and taking no part in public affairs, an edict, harsher and more sweeping than any of the former, was issued. It enacted that wherever Christians should be found still adhering to their superstition, they should be compelled to sacrifice or die. Whole communities in towns and cities were literally called over individually by name and offered the alternative. It is clear, indeed, that such a measure could not be executed to the full extent of its intended malignity; but it left Christian people at the mercy of savage magistrates, and the annals of martyrdom are filled with accounts of wide-spread and cruel suffering. But systematic persecution like this exhibited the numbers of the Christian body; and the inflexible courage of Christian men and women made an impression which must have added enormously to their influence and consideration in the State. Soon it will be seen that this influence was taken openly into account in the decisions of history.

<small>The Fourth Edict</small>

CHAPTER III.

FROM DIOCLETIAN TO CONSTANTINE.

IN the turbulent events of the next few years, when persecution was at its height, and the immense resources of the empire were directed against the Church, a force was gathering in the Western provinces which was destined to shatter the opposing power, and to place the Christian Church in a commanding position by the side of the imperial throne.

Constantine, the son of Constantius Chlorus and Helena, on whose action great events depended, was <small>Constantine escapes from Nicomedia</small> residing at the court of Nicomedia when Diocletian resigned. When he was passed over in the choice of the Cæsars, his position became critical. He obtained permission from Galerius to rejoin his father in Gaul. Fearing treachery or a withdrawal of leave, Constantine started on his journey on the evening before the day fixed for his departure. He took the precaution of maiming or carrying off the horses at the various stages of the road, to prevent all possibility of pursuit, and reached in safety the camp of Constantius at Boulogne, in time to share the last expedition of his father against the Picts. On the death of Constantius, <small>Elected emperor by the troops</small> which occurred shortly afterwards, Constantine was saluted emperor by the troops. This event, so critical and momentous in the history of the Church, as to form a very striking point in the new phase into which Christianity was entering, took place at York. It was the first act which distinguishes the city of Paulinus and Alcuin in ecclesiastical history. Galerius was induced to recognise the accomplished fact, and to forward to Constantine the imperial purple with the title of Cæsar, the higher dignity of Augustus being withheld.

Almost at the same moment Galerius was foiled in another quarter. Again, though in a different sense, the foe was of his own household. Discontent had arisen in Rome, partly owing to the loss of its imperial position, partly to the heavy taxation which had been imposed upon it, partly because Galerius had reduced the numbers of the Prætorian guards. The citizens only required some one to give expression to their grievance, and to restore their lost privileges.

Maxentius, son of the ex-emperor Maximian and son-in-law of Galerius, accepted the perilous task. His first step was to recall his father Maximian to his ancient dignity. The name and prestige of their old general drew to his standard the troops of Severus, who was forced to die by his own hand at Ravenna. And when Galerius marched into Italy to avenge the insult to his power, he, too, found resistance everywhere, and was glad to escape the fate of Severus, and to secure his retreat to Bithynia.

<small>Maxentius in Rome</small>

A contest for power between Maximian and his son followed. Maxentius triumphed, and his father fled to the court of Galerius at Nicomedia. In this way the stage was cleared for the great conflict. Maxentius for the moment was master in Italy, Constantine supreme in the West, watching events calmly. Maximin (Daia) on the Danube, and the beaten and baffled Galerius in the East.

<small>A great conflict imminent</small>

A swift and tragic end now befell Maximian. His thirst for power found little satisfaction at Nicomedia. He was present, together with Diocletian, at Carnuntum, a place on the Danube, where Galerius created Licinius emperor in place of Severus. Hence he carried his insatiable ambition to the West, and there plotted against his son-in-law Constantine. Fausta proved to be truer wife than daughter, disclosed her father's treachery, and delivered him to the death which his crimes had deserved.

The end of Maximian

The life of Galerius also was drawing to a close. The Church historians are careful to note the cruel and prolonged tortures, which seemed to be a retribution for the widespread misery and pain which he had brought upon the world. But before he died, some feeling of remorse struck him, and he issued an edict, carefully guarded indeed, but still favourable to Christianity. 'It had ever been his aim,' he says, 'to maintain the ancient discipline of the Romans; he had urged the misguided Christians to return to their old allegiance. Some, indeed, had yielded to the terrors of the earlier edicts, and now paid adoration to the gods of Rome, but most were obstinate (*cum plurimi in proposito perseverarent*); still, as an act of clemency, he would allow them to leave their prisons, and rebuild their churches, and meet for worship, provided' (and this surely is a clause to leave Galerius free in case of recovery) 'they do nothing against good discipline.' He ends by demanding the prayers of Christians for his restoration to health.

Death of Galerius

This edict is a significant event in Church history, not for its immediate results, which must have been transitory[1]—for Galerius died a few days after its promulgation—but far more because it implies the failure of persecution. It is a tribute to the strength of Christianity, and even points to belief forcing itself upon the emperor, or upon those who influenced his counsels.

The meaning of the favourable decree of Galerius

There had been a real and not a metaphorical contest between the two empires. The Church was literally the conqueror. The success of course was not complete as yet. The decree of Galerius was a wave of advance which would recede for a while. But when the long train of Christian confessors marched forth from the prisons and the mines, maimed in the conflict, but still resolute, it was as real a triumph of one power over another as when Cæsar rode up to the Capitol laden with the spoils of the East. Persecution had resulted so far only in displaying the numbers of the Church, and in showing that her spiritual force and her organisation were superior to those of her adversary.

Maximin, who now shared with Licinius the government of the eastern empire, though possibly he did not formally revoke the favourable edict of Galerius, and though he certainly permitted the release of Christians from the prisons and the mines and made no hostile sign for a few months, before long caused the persecution to revive. But a different system was pursued. In order that at least it might have the appearance of a popular movement, the various

The plan of Maximin

---

[1] See Eus. *H.E.* ix. 1, who describes the result of the temporary lull, the return of Christians to their homes. 'All on a sudden, like a flash of lightning blazing from dense darkness, in every city one could see congregations collected, &c.'

communities were permitted or incited to petition the emperor against the Christians. In accordance with these forced addresses the emperor prohibited the assembling of Christians in their churches. He even anticipated the system of Julian by reorganising the heathen hierarchy somewhat on the model of the Christian episcopate. High priests were constituted in the cities, who were to offer daily sacrifices. They were to be robed in white—a mark of the highest distinction. It was part of their charge to prevent the erection of churches and the meetings for Christian worship; they were to compel Christians to do sacrifice, or in default to hand them over to the courts, where the cruel mercy of mutilation rather than death was found to be the more formidable sentence. Lactantius describes with indignant pathos the barbarous cruelty, the rapacity, the gross and unbridled sensuality of this heartless and inhuman despot. Among other acts of indecent cruelty, not the least unseemly was his treatment of Valeria, widow of Galerius and daughter of Diocletian, and of her mother, Prisca. These two ladies had taken refuge at the court of Maximin. But when Valeria bravely repelled his solicitations for marriage, he banished the wife and daughter of emperors from his court, driving them from place to place, notwithstanding the indignant protests of Diocletian, until at length they perished at Thessalonica under Licinius.

This was not the only painful insult to which Diocletian had been exposed in his retreat at Salona in
<small>Death of Diocletian</small> Dalmatia. He had indeed found there a charming and secure repose from the weariness of supreme rule. He had beguiled his days with

building palaces, with gardening, and with the pursuits of a cultivated leisure. But he could not shield himself from the vexation of being witness to the ruin of his own political fabric, and of seeing his wise counsels set at nought by his successors. Circumstances forced him to turn persecutor again, to do the very thing which he detested, to resume the blunder which had driven him from the throne. Then rumours of personal insult reached his seclusion. The statues and portraits of this new founder of the empire were overthrown and destroyed by the Augusti whose fortunes he had initiated. These accumulated grievances made his life unendurable, wore out his strength, and brought him to death. After nine years of retirement Diocletian died in A.D. 313.

At Antioch—the cradle of Hellenic Christianity—a persecuting measure of novel and impious ingenuity was adopted, which seems to show the growing effect of Christian education. Theotecnus, the governor of that city under Maximin, with the sanction of the emperor forged certain 'Acts of Pilate,' a tale of infamous slander intended to disparage and confute the Christian message. This document was published throughout the empire and delivered to the schoolmasters to be studied and learned by their pupils—an educational system deliberately founded on a lie.

Christianity misrepresented in schools

Meantime the coarser methods of terror were relentlessly pursued. We read especially of Christian leaders in thought and teaching, and the most influential rulers of the Church, being slain by wild beasts or by the sword. Among these are recorded Lucian of Antioch, priest and scholar, Silvanus, an aged Bishop, and Peter, Bishop of Alexandria.

But deliverance was at hand. Events were drawing to a head in the West which were destined to take off this burden of persecution from the Church and to bring it into entirely new relations with the State.

CHAPTER IV.

CONSTANTINE.

THE first care of Constantine had been to crush the barbarians who had risen in rebellion on the Rhine frontier and in Britain. He now determined on a great adventure. The population of Rome and of Italy had endured for five years the savage lust and the hateful oppression of Maxentius. It is well to remember, on the eve of the impending change, how despotism of this cruel and sensual kind, absolutely without any check or restraint, was soon to become impossible. The higher motive was already beginning to influence events. The injured citizens appealed to Constantine, who resolved to cross the Alps and attack the tyrant. On whatever grounds the conflict began, eventually it became a struggle between paganism and Christianity. Constantine is represented as wavering for a while between two opinions. It was a momentous choice for the world as well as for Constantine. His decision in favour of Christianity is one of those critical and determining acts which mark the beginning of a new epoch.

The great resolve of Constantine

It was at this time that the famous vision appeared which confirmed the emperor in his choice. The army was on the march, when one day, early in the afternoon, Constantine beheld a shining Cross in the heavens above the declining sun. On the Cross appeared an inscription in Greek letters, 'by this conquer' (ἐν τούτῳ νίκα). This was in sight of the whole army. The story is given in contemporary historians, and was related to Eusebius by Constantine himself on oath. Nor is there any good reason to doubt the occurrence. In its main features a similar phenomenon has been not unfrequently observed;[1] and the *labarum* or sacred symbol, made in commemoration of the event, should be taken in evidence.

<small>The sign of the Cross</small>

Constantine crossed the Alps by the Mont Cenis pass. The campaign was full of risk for his troops. In numbers they were far inferior to the enemy. Constantine was at the head of forty thousand men, Maxentius commanded at least four times as many. But in discipline and hardihood there could be no comparison between the Gallic legions fresh from campaigns on the borders of the empire, and the troops of Maxentius enervated by the luxury of Italian cities. For the first time, too, in history the Christian cause inspired an army. To thousands of Constantine's soldiers that advance from the passes of the Alps to the gates of Rome was a symbol of the Christ going forth conquering and to conquer. It was indeed a visible token of the progress of Christianity. More than a hundred years before Tertullian had openly spoken of

<small>The march of Constantine</small>

---

[1] For a remarkable parallel, see Whymper's *Scrambles amongst the Alps*, ch. xxii.

the Christian body as a force in the State. 'If we chose to put forth our strength in open war, would there be lack of numbers to fill our ranks? we are but of yesterday, and yet we have occupied all that belongs to you, your cities, your islands, your camps and council-chambers, your very palace, the senate, and the forum.'[1] And now the time had come when the Church was too powerful an element in the imperial system to be ignored by the contending powers. It is the part of genius in every age to detect and turn to account new forces. Constantine had the skill to do this; he triumphed by means of an open profession of faith and alliance with Christianity. But to the Christian in the retrospect, if not at the moment, there could only be one interpretation of the campaign. The unequal contest crowned with success, the preservation of Constantine's own life in spite of his conspicuous and daring courage, lastly the mad improvidence of Maxentius, who at Ponte Molle lost the battle before the troops engaged, could only mean the imminent rule of Christ in his Church over mankind. It meant the Kingdom of God coming with power.

Two victories, at Susa beneath Mont Cenis, and before the gates of Turin, placed the north-west of Italy at the feet of Constantine. In the east, Verona, strongly placed and strongly held by the troops of Maxentius, proved a formidable obstacle. It was invested, however, by the invading army; and when Pompeianus advanced to relieve the city he was met by Constantine, who, by a masterly display of generalship, completely defeated the opposing forces

Constantine is victorious

---

[1] Tertull. *Apol.* ch. xxxvi.

in a battle which raged from evening to the dawn of day.

Though immense resources still remained at the disposal of Maxentius, he had neither the skill nor the courage to use them. He was only induced to leave the city on the strength of a very ambiguous oracle: 'that on that day the enemy of Rome should perish.' Maxentius gave his own solution to the dark saying and took the field.

Constantine found the defending army posted at Saxa Rubra, about nine miles from Rome, their rear resting on the Tiber near the Pons Milvius, now Ponte Molle. *The battle of Pons Milvius* Impetuous charges of the Gallic horse put to flight the cavalry of Maxentius and exposed the infantry. The rout became general and confused. Maxentius himself was carried in the crowd of fugitives to the Tiber, where he sank in the deep mud and perished miserably. Some may remember the famous picture in the Vatican galleries by Raphael or his school, in which this decisive scene in Christian history is nobly represented.

One of Constantine's measures on assuming the sovereignty of Rome and Italy was the suppression of the Prætorian guard—the powerful body which had so often made and unmade emperors in the past. One result of this was to leave Rome unprotected and without power of resistance against the encroachments of the empire. Another was to hand over Rome to the Christian Church with her great name and her immemorial traditions of empire—a factor in history of hardly less moment than the battle of Pons Milvius itself.

The outward sign of this great revolution was a statue of himself, which Constantine caused to be erected. The Emperor was represented holding in his right hand a Cross, and on the pedestal beneath an inscription ran as follows: 'By virtue of this salutary sign, which is the true symbol of valour, I have preserved and liberated your city from the yoke of tyranny. I have also set at liberty the Roman senate and people, and restored them to their ancient greatness and splendour.' Such an inscription reflects the attitude of Constantine towards Christianity at this crisis. He had taken the Christian side, but he was still but a novice, a catechumen in Christian truth.

Constantine professes Christianity in Rome

Towards the end of the year Constantine left Rome for Milan, where he met Licinius. This meeting resulted in the issue of the famous edict of Milan. Up to that hour Christianity had been an *illicita religio*, and it was a crime to be a Christian. Even in Trajan's answer to Pliny this position is assumed, though it forms the basis of humane regulations. The edict of Milan is the charter of Christianity; it proclaims absolute freedom in the matter of religion. Both Christians and all others were to be freely permitted to follow whatsoever religion each might choose. Moreover, restitution was to be made to the Christian body of all churches and other buildings which had been alienated from them during the persecution. This was in 313 A.D.'

The edict of Milan, A.D. 313.

The conference at Milan, and the alliance between Constantine and Licinius, roused Maximin to action. He left Syria at the head of his army in the depth of winter, and reached Bithynia by forced marches after sustaining a grievous diminution in the numbers both of men and baggage animals. Byzantium capitulated after a short siege. Meantime Licinius was pressing forward to meet his rival. The decisive conflict took place near Hadrianople. It is said that on the night before the battle Maximin made a vow that if victory were to be on his side, he would show his gratitude by the extirpation of Christianity. Licinius, on the other hand, warned by a vision, joined with his army in prayer to the Supreme God. In the battle which ensued, the troops of Licinius, notwithstanding their numerical inferiority, were completely victorious. Maximin fled, exchanging the imperial purple for the dress of a slave. In this disguise he made his way to the mountains of Cilicia, and took refuge in Tarsus; where, being pressed by the enemy, he drank poison and died in great agony. Thus perished the last of the persecuting emperors. Licinius entered Antioch without opposition. He gave orders for the execution of the near relatives and the chief ministers of the late emperors Galerius and Maximin. Candidianus, the illegitimate son of his benefactor Galerius, and the young children of Maximin were included in that proscription. It was at this time that the empress Valeria and her mother Prisca were put to death at Thessalonica by the orders of Licinius, as has been narrated. (See p. 25.)

Defeat and death of Maximin

It was a wonderful reversal of events. The ten years' warfare (such it seemed to have been) had ended in a glorious victory for the Christian cause. Language was inadequate to express the exultation of the Church. 'Of a truth the Lord hath destroyed them and blotted them out,' writes Lactantius, 'let us, therefore, celebrate the triumph of God with rejoicing, and with praises tell of the Lord's victory, with prayers night and day let us celebrate it.'

So far little has been said of controversy within the Church itself. To enter deeply into such questions is indeed foreign to the purpose of this work. But one controversy which shook and threatened to shatter the African Church cannot be passed over in silence.

<small>Church controversy in Africa</small>

Africa had suffered more than the other provinces in the late persecutions. The fierce, unyielding, and passionate type of Christianity which there prevailed had burst forth into fanatical zeal. And when the storm had passed, many priests and ministers of the Church who had faithfully kept their trust and refused to deliver up sacred vessels, copies of the Holy Scriptures, and service books, declined to re-admit into full communion those weaker brethren—*traditors*, as they were called,—who had yielded to the threats and perils of persecution and surrendered the sacred deposits. This question divided the African Church. The quarrel culminated in the election to the Bishopric of Carthage. Cæcilian had been regularly appointed Bishop and consecrated by Felix, Bishop of Aptunga; but the election was impugned on the ground that Felix was a traditor. A council of the opposing faction met in Carthage under the presidency of Donatus, Bishop of Casæ Nigræ. On the refusal of Cæcilian to acknowledge their jurisdiction, they proceeded to elect a rival Bishop of Carthage. In this crisis an appeal was made to the emperor Constantine, who referred the question to a council of Bishops which he convened at Rome.

The decision was given against the Donatists, the name by which the severe and fanatical faction of the African Church began to be known. At the Council of Arles (314), as in every other instance, the Donatists were met by adverse decisions. But the spirit of fanaticism rose higher at every rebuff, till at length it became necessary to use against it the engines of the civil power. Exile and confiscation only served to exasperate and solidify those who remained, and no external pressure availed to crush out Donatism. On the contrary, an extreme sect of this fanatical faction broke into greater excesses. The Circumcellions, as they were termed, rose in open insurrection against the Roman government. They proclaimed wild theories of equality, to which they gave effect by means of bloodshed and robbery. The excitable African character of the sect showed itself sometimes in a rigid asceticism, sometimes in the most violent excesses, and in reckless desire for martyrdom. The history of this strange religious enthusiasm carries us considerably beyond the reign of Constantine. The Circumcellions received a crushing defeat in the reign of Constans; but the Donatists continued to exist and to flourish as a sect till a far later period. Even in the reign of Honorius they could boast of an equally divided allegiance with the Catholics.

The fanaticism of the Donatists

There are several points of interest in these events beyond the immediate dispute. First, the appeal of the Donatists to the emperor on a question of doctrine and internal discipline deserves no-

The significance of these events

tice, though the appeal was made not by the Church, but by the adherents of a schism. Then the assemblage of a council at Rome on a momentous question like this marks an era in the history of the Roman Church. It is, however, easy to exaggerate the historical importance of the incident. It tells in favour of the indestructible prestige of Rome, not in favour of the supremacy of the Roman Church. In the Council of Arles some notable decisions were given, which marked the changed relations between Church and State. For instance, a soldier who deserted in time of peace was to be deprived of the Communion; scholars educated at the public expense were to bring letters from their Bishop to prove that they belonged to the Christian Church.

But in various directions Christianity began to exercise a decided and a softening influence on legislation. In accordance with a natural feeling, crucifixion, now surrounded by the holiest associations, ceased to be a legal mode of execution. Laws were passed against the exposure of infants, a frequent and allowed practice in pagan civilisation. In the punishment of guilt the principle of equality before the law was recognised; no regard was to be paid to the rank or dignity of the offender ('honorem reatus excludit'). Branding on the forehead was prohibited, expressly on the ground that no dishonour ought to be done to the dignity of the countenance, framed as it was in the image of God. The crimes of seduction and rape were visited with a severity which contrasted sharply with the pagan palliation of these offences. No rigour of vengeance for these crimes would seem too harsh in the eyes of a generation which had suffered

Effect of Christianity on the laws

the sensual and cruel indignities of Maximin and Maxentius. On the other hand, celibacy, involving legal disabilities in the ancient code, ceased with Christianity to bear that character, and in some of its aspects was raised to the rank of a supreme virtue. Public relief was to be administered in districts suffering from famine, lest by hunger men should be driven to commit crimes. The severity of prison life and treatment was alleviated by law.

In this way the first gleam of Christianity, by an instant effect, sent a ray of gentleness and light through the whole of human life in its most painful phases and its most hopeless and miserable regions.

Slavery, indeed, continued to be a social institution. Its aspect in the new light of Christianity had not yet touched the human conscience; and, indeed, there were reasons against a sudden abolition. Trade and commerce in the ancient world were mainly administered by slaves; to abolish slavery would be to disorganise commerce. The great lesson of the dignity of labour was to be gradually taught; but still the tendency was in favour of freedom. Encouragement was given to the liberation of slaves, and regulations were framed for carrying it out in the presence of the priest or of the congregation.

Slavery and Christianity

Imperial edicts were issued in favour of the clergy, who now became a privileged order in the State, a result by no means of unmixed advantage to the Church. Ruined churches were rebuilt, and the confiscated revenues were restored to Christian corporations. As for polytheism, the public worship of the gods was not prohibited, though the celebration of secret rites at home was disallowed, as tending to the practice of magic and of immorality.

And yet, notwithstanding the rapid and astonishing success of Constantine, paganism was still a considerable force in the empire, and its cause did not appear desperate as yet. Christianity had lost as well as gained by the revolution; and the change of imperial favour had clashed with many interests. These interests and the indignant spirit of paganism gathered to a head and remained a source of danger to the government of Constantine.

Paganism still a force in the empire

It became clear, too, that Licinius was prepared to use all these elements of discontent in a struggle for empire with Constantine. He changed his attitude towards the Christians, who were dismissed from the imperial service in the army and in the palace. Bishops were forbidden to meet in synod; even such offices of humanity as visiting prisoners in their cells, an act which may be claimed as distinctively Christian, were declared illegal. Once again men were put to death for their religion. Perhaps the policy of these acts, not discerned at the time, was simply to proclaim an open opposition to Christianity, and to gather under one standard all the opposing forces.

Struggle between Licinius and Constantine

The alleged pretexts of the war may be dismissed. The issue was once more between Christianity and paganism. The good fortune (*felicitas*) of Constantine followed him in this campaign. Licinius was defeated first at Cibalis on the river Save, and a second time, after a desperate encounter, at Mardia in Thrace (314). Constantine, however, granted terms to his adversary, and for eight years the empire enjoyed internal peace.

But the causes of dissension remained behind. Once more (323) the question between paganism and Christianity was to be tried on the field of battle, and their armies confronted one another on the plains of Hadrianople. Again the skill of Constantine and the trained valour of his troops proved superior to the undisciplined levies of Licinius; while at sea Crispus, the eldest and ill-fated son of Constantine, destroyed the enemy's fleet in the crowded waters of the Hellespont, sowing thereby the seeds of his father's jealousy. Byzantium fell, but not without a vigorous resistance; and, after one more crushing defeat on the site of the modern Scutari, Licinius submitted himself to the mercy of Constantine. He was permitted to live at Thessalonica; but his death soon followed; whether in a military tumult or by express order of the senate, is uncertain. There can, however, be little doubt that the death of Licinius was required by the policy of Constantine.

Licinius defeated

What we notice in the whole of these events is the enormous power which still belonged to paganism. The balance still wavered between paganism and Christianity. This alone accounts both for the clemency shewn to Licinius after his defeat, and for the doom which overtook him so speedily at Thessalonica. It was only the consummate strategy of Constantine which determined the event. A less skilful arrangement, or a less resolute attack at Hadrianople or at Scutari, might have changed the course of history.

Constantine had now, by a marvellous succession of

victories, placed himself in a position of supreme and undisputed power. At this juncture it is of interest to observe that, just as the quadruple system of Dio-cletian was essential for the breaking up of paganism, so the restored monarchy of Constantine was required for the consolidation of Christianity; and again that the divided empire, which followed the reign of Constantine, served to sustain Catholicity at least in one half of the world. Each change of system seemed to favour the advance, the expansion, and the purity of the Church.

The changes in the empire favourable to Christianity

The foundation of Constantinople was the outward symbol of the new monarchy and of the triumph of Christianity. It was impossible for Rome, in the changed condition of the world, to continue to be the centre of power. Nicomedia was stained by the records of persecution; but the choice of this incomparable position for the new capital of the world remains the lasting proof of Constantine's genius. It was the first of Christian cities. It was Christian from its foundation, and unlike Rome or Antioch or Alexandria, had no records of pagan tradition or custom to erase before the new faith prevailed. The magnificence of its public buildings, its treasures of art, its vast endowments, the beauty of its situation, the rapid growth of its commerce, made it worthy to be 'as it were a daughter of Rome herself.'[1] But the most important thought for us is the relation of Constantinople to the advance of Christianity. That the city which had sprung into supremacy from its birth and had become the capital of the conquered world, should have excluded

The new Rome

[1] *De Civitate Dei*, v. 25.

from the circuit of its walls all public recognition of polytheism, and made the Cross its most conspicuous ornament, and the token of its greatness, gave a reality to the religious revolution. The religious as well as the imperial centre of the world had been visibly displaced.

But Constantine's intense desire for unity in Church as well as State was disappointed. The opposing forces of paganism had no sooner been reduced to silence than a formidable heresy sprang up within the bosom of the Church.

CHAPTER V.

THE COUNCIL OF NICÆA—ATHANASIUS.

THE history and significance of Arianism will be fully treated in another volume of this series. But even in a general sketch of the period some notice of this important movement is required.

The great storm which Arianism excited has not in truth subsided yet. The Council of Nicæa was only an incident in the struggle. The contention raged round the central figures of that council long afterwards, and Athanasius and Arius have still their representatives in modern theology.

Arianism

Of Arius himself the first thing we know is that he was a scholar of the presbyter Lucian at Antioch. He is described as being a diligent but narrow and unenlightened student of Holy Scripture, by no means fitted through force of intellect to create an epoch of religious thought. He was placed in charge of a parish in Alexandria named Baucalis, where he gained so high a reputation by his asceticism and by his popular manners that, when a vacancy occurred in the see of Alexandria, the election all but fell upon him instead of his opponent Alexander.

Briefly stated, the purport of the teaching of Arius was to deny the co-equality and co-eternity of the Son with the Father. The origin of the heresy may be traced partly to unduly pressing by the rules of human logic the analogy of the human relation between father and son, and partly to the supposed danger of polytheism in the statement of two uncreated Persons. Arius stated, indeed, that the Father created Christ, but that He created Him in order that through Him He might create all things. Moreover, he represented Christ as widely, nay, infinitely separate from all other created beings; he even ascribed to Him the name of God (because he found that name ascribed to Him in the New Testament), and he affirmed that Christ was 'born before all time as perfect God, only begotten, unchangeable.' It was only the subtlety of the Greek language that enabled Arius to make such distinctions. He was able to express the idea that Christ was born before all time, and yet 'there was when he was not' ($\mathring{\eta}\nu$ ὅτε οὐκ $\mathring{\eta}\nu$), avoiding the use of the word for time. But of course it was impossible to uphold such fine distinctions. It was the rift within the lute. Popular speech broke down the nice definitions of the scholar, and asserted the inferiority of the Son as touching the Godhead.

Arius took especial pains to popularise his system. He wrote a collection of songs for sailors, millers, and pilgrims, so that the deepest and most sacred expressions of Christian theology were bandied to and fro in taverns and market-places, as the watchwords of opposing factions.

The opinions of Arius were condemned in a council of Libyan and Egyptian Bishops at Alexandria, in the year 321 A.D. Still the contest went on with increased bitterness. Attempts were made to compromise the matter, especially by Eusebius, Bishop of Cæsarea, the well-known historian, a man of the very highest reputation in the Eastern Church as a learned and accomplished theologian. Eusebius 'dreaded the intrusion of profane passions into such investigations, which required, beyond all others, the purity, calmness, and quiet of a soul consecrated to God.'[1] 'We men,' he argued, 'are unable to understand a thousand things that lie immediately at our feet. Who knows, for instance, how the soul became united to the body, and how it leaves it? ... Why then do we, when we see ourselves surrounded here by so many difficulties, presume to search after the perfect knowledge of the essence of the Eternal Godhead?'

But it was too late to allay the storm. At length a remarkable intervention took place. For the first time in the history of the Church, the civil power, seeing the danger of intestine strife among Christians, stepped in to settle a controversy concerning the Faith. With Constantine the empire had become Christian. It was his earnest wish and his policy to unite his dominions by the bond of a common religion. But the Arian schism threatened to split his subjects into opposite camps. It was a danger to the empire as well as to Christianity.

The Council of Nicæa

[1] Neander, *Church History*, iv. 13. (Eng. Trans.)

First he wrote to the two leading parties in the struggle—to Alexander, Bishop of Alexandria, and to Arius. But his letter showed little grasp of the point in dispute, and little knowledge of human nature, and proved of no effect.

When this failed, he looked around for other means of restoring peace to the Church and empire. Questions that had agitated particular Churches had frequently been settled by synods composed of the provincial Bishops. But this question concerned the universal Church. The solution of it therefore seemed to lie in a general assembly of all the provinces. Accordingly he summoned the first œcumenical council at Nicæa in Bithynia, now a miserable village called Is-nik (325).

No complete account of the proceedings of the council has been preserved; but the letters of Athanasius, and the history of Eusebius, who attended the council, have preserved many facts concerning it, and the so-called Nicene Creed gives the leading results.

Eusebius of Cæsarea took a prominent position in this great debate. Two reasons are sufficient to account for this: he was the most learned man of his time; he was the confidant of the emperor. Though Eusebius had not been a partisan of Arius, he endeavoured to give him fair play. He represented the party of moderation, and, if such were possible, of compromise.

Eusebius

But the most remarkable personage present at the council was Athanasius. At that time he was not more than thirty years of age, possibly not more than twenty-five. He held no more dignified position than that of Archdeacon to the Bishop or

Athanasius

'Pope Alexander; but he had already acquired a marvellous ascendency. Alexander had detected the great promise of his boyhood, and when he grew up, he had taken him to live ' as a son with his father.'

Alexandria was the meeting-place of creeds and of all systems of philosophy, art, and literature. All phases of Christianity were represented there—mysticism, neoplatonism, the tendency to asceticism, the practice of monasticism. In these surroundings the keen intellect of Athanasius grew.[1] Soon he became the leading and the most resolute opponent of Arianism, and at the Council of Nicæa he stood by the side of the Bishop, advising, suggesting, and keenly observant of every turn and argument in the debate.

His after life, which extended far into the history of the fourth century, was full of interest and adventure. He stood almost the sole champion of truth in the midst of menace and slander and of danger to his life. 'Athanasius contra mundum,' 'Athanasius against the world,' is hardly an exaggerated phrase.

The triumph of the orthodox cause at Nicæa was expressed by the reception of the symbol which, with the additions made afterwards at the Council of Constantinople, has descended to us as the Nicene Creed. That Creed became the highest symbol and standard of faith in the centuries which followed. And, though inferior to the noble simplicity of the Apostles' Creed, though 'scarred by controversy,' and though to the subtle Greek mind not absolutely unambiguous and precise, yet it is an admirable exposition of the Catholic faith, and worthy to be the rallying point of the

---

[1] Neander, *Church History*, iv. 17.

Churches. But the Council of Nicæa failed entirely to root out Arianism. It left as its legacy a long and bitter controversy, and the central figure round which the conflict raged was Athanasius.

The emperor Constantine at first commanded obedience to the Nicene decisions, but was won over to the side of the Arianisers, chiefly through the influence of Eusebius, Bishop of Nicomedia, who was a personal friend of Constantia, the emperor's sister.

<small>Charges brought against Athanasius</small> Various charges, quite unfounded, and even of an absurd and impossible character, were brought against Athanasius, who now succeeded Alexander as Bishop of Alexandria. He had, it was alleged, prevented the sailing of the corn ships from Alexandria to Rome; he had taken on himself authority to tax the Egyptians for Church purposes; again, he had sent a purse of gold to Philumenos, a rebel. It is easy to detect the undercurrent in these charges—the attempt to represent Christianity as high treason. When they were easily confuted, another was added. 'He had caused an attendant priest to enter a church, where a schismatic clergyman was offering the Holy Eucharist; the office had been interrupted, the altar overthrown, the chalice broken.' Athanasius was able to show that there was no church in the place named in the indictment, and that on the day mentioned no celebration of the Eucharist took place. A still graver accusation, but one as unfounded as the others, and still more easily confuted, charged him with the murder of one Arsenius. Athanasius was able to produce the murdered man in court, to the confusion of his enemies.

Notwithstanding this triumphant acquittal, so great

was the Arian influence at court, and so persistent the enemies of Athanasius, that a new charge was brought against him of preventing the sailing of the Alexandrian corn ships to Constantinople. The emperor, feigning belief in the accusation, with the hope perhaps of securing peace for the empire, banished Athanasius to Trèves in the year 336. Many readers, who have visited that quaint and interesting old Roman city on the banks of the beautiful Mosel, will like to associate it with the story of the great and saintly Athanasius.

In this year the momentarily triumphant opponent of Athanasius, the author of much confusion and evil to *Death of Arius* the Church, Arius, himself perished at Constantinople by a sudden and shocking form of death. He was about to be received into communion with the Church at Constantinople, to the scandal of the Catholics, by the compulsion of the emperor himself, when the end came by the stroke of a sudden malady, which seemed to Athanasius and others at the time to be a manifest token of the divine displeasure.

In the following year (337) died Constantine the *Death of Constantine* Great, having been baptized a few days only before his death.

It is difficult to estimate in a few words the influence of Constantine on the history of the Church; *His influence on the Church* but some lines of thought may be indicated. 1. The association of the Church with the imperial power brought with it evil as well as good. If freedom from persecution was a gain, dangers of a more subtle, but not less fatal, character supervened. 2. It at once became apparent that the religious views of an emperor might exercise a paramount, which would often be a dangerous, influence on Christian opinion. 3. The prominent place instantly taken by Church interests in the councils of the State foreshadowed the inevitable results of this contact; actual separation between Church and State became henceforth impossible. 4. One result of this 'establishment' of Christianity was the strain which it put on the simplicity of the Christian life. We begin to hear of wealthy endowments, stately and magnificent churches, growing ecclesiastical privilege, and of a clergy exposed to the temptations of dignity and riches rather than to those of poverty and scorn. 5. The foundation of Constantinople and the transference of power to the East greatly tended to the independence of the Roman Church, and was the beginning of the separation between East and West.

CHAPTER VI.

THE SONS OF CONSTANTINE.

At Trèves Athanasius formed a friendship with Constantine, the namesake and eldest surviving son of the late emperor. Constantine the younger shared the sovereignty of the world with his brothers Constantius and Constans—Constantine ruling the western provinces, Constans Italy and Africa, and Constantius the eastern portion of the empire.

Accession of the three emperors

The succession of the three sons of Constantine was signalised by the cruel massacre of all their nearest kindred, with the exception of two nephews of the late emperor—Gallus, who was thought to be dying, and Julian, afterwards emperor, and called 'the Apostate' by Church historians, who was saved by the intervention of Mark, Bishop of Arethusa.

This crime is laid to the charge of Constantius alone by the testimony of Julian, of Athanasius, and of the historian Zosimus.

Constantine's career was short. In 340 he was slain in battle near the walls of Aquileia in the course of a campaign against his brother Constans. This event was followed by the partition of the empire between the two surviving brothers.

In 338 Athanasius was restored to his bishopric with the consent of the three emperors. His return was welcomed with signs of the most enthusiastic joy by the citizens of Alexandria. But his Arian enemies allowed him no rest. Rival claimants were put forward for the see of Alexandria; first Pistus, and, when he was completely discredited, Gregory of Cappadocia. Gregory, supported by the whole strength of the Arian, which was also the imperial party, forced his way through scenes of bloodshed and desecration to the episcopal throne. For the second time Athanasius fled. On this occasion, setting sail for Rome, he laid his case before Pope Julius for decision by a council.

Athanasius returns to Alexandria

Again in exile

It is impossible not to observe the growing influence of Rome. Up to this point and beyond it that influence was natural, legitimate, and limited. Many reasons converged to create and extend the authority of the Apostolic Roman see: the prestige of the metropolis of the empire, its historic fame, the

The growth of the Roman see

desertion of it by the imperial courts, the sanctity of its Apostolic founders, the blood of its martyrs, and the traditions already venerable of that Church: all these and other conditions gave the Church of Rome a naturally leading position in Christendom. The growth and the decay, the good and the evil of this influence form in themselves an interesting chapter in ecclesiastical history.

The visit of Athanasius to Rome was productive of far-reaching results, and that in an unexpected way. *Influence of Athanasius in Rome* The Bishop or Pope of Alexandria was accompanied by two monks of the Egyptian deserts. Their strange and uncouth garb, their absorbed looks, the intensity of their devotion, attracted the gaze and curiosity of the citizens of Rome. Athanasius described the practices of the ascetic life—a growth of Oriental piety then unknown in western Europe—and narrated in detail the story of the celebrated hermit St. Anthony. A noble Roman lady named Marcella, afterwards an intimate friend of St. Jerome, was among the audience. She was captivated by the description, and became the founder of a convent in Rome. The seed of monasticism thus planted yielded in after years a rich harvest in this place. In other ways, too, this master-mind made a deep impression on the Church in Rome, which, in Milman's words, became 'the scholar as well as the partisan of Athanasius.'

The Eastern Bishops had declined to be present at the Council of Rome which formally purged Athanasius of the charges laid against him. This may be noted as an instance of the widening breach between the Churches of the East and West. The latter had remained almost entirely free from the taint of Arianism which had deeply infected the Eastern Church.

A further example was afterwards exhibited at the Council of Sardica (347), a city of Mœsia near the frontier line of the Eastern and Western empires. The Oriental Bishops reached the city indeed, but refused to take part in the council except on impossible conditions, and eventually left Sardica and formed a council of their own at Philippopolis. The Western Bishops continued their session. Among the canons passed at the Council of Sardica was one permitting, in certain circumstances, an appeal to Rome, a canon which, as Professor Bright remarks, approached dangerously near to giving a supremacy to the Pope.

The Council of Sardica

And now news came from Alexandria of the death or the murder of the usurper Gregory, and Athanasius was once more allowed to return to his see. It is said that Constans exacted this permission from his brother Constantius under the threat of war—a signal instance of the influence which ecclesiastical affairs were beginning to have on the destiny of the empire—an influence which forty years previously would have seemed quite incredible.

Athanasius again returns

For the moment the attitude of Constantius to Athanasius was gracious and affable: he admitted him to a personal interview at Antioch, and wrote letters in his favour to the authorities in Egypt, ecclesiastical and civil. But a change was at hand. In the year 350 an event occurred which deprived Athanasius of a powerful friend, and placed the whole civilised world under the rule of a single Arian despot. This was the death of

Constans. The emperor of the West was staying in the neighbourhood of Autun, surrounded by troops, devoting himself to the chase and other pleasures, when one of his generals, Magnentius, a German by birth, formed a conspiracy, assumed the imperial purple, and forced Constans to put himself to death.

<small>Constantius sole emperor</small>

In less than two years Magnentius was defeated at the battle of Mursa by Constantius, whose first act as sole emperor was to direct a cruel persecution against the Catholic Christians in several parts of the world.

At a council held at Arles under his auspices, Athanasius was condemned; and at Milan, now the acknowledged capital of the West, an interview took place which vividly illustrates the danger of this imperial connexion for the Church. Constantius summoned a council of Western Bishops to meet at Milan. With his own hand he drew up an edict against Athanasius, supported by such theological arguments as he was master of. This document was presented to the assembled Bishops. The emperor did not at first appear in person, but remained concealed for a while behind the tapestry hangings, which were suspended at the end of the council chamber. But when the murmurs of dissent, which greeted the reading of the edict, broke upon his ear, he burst impatiently into the assemblage, exclaiming, 'This doctrine which you reject is my doctrine: if it be false, as you say, how comes it that heaven has given success to my arms, and placed the world in my power?'

Fortunately a Christian Bishop was found bold enough to refute an argument which was only formidable because it came from imperial lips. 'Your success,' said Lucifer, Bishop of Cagliari, 'proves nothing: Scripture is full of instances of apostate kings whom God did not overthrow at once,' and he cited the instances of the Midianites and Amalekites, of Saul and Solomon; then turning to the arguments of the edict he continued, 'Your doctrine is the doctrine of Arius himself, neither more nor less, and those who support it are the precursors of anti-Christ.' Though the council ended by the exile of Lucifer and other faithful Bishops who had refused to condemn Athanasius, and by the forced and formal assent of the rest, the firm and dignified resistance offered to the tyrant was a substantial victory for the cause of truth.

The significance of the scene, however, cannot escape us. Here was an emperor, who had not advanced so far in Christianity as to become a catechumen, endeavouring to force heretical theology by crude arguments on an assemblage of Bishops, and daring to say: 'That which I will is a canon of the Church,'[1] and again: 'Have I chosen you to be my advisers that I may be prevented from doing what I choose?' It was a moment of peril and ominous for the future.

But, on the other hand, it may be thought a providential circumstance that, at this beginning of the connexion between the empire and the Church, the Church was brought into open conflict with the emperor, and was not persuaded by the flattery of court favour to yield herself a bondslave to the civil power. An orthodox emperor might have been more dangerous to the infant liberty of the Church than a declared Arian

---

[1] ὅπερ ἐγὼ βούλομαι τοῦτο κανών, ἔλεγε, νομιζέσθω.

like Constantius. The adjustment of the relations between Church and State had already become a grave and difficult question; and one of the chief points of interest in this period of Church history is to watch the great experiments by which a solution of that question was attempted.

We now return to Athanasius. The partisans of Constantius required no formal edict or imperial command to attempt the Bishop's overthrow. Several emissaries from the court reached Alexandria, and after a treacherous calm of a few weeks, a preconcerted attack was made on the church of St. Theonas, where Athanasius was assisting at a midnight service. The church was surrounded by troops. An impressive scene followed. The Bishop seated on his throne desired the deacon to read the Psalm—the 136th—and the people to respond 'for his mercy endureth for ever.' The Psalm was scarcely finished, when the soldiers rushed into the church, trampling down, wounding, and slaying the worshippers. Athanasius himself, after remaining almost to the last, miraculously escaped, and retired to the convents and cells of the Egyptian deserts.

Athanasius driven by violence from Alexandria

Then a bitter trial came upon him. The Arians introduced into the see of Alexandria an adventurer of coarse manners and evil repute, named George of Cappadocia. For more than five years the orthodox Christians of Alexandria were exposed to a brutal and systematic persecution only terminated by the murder of George at the hands of the pagan population, whom his arrogance and oppression had equally exasperated. This was in A.D. 362.

George of Cappadocia

In the previous year Constantius had died. By the Council of Ariminum (Rimini) A.D. 359, he had made one more attack on the purity of the Nicene faith. By the subtlety of Valens, an Arian Bishop, that important council had been induced to accept a Creed which in specious language conveyed heretical teaching. When that Creed was by the emperor's influence pressed upon the Eastern and Western Churches, in the words of Jerome, 'the whole world groaned and marvelled to find itself Arian.'

Council of Ariminum

It may be convenient here to anticipate events by briefly tracing to its end the noble career of the saintly Athanasius. He had returned to Alexandria under an edict of toleration issued by the emperor Julian. There he succeeded by the wisdom of his rule and great personal influence in maintaining quiet in that turbulent city. Nor was his pastoral activity confined to the narrow limits of Egypt. 'The age, the merit, the reputation of Athanasius,' says Gibbon, 'enabled him to assume in a moment of danger the office of ecclesiastical moderator.' The danger of a schism, which the misguided decision of Ariminum might have occasioned, was averted by the gentleness and wisdom of Athanasius. But all this was quite contrary to the intention of the emperor Julian, who succeeded Constantius. He issued a hostile edict against Athanasius, whose life at once became in danger. For a fourth time he fled, waiting till 'the little cloud,' as he termed it, of Julian's power should be dispersed.

The sequel of Athanasius' career

The Nile boat which was carrying Athanasius into exile was closely pursued by the pagan governor of Alexandria. By a clever manœuvre, the boat of Athanasius turned and met its pursuer. As they passed their enemies, they were asked, 'Have you seen Athanasius and his friends pass on the river, and are we near to them?' 'Yes,' exclaimed one, standing out from the crowd of sailors, probably the Bishop himself, 'we saw them close to this spot; they cannot be far distant.' So he eluded further pursuit.

The cloud of the pagan reaction under Julian soon passed away, and Athanasius was enabled to return, this time for a season of long and almost uninterrupted peace. He devoted himself to writing books, to the administration of his diocese, to correspondence with his friends, to the care, it may be said, of the universal Church, of which St. Basil calls him 'the very summit, a man of truly grand and Apostolic soul, who from boyhood had been an athlete in the cause of religion.'

Athanasius died peacefully in his own home, after a life of persecution and exile. The exact date is stated to be Thursday, May 2, 373.

Undoubtedly no figure in ecclesiastical history stands out with more impressive grandeur or more clearly than that of Athanasius; no one has rendered higher or more difficult and varied service to the cause of truth and of Christ. Other leaders in a great crisis may have been more learned, more powerful in speech and argument, of quicker intuition, of deeper contemplation; but no one, since St. Paul, had singly filled a wider space in contemporary Church history, no one had risen nearer to the Apostolic ideal in zeal for Christ, in activity of service, and in courageous defence of the faith as delivered to the saints.

CHAPTER VII.

THE EMPEROR JULIAN CALLED THE APOSTATE.

WE now proceed to narrate the dramatic story of the emperor Julian. That story is a romance and a tragedy.

The interest of Julian's career

The romance of a young and gallant prince passing through many vicissitudes of fortune, from imminent peril of death to the imperial throne; the tragedy of an absolute earthly ruler fighting with self-chosen weapons against the Kingdom of Christ, and by his own self-will devoting himself to ruin. It was a career which deeply affected Christianity—the last desperate struggle of a dying paganism which sealed the certainty of the triumph of the Church.

Besides the great Athanasius, the names of Gregory Nazianzen and of Basil are closely linked with the history of Julian. The threefold record will give us interesting glimpses of the Church life and of the better side of paganism which were so strangely mingled in those dark and terrible days of conflict.

We must go back once more to the time of Constantine's death. It will be remembered that, besides the three Augusti, two only of the imperial family were allowed to live—Gallus and Julian, sons of Julius Constantius and nephews of Constantine the Great.

It will not be necessary to follow in detail the career of the unfortunate Gallus. The two brothers

Gallus

were nurtured and educated under the careful and suspicious supervision of the emperor Constantius. At length, after six years of thinly disguised imprisonment in a Cappadocian fortress, Gallus was allowed to share the government of the world with the title of Cæsar. His rule was a cruel and impolitic despotism, which was aggravated by the inhuman ferocity of his wife, the princess Constantina, who is described as a very tigress in her thirst for blood.

The massacre of two emissaries of the emperor Constantius, sent to make enquiries at Antioch where Gallus held his court, sealed the fate of that prince. He was summoned under a pretext of friendship to the imperial presence at Milan; and signs of his impending fate might be discerned in the coldness or insolence of his reception at the various cities through which he passed. Before long he found himself deprived of his guards, stripped of the ensigns of a Cæsar, a helpless prisoner in the power of Constantius, who ordered his execution at Pola, a fortress in Istria.

Julian was now left sole survivor of the family of Constantine, with the exception of the emperor himself.

<small>Julian at Milan</small> He had a difficult and dangerous part to play. He was summoned by the murderer of his brother to the court at Milan, where, it is said to his credit, no word passed his lips which could be interpreted as a condonation of that crime. At the same time, with an address and caution beyond his years, he was able to avoid the pitfalls prepared for him by the intriguing ministers of Constantius, who were ever on the watch to give an evil significance to his language or his silence. Fortunately he had a friend at court. Eusebia, the emperor's wife, whose gracious disposition has won the praise of all historians, espoused the cause of Julian. It was probably by her intervention that

Julian was permitted to retire from Milan and to reside at Athens.

At that time Athens was, as we should term it, the university of the civilised world. All the political influence of former days and the pride of empire had of course long passed away from it; but it was still the home of the Muses. All that was best in the literature and philosophy of that declining age was to be found there. To Julian, therefore, who was an enthusiastic lover of the Greek language and of Greek speculation, Athens offered the strongest attraction. It is important to remember this; for the paganism, with which Christianity was soon to be confronted, was not the coarse and popular paganism which it had supplanted, but a refined and philosophic system which was intended to appeal to the nobler instincts and cultivated tastes of mankind.

He studies at Athens

Up to this time Julian was professedly a Christian. He had been the pupil of Eusebius, the Arian Bishop of Nicomedia; he had been carefully, almost rigorously, initiated into the ritual and usages of the Church; he had taken part in the services as a reader. But Christianity as it had been presented to him by Arian teaching, and in the lives and aims of Constantius and his courtiers, had no attraction for Julian; it had not touched his heart.

Julian's education

For this reason some modern historians have hesitated to add the title of apostate to Julian's name. Indeed no one can rightly be called an apostate who has not been an adherent or willing servant of a leader or a master; and it cannot be said of Julian that he was either an adherent of

The title of apostate

Christ or His true servant. He had been forced into a service which had been misrepresented to him and which he found irksome. He never gave his heart to Christ or the enthusiasm of his nature to the Christian cause. Already in secret he had yielded to the fascination of pagan teaching and of mystic rites, and had become a worshipper of the gods of Greece after the idealised fashion of the modern philosophy; but the time had not arrived for an open declaration of his real belief.

Meanwhile an opposite influence presented itself to him in the schools of Athens. Among the most distinguished of his fellow-students were two Christian scholars, whose close and loving friendship forms one of those touching human episodes which break in upon the severity of history with a gentle and domestic interest. These were Basil of Cæsarea and Gregory of Nazianzus. In the light of their learning, deep as his own, and in their no less vivid enthusiasm for the great classical writers, Julian might observe a Christianity which was as keen as philosophic paganism in the search for truth, and as receptive of the highest results of Hellenic thought.

Basil and Gregory fellow students of Julian

These devoted Christian youths became intimate with Julian; and it is said that, long afterwards, when Julian gained the summit of imperial power, the vast influence, the noble career, and the unsullied fame of these great Churchmen, more than anything else moved the master of the world to jealousy. Julian left Athens with the deepest regret, and never ceased to regard it with a loving and tender reminiscence.

With the fate of his brother Gallus before him he must have obeyed the emperor's summons to Milan with some misgivings. When he arrived at court he was despatched to Gaul to take the command in that province, and to ward off the attacks of the barbarian tribes on the Rhine frontier. It was a post in which it was dangerous either to succeed or to fail. Julian, however, soon developed conspicuous military talents and endeared himself to his soldiers. Thrice he crossed the Rhine and each time the campaign was crowned with success. Thousands of Roman citizens were rescued from a shameful imprisonment among the barbarian Alemanni, and when the triumph of his arms was complete, the peaceful administration of Julian restored the blessings of order and prosperity to the province.

Julian despatched to Gaul

A story is told of the first of these victorious campaigns, which shows how the leaven of Christianity was at work in the Roman armies, and brings an interesting and familiar name before us.

One day, when the imperial bounty was being distributed to the army, a young soldier stepped out from the ranks, and marching straight up to Julian exclaimed, 'Cæsar, hitherto I have served you; now let me serve God. Let him who wishes to fight under your banner take your pay; as for me, I wish henceforth to be Christ's soldier alone. Fighting is no longer lawful for me.' Taunted with cowardice, the young soldier offered to pass through the enemies' ranks unarmed in the name of the Lord Jesus and with the sign of the Cross. It so happened that that very day ended the campaign, and the proof of valour was

St. Martin of Tours

not exacted. Julian, however, made enquiry about the young soldier, and was informed of his affectionate nature, of his charity, and of the love which his comrades bore him. He was told, also, how one bitterly cold night this soldier had divided his military cloak into two halves, and had given one half to a shivering beggar; in the night the Christ had appeared to him clothed in that half cloak, saying: 'It was Martin that clothed me.' The story is familiar, but it is not remembered by all as an incident in the campaign of the pagan Julian.

The success of Julian was by no means grateful to the emperor Constantius, who began to employ against him the policy which he practised on Gallus. A demand came to Julian to despatch some of his best troops across the Alps to the East, where Constantius was preparing for his war with Persia. Julian perceived the danger; but to disobey the commands of the emperor seemed impossible. The devotion of his troops came to his aid. They surrounded the palace where he resided at Lutetia, the modern Paris, and first with low and isolated voices, then with a chorus of tumultuous cries, called on Julian to assume the titles of Augustus and emperor. After a certain show of resistance Julian accepted the situation. The conciliatory letter which he addressed to Constantius was answered by a peremptory message to lay down the title which he had assumed, and to trust himself to the clemency of the emperor. To such a letter the only possible response was war.

The jealousy of Constantius

The march of Julian against Constantius

This was the occasion which Julian took of publicly

renouncing Christianity, so that the campaign, which he instantly commenced against Constantius, bore to a certain extent the character of a reaction in favour of paganism. Symptoms of such a reaction had already appeared, and perhaps had given hopes to Magnentius in his desperate conflict with Constantius.

We will not linger over Julian's gallant and adventurous march, with a flying column, as we should term it, detached from its base and from the main division of his army, through the unknown depths of the Black Forest, and across the Alps, to a point on the banks of the Danube between Ratisbon and Vienna, and thence by the river to Sirmium in Illyricum, one of the chief imperial residences. Everywhere he was received with joy. Constantius turned back from the Persian war to meet his adversary, and the frightful prospect of imminent civil war disclosed itself to the world. Happily for the peace of the empire, Constantius caught a fever in a town where he halted not far from Tarsus, and there died. He was succeeded by Julian, who now, at the age of thirty-two, became sole master of the Roman world (361).

<small>Constantius dies</small>

It was a critical and dramatic moment in the history of mankind. Once more Christianity and paganism confronted one another; but the circumstances and conditions of the conflict had changed. Formerly paganism had endeavoured to hold back the advancing tide of Christian influence; but Christianity had won the victory. Constantine had avowedly fought his way to supreme power in the name of Christ, and he upheld with all the authority of the

<small>Julian succeeds to the empire</small>

State the religion which had carried him to victory. Still that revolution was not effected without wounding and destroying many interests, and without exciting deep antipathies. There were many anti-Christian influences which were strong enough at any favourable moment to create a formidable reaction.

The paganism of Julian Julian took advantage of the lingering prejudice in favour of the old religion, and gave all his energy to promote a revival of paganism. But the paganism which Julian sought to restore was very different to any form of religion which the world had yet seen or known. In one important particular, at any rate, it differed from the ancient idea of a religion which confined special gods and special observances to particular countries. Julian's paganism was to be a catholic paganism, and in this, as in other elements, the influence of Christianity may be traced.

He accepted the Greek and Roman polytheism, and the Homeric Olympus, but he allegorised these conceptions after the manner of Alexandrian philosophers. He acknowledged, indeed, a supreme eternal cause of the universe; but that cause was invisible and inaccessible to the human intellect, and was only to be reached by the ministers and interpreters of the supreme deity, known to men by the familiar names of Jupiter, Mars, Minerva, or Venus. Lastly, the celestial bodies were, he held, rightfully objects of worship; amongst them the Sun held sovereignty, and was in a special sense the favourite divinity of Julian.

Such was the religion which Julian attempted

to oppose to Christianity. It awoke no enthusiasm, because it contained no principle. It made no response to human needs or to the human conscience. Julian, pure-minded and even ascetic in his own views and life, was disappointed to find that the revival of paganism only meant renewed license to indulge in the coarse ritual of the heathen gods.

The two directions in which Julian delighted to make a display of his convictions were, a profuse expenditure on sacrifices to the gods, and an exaggerated devotion to those philosophers and mystics who had been his teachers and religious guides. So bitter was the resentment which he felt against the Christians, that any cult or worship which they opposed was taken under his protection.

This feeling became the occasion of one of the most remarkable events in his reign. Because a Christian prophecy had foretold the utter destruction of the Temple at Jerusalem, and had declared against its restoration, Julian determined to rebuild the Temple. He assumed a friendly attitude towards the Jews, for no other reason except that they were enemies of the Christians.

<small>Julian's attempt to rebuild the Temple at Jerusalem</small>

What follows is attested not only by the Christian writers, Ambrose, Chrysostom and Gregory Nazianzen, but by a more impartial witness, the heathen historian Ammianus Marcellinus.

The Jews hastened with great alacrity to carry out the emperor's wish. Men and delicate women, rich and poor alike, vied with each other in preparing the foundations of the Temple. 'But,' says Ammianus, 'whilst Alypius, assisted by the governor of the province, urged with vigour and diligence the execution of the work, horrible balls of fire breaking out near the foundations with frequent and reiterated attacks rendered the place from time to time inaccessible to the scorched and blasted workmen, and the victorious element continuing in this manner obstinately and resolutely bent, as it were, to drive them to a distance, the undertaking was abandoned.'

We leave the story as we find it: whatever explanations may be offered, few historical incidents are better authenticated, and few are more significant.

Julian had persuaded himself that his mission was to destroy Christianity. But he did not propose to Julian abstains from persecution persecute, both because he was not naturally cruel, and because persecution as a political measure had been tried and failed. It had increased the number of martyrs, deepened the enthusiasm for the faith, and drawn fresh adherents by the attraction of danger. So Julian determined not to persecute; the 'Galilæans,' as he contemptuously terms the Christians, were only to be deprived of those favourable exemptions from taxation and civic duty granted them by Constantine. They were to restore or rebuild the pagan temples which they had destroyed; they were to render back the sites on which the temples stood, and the sacred vessels which they contained.

But whatever resolve Julian might make about refraining from persecution, he soon found that the process of destroying Christianity involved it. His measures as to the restoration of pagan temples became the occasion of cruel and irritating persecution. In many cases churches had risen on the sites of temples, and the temples could not be rebuilt except at enormous expense. The zeal of provincial magistrates and populations carried out what they conceived to be the emperor's wish, by the oppression of many Christians; if the Christian was quite ruined, Julian was ready with his sneer, 'It is the condition which their Master called "blessed."'

Persecution becomes inevitable

Another curious and petty mode of persecution, and one which raises an interesting question, was the prohibition to Christian teachers of the great classical works of Greek and Roman authors. 'If they do not believe the gods,' he decreed, 'let them not read the books which describe their deeds.'

Christians debarred from reading the classics

Julian's object was doubtless to lower the standard of Christian education and to reduce the Galilæans to the status of a despised and illiterate sect. Even pagan historians feel a sense of shame in recording this unjust and illiberal measure. St. Augustine speaks of it in indignant terms. In a fine passage of the *De Civitate Dei* addressed to those who formed *a priori* schemes about the Advent of Christ, and tried to round off the number of persecutions, so as to make them tally with their theories, he asks: 'Is not he a persecutor of the Church who prohibits a liberal education?'[1] The Christian response to these measures was a noble one. Within a few months, works were composed by Christian scholars setting forth the history and the verities of Christianity in dialogues or poems modelled on the style of Homer, Euripides, or Plato.

---

[1] An ipse non est ecclesiam persecutus qui Christianos liberales literas docere ac discere vetuit?—*De Civ. Dei*, xviii. 52.

This striking and unexampled effort in literature has had no slight influence in deciding the future of Christian education. It is in great measure owing to the position taken by Gregory Nazianzen, Basil of Cæsarea, and other great scholars of this epoch, that Christianity is not a narrow enthusiasm, but a Church divinely built upon a foundation broader than all human knowledge.

But the opposite view, condemnatory of all pagan literature and its influence, found vigorous defenders in this age as it has at other epochs. The depreciation of secular learning has been an animating principle in schools of Christian thought as widely opposed in time and characteristics as the monasticism of Egypt and the Evangelical school of the eighteenth century. The historian Socrates found it necessary to put forth an elaborate defence of teaching from the great pagan writers. 'Christ,' he says, 'has taught us to become approved money-changers' (an expression not elsewhere found) 'in order that we may prove all things and hold fast that which is good.' He cites also the instance of St. Paul and of 'the ancient doctors of the Church.'

Among the scholars who took part in this literary movement against the decree of Julian, and who claimed for Christianity the whole range of human learning, and refused to place it outside the highest results of Hellenic wisdom, the two Apollinarii, father and son, the one celebrated as a grammarian, the other as a rhetorician, were especially distinguished. The elder Apollinarius translated the Pentateuch and paraphrased the historical books of the Old Testament in Greek verse, using all the different metres, says Socrates, 'in order that no form of expression peculiar to the Greek language might be unknown or unheard of among Christians.'[1] The younger Apollinarius explained the teaching of the New Testament in the form of Platonic dialogues. But nowhere did Julian find a more able and strenuous resistance to his illiberal method of persecution than in his former fellow-students Gregory Nazianzen and Basil of Cæsarea. St. Gregory has left many poems, some descriptive of his own career and of contemporary events, some on abstract subjects of Christian thought, which, though falling short of classic correctness and beauty, have a charm of their own recognised by modern criticism.

St. Basil wrote a special address to the young, showing how they may study Greek literature to advantage. He takes the view already adopted by Eusebius, that all that is good in pagan literature was an echo of the inspired teaching of the Old Testament. The whole movement is full of interest, and suggests modern parallels in many points; with Synesius of Cyrene, for instance, there is the same tendency to push classic influence and modes of thought to an extreme which is observable in some phases of the Renaissance in Europe.

Julian's brief reign of eighteen months (from November 361 to June 363) was divided between a residence at Constantinople, a residence at Antioch, and his campaign on the Euphrates against the Persians. It would lie beyond the limits of our subject to go minutely into the details of Julian's active and interest-

[1] Socr. Bk. iii. ch.16.

ing career. It is enough to say that, notwithstanding his self-denial and energy as a ruler, and his military skill and brilliant rhetoric, troubles grew thick upon him.

At Antioch the greater part of the population was hostile to him, and he was exposed to petty annoyances of looks or muttered words which it was impossible to restrain or to punish. Julian was drawn more and more into the hateful necessity of persecution. Christians were excluded from civil employment in the imperial service. Soldiers who declined to take part in the idolatrous rites with which Julian surrounded the military life were put to death. The great temple of Apollo near Antioch was burnt to the ground, probably by accident; but Julian attributed the calamity to the fanaticism of the Christians. The order was given to demolish Christian churches. Several Christians were brought to trial, and were cruelly tortured and slain. Their constancy amazed and baffled their judges. One, Theodoret by name, in the midst of his tortures calmly prophesied the death of his judge; and of the emperor he said: 'An unknown hand shall take his life, and his body shall lie unburied in a foreign land.' Within a few days the first part of the prophecy was fulfilled. Count Julius, Theodoret's judge and a near kinsman of the emperor, died in agonies. The rest of the prophecy lingered in men's minds till it was fulfilled in the Assyrian deserts.

Julian at Antioch

It is not necessary to describe at large Julian's disastrous campaign on the Euphrates and the Tigris. Nor does that campaign immediately affect the history of the Church except so far as it terminated the career of her last pagan persecutor.

Julian's last campaign and death

Julian had proved himself a brilliant commander in his Gaulish campaigns, and in his daring march for empire from the Rhine to the Danube. In the present expedition his old soldierly qualities remained, but as a general he made fatal mistakes. At the instigation of a Persian spy he burnt his ships and provisions on the Tigris, marched into the heart of the waterless deserts, was there abandoned by his treacherous adviser, and exposed to the onslaught of the enemy's cavalry. After some days of unspeakable hardships and privations Julian determined on a retreat. In one of the skirmishes with a body of Persian horse he rushed unarmed to the front and was fatally wounded. A scream of agony escaped him, which, so far as it shaped itself into articulate words, was interpreted to mean, 'O Galilæan, thou hast conquered!' or else, 'O Sun god, thou hast deceived me!' The scholar will recognise that in Greek the two sentences would have a far closer similarity of sound than in English.

Such was the end of Julian, and such the success of his attack on Christianity. In some ways this great trial of the Church was not without its results for good —the removal of dangerous exemptions from ecclesiastics, the cutting down of unseemly state and wealth in the Church, the spread of Christian teaching by the partial assumption of it into his system by Julian, the purification and strengthening of the Church by the excision of weak and cowardly members.

CHAPTER VIII.

ST. BASIL AND ST. GREGORY.

It is a relief to turn from Julian to his two fellow-students in the schools of Athens—Gregory Nazianzen and Basil. The careers of these two noble champions of the faith against the influence of pagan and Arian emperors make an instructive and stirring contrast to the life and work of Julian.

Gregory and Basil were born about 330. Both were natives of Cappadocia; the parents of Basil living at Cæsarea, then the capital of the province; those of Gregory at the little town of Nazianzus in the south-west of Cappadocia, of which place Gregory's father was Bishop.

The life-long friendship began when Basil and Gregory were schoolfellows together at Cæsarea, under the tutorship of Carterius, afterwards, it is thought, the instructor of Chrysostom, and always tenderly loved and remembered in after days by Gregory. From Cæsarea in Cappadocia, Gregory and his brother Cæsarius—afterwards a celebrated physician—passed to the city of the same name in Palestine to pursue the study of rhetoric. Shortly before that time the empress Helena had discovered, or believed she had discovered, the true Cross on Calvary, and the young students at Cæsarea would doubtless visit at Jerusalem the noble church which had been lately consecrated on the spot. Still eager in the pursuit of knowledge, Gregory went to Alexandria

Early life of Gregory and Basil

then the seat of the most refined culture and the most advanced learning of the age. After a short residence at Alexandria he became anxious to visit a city of still older renown and greater memories. Like Julian, Gregory was attracted to the schools of Athens, which was still the eye of Greece, the centre of Hellenic culture.

At Athens Gregory and Basil met again. It is amusing to read how Gregory saved his old friend from the annoyance of rough practical jokes, to which freshmen were exposed at Athens as they have been at more modern seats of learning. As fellow-students they lived in the closest intimacy, sharing one room, studying the same books, and stimulating each other to aim at the highest ideal of Christian scholarship. Here Basil especially became intimately acquainted with Julian. They studied together, as Basil afterwards reminds the emperor, not only the models of classical eloquence and poetry, but also the Holy Scriptures. It is interesting to remember in after life this intercourse of the scholar emperor and the scholar saint.

Student life at Athens

Gregory and Basil achieved the highest reputation at Athens. Distinguished and lucrative careers were open to either of them, but each resolved to devote all to the cause of Christ. Each, however, had his temptations and his weaknesses.

The classical writers of Greece and Rome still possessed a great, perhaps a dangerous, attraction for Gregory. As for Basil, a wise and loving elder sister—Macrina—detected an intellectual pride which kept him back from entire self-

Basil adopts a monastic life

abandonment to Christ. A letter of his brother has been preserved, which implies that Basil had adopted the manner and airs of a fine gentleman. But the spirit of devotion prevailed, and Basil determined to retire from the world and live a secluded life with a community of like-minded brethren. First, he visited the celebrated hermits and ascetic communities in Palestine, Syria and Egypt; then he resolved to carry out his plan of life in a quiet spot on the banks of the river Iris in Pontus.

This age of Church history was the age of great experiments in the Christian life; and Basil's experiment, with its teaching for the future, deserves to be carefully noted.

Basil decided for the life of a community as against the solitary life with much reason. 'What discipline of humility, of pity, or of patience,' he says, 'can exist if there be no one on whom those virtues are to be practised?' In a letter to Gregory, inviting him to join his society, Basil gives a charming account of his monastic home, with an appreciation of natural scenery, which seems to be a gift of Christianity. 'My mountain is lofty, covered with thick woods, watered on the north with clear streams. At its foot extends a vast plain made fruitful by the mountain rivulets, so closed in by stream and mountain, as to make it like an island.' 'And it was,' he said, with recollections of his Homer, 'as beautiful as the island of Calypso.'

Gregory, however, had duties at Nazianzus in assisting his aged father in his episcopal labours, helping too in domestic management, in which he finds intolerable difficulties. 'To govern servants,' he says, 'is a very net of ruin.' He visited Basil, however, and was charmed by the scene of mingled industry and devotion. Soon after this Gregory was ordained, not voluntarily, but, as happened sometimes in those days, suddenly by compulsion on the part of the congregation. Such forced ordinations—we hear too of forced baptisms and of forced episcopal consecrations—are among the most remarkable ecclesiastical incidents at this period of Church history. It is another instance of the Church feeling her way to a more perfect discipline.

Gregory assists his father at Nazianzus

Once ordained Gregory made it a principle to fulfil his duties as priest to the utmost of his powers. The address which he delivered on pastoral work, afterwards amplified into a treatise, has remained a standard authority on this subject through all the Christian centuries. Soon the terror of Julian's accession fell upon the Church. His cruel and illiberal edict against the use of classics by Christian teachers was deeply felt by the two friends. But a more bitter and nearer visitation was at hand. Julian passed through Cæsarea on his march to Persia. He found a Christian population, and the last heathen temple levelled to the ground. He levied an enormous fine on the city, but was nobly resisted by Basil. Then he left Cæsarea, threatening a terrible vengeance on his return from the Persian expedition.

St. Basil became Bishop of Cæsarea, a position of great and wide importance and supremacy. By him St. Gregory was appointed Bishop of Sasima, a small and unattractive spot, but chosen as the seat of a Bishopric that it might be a sort of eccle-

St. Basil Bishop of Cæsarea

siastical outpost in a dispute on the question of episcopal jurisdiction. This position was distasteful to St. Gregory, and produced a coolness for a while between him and St. Basil.

Basil's weak and tortured frame was the first to succumb to death. His episcopal rule had been surrounded with difficulties and dissensions, but his splendid resolution triumphed over all. He was threatened by the emperor Valens, but his noble Christian courage not only compelled the emperor to retract his edict of banishment, but preserved for his city the purity of the Catholic faith.

St. Gregory was summoned to the see of Constantinople, where he presided at the œcumenical council held in the year 381. He had a hard fight against the Arian faction in Constantinople under the emperor Valens, but better times came with Theodosius. Eventually St. Gregory left Constantinople, after delivering an impressive valedictory address, and retired to his native Nazianzus, where he died in about the sixtieth year of his life.

The teaching of these two lives

The life and works and examples of these two great Saints have left an indelible impression on the Church. Their history, of which our limits have afforded only a meagre outline, is full of deep and modern interest. In the course of it important questions were raised, such as the Christian study of the classics, the pastoral duties of the Christian minister, the ties of friendship and religion, the attitude of a Catholic Bishop to an unbelieving emperor—questions which we may learn to decide in the clear light of ancient ecclesiastical history, and by the eloquent words and devoted lives of two of the greatest and saintliest of holy and heroic men whose linked memories are a heritage of the Church.

CHAPTER IX.

JOVIAN, VALENTINIAN, VALENS.

THE death of Julian left the army in a miserable and even desperate position. It became necessary to elect a new general and a new emperor. For a while it seemed possible that the spirit of faction would seal the ruin of the unfortunate expedition. But while the leaders of the army were discussing rival claims, a shout was raised in the rear in favour of Jovianus, an officer of medium rank. The favourable but almost accidental cry of a few soldiers was carried from rank to rank and resulted in the choice of Jovian as emperor, an election furthered, it is said, by the confusion occasioned by the similarity of sound between the names of Julian and Jovian, which created a momentary belief among the veterans of the late emperor that their favourite leader had returned to life.

<small>Jovian elected emperor</small>

The emperor thus elected by a knot of the inferior officers and common soldiers of a retreating army was a Christian, a circumstance which seems to imply that the sentiments of Julian, and his bitter hostility to Christianity, had not deeply penetrated the mass of his soldiers. Many signs pointed in the same direction throughout the empire. Altars which had smoked with innumerable victims were left cold and dishonoured. The massive and half-finished remains of magnificent heathen temples stood witnessing to the momentous change. In the army the pagan emblems once more gave place to the Christian symbol of the *labarum*.

<small>The change from paganism</small>

The new emperor had a task of immense peril and difficulty before him. He had to achieve the rescue of his famished and despondent troops from the interminable deserts, and from the pursuit of the enemy. Gibbon has truly marked this as an important epoch in the decline and fall of the Roman empire, when Jovian concluded a shameful, though perhaps a necessary, treaty with the Persian monarch, by which he abandoned five provinces and the impregnable fortress of Nisibis to the victorious Sapor. It is not, however, true to assert, as Gibbon does, that this was the first occasion on which the limits of empire were contracted.

The impenetrable silence in which the Persian expedition had been involved was at length broken by the news of Julian's death, and the succession of Jovian. That news was variously received. At Antioch it produced the liveliest satisfaction. There the Christian emperor was welcomed with delight. St. Jerome describes his boyish recollections of the scene when the news reached his native town. He witnessed the desertion of the temples, and the sudden cessation of heathen sacrifice. He records, too, the saying of a pagan bystander which he overheard: 'Why do the Christians call their God long-suffering? Here He has not lost a single day in taking vengeance.'

It is unhappily characteristic of the history of

Christianity, that the removal of external pressure or persecution opens the field to internal dispute. Jovian was surrounded by the advocates of the different Christian parties, each eager to secure the imperial interest for his own faction. He took the wisest possible course. He summoned Athanasius to his presence, and asked his counsel. It was a policy which disappointed a crowd of Arian Bishops who had expected another Constantius, and whose sole object was to obtain a share of court favour.

<small>Jovian's Church policy</small>

St. Athanasius had written to Jovian, referring him to the Nicene Creed as the standard of faith, and on his arrival at court had urged the emperor to adopt a policy of toleration and religious freedom. Consequently both Arianism and pagan philosophy, no longer basking in the sun of imperial protection, began to pine away and disappear. Jovian proceeded to restore to the Churches, with some restrictions, those favours and immunities which they had enjoyed before the reign of Julian.

Altogether the firm and prudent attitude of this rude soldier suddenly elevated to supreme power was a precedent which promised well for the future relations of Church and State. We seem here to have an admirable adjustment between those relations, neither displacing the other, but each regardful of mutual interests; the empire supporting and drawing spiritual strength from the Church, and in spiritual matters ruling and judging by the advice and wisdom of her chief pastor; the Church in all temporal things submitting herself to Cæsar's rule.

But the career of Jovian was destined to be short

and tragic. The difficulties of his position seemed to be surmounted. He was passing though Asia Minor on his way to Constantinople. His wife Charito with her youthful son was hastening to meet him, when the tidings met her that her husband was no more. He had reached a halting place, Dadastana, on the confines of Bithynia and Galatia; the night was intensely cold, his lodgings happened to be in a newly built house, the walls of the chamber in which he slept were damp and a large fire was lighted. In the morning the emperor was discovered to be dead. Either the exhalation from the damp walls or the fumes of the charcoal had been fatal to him.

<small>The death of Jovian</small>

St. Augustine in the 'City of God' remarks: 'It was well for divine wisdom to load Constantine with prosperity, to show it can recompense its servants; it was well too to smite Jovian in spite of his piety, that men should learn not to follow the Christian faith in the hope of earthly gain.'

For ten days the Roman empire was without a head. Several names were proposed, but none met with the unanimous approval of the high officials who had met in council, until the name of Valentinian was mentioned. Valentinian, the son of a distinguished general, had himself served with merit on the Rhine and in the campaigns against Persia. He was a Christian and had run some risk in consequence of his sincerity in the reign of Julian. The heathen historian, Ammianus Marcellinus, praises the proved courage of Valentinian and the purity and simplicity of his life. But one dark stain, which the

<small>Choice of a new emperor</small>

possession of supreme power rendered darker and more injurious, marked the character of Valentinian. He was subject to fits of furious and indiscriminating passion which hurried him into acts of inexcusable cruelty. The administration of the empire under this prince became a reign of terror. A brighter side of his policy, which especially commended itself to his heathen biographer, was his impartiality in all matters of religion. We shall see, however, how impossible and, indeed, how criminal it is for a Christian ruler to preserve this attitude when the usurpations of heresy demanded the interference of the civil power.

The election of Valentinian was confirmed by the army. It is a sign of the confusion and indecision of religious thought at this crisis that the ceremony was deferred until the arrival of a day esteemed propitious in the light of pagan superstition. In obedience to the demands of his soldiers Valentinian appointed a colleague—not, however, one who would have been the choice of others—his own brother, the feeble and incompetent Valens. In the division of empire Valentinian took for his share the more difficult task of governing the West with Milan for his capital; the East, with its centre at Constantinople, was left to Valens.

<small>Valens</small>

Valentinian did not entirely reverse the policy of Julian towards the Christian Church. He withdrew, indeed, from the heathen temples the Christian endowments conferred on them by Julian, but he did not restore them to the Church. The Christian priesthood was no longer permitted to carry

<small>Valentinian's Church policy</small>

with it immunity from taxation—the dangerous gift of Constantine.

In Church questions he endeavoured to separate himself entirely from religious controversy. When he was met on his way to Italy by a deputation from the Bishops of the Hellespont and of Bithynia, requesting him to summon a council: 'I am but one of the laity (or people),' he said, 'and have therefore no right to interfere in these transactions. Let the Bishops to whom such matters appertain assemble where they please.'[1] It is important for us in these days to take note how impossible it is for a Christian ruler to adhere to such resolutions.

Almost immediately after his arrival at Milan Valentinian found a state of affairs in the Christian Church which demanded his intervention. Auxentius, Bishop of Milan, had throughout his career belonged to the Arian party, and it was by the influence of the Arian Constantius that he had been placed in his see. But now that Arianism had ceased to be fashionable at the imperial court in the West, Auxentius professed a change, and declared himself on the Catholic side. This sudden and suspicious conversion failed to secure the confidence of the Christians in Milan, who took up an attitude of mistrust and resistance. At that time Hilary, the celebrated Bishop of Poitiers, was visiting the Churches of Italy with the view of reconciling with their flocks certain Bishops who in an unguarded moment had subscribed the erring Creed of Ariminum. In many cases such reconciliation was easy and delightful; the Bishops had erred from ignorance rather

Non-intervention impossible

[1] Sozomen, vi.-vii.

than from any deliberate opposition to the Nicene Creed. But at Milan Hilary took the side of the Catholic Christians in their resistance to the time-serving Bishop Auxentius.

Valentinian wished to stand aloof. But his counsellors forced upon him the necessity of putting an end to a state of affairs which threatened the public peace. Accordingly, Valentinian commanded all Christian people to submit to Auxentius, and to frequent only the regularly consecrated churches. Discovering the impossibility of enforcing this decree, he next proposed a measure equally distasteful, and equally impracticable, namely, the appointment of a commission of Bishops and lay officials to settle the question. The end of the affair was that Auxentius gained so great an influence over the emperor that Hilary was ordered to quit Milan.

From Gaul, Hilary addressed a letter to Valentinian, in which he nobly maintains the independence of the Church in her own province, and the danger of seeking an unworthy alliance with the civil power. It is a model treatise on the true relations between Church and State.

Another incident, into which we shall not enter at length, presents some suggestive details to the Church historian.

On the death of Liberius, Bishop of Rome, the question of his successor gave rise to a fierce and even *An ecclesiastical dispute in Rome* sanguinary conflict between the partisans of Damasus and Ursinus, rival candidates for the see. In the end, the party of Damasus prevailed. But in the course of the contention, the authority of the civil governor had been overridden, the emperor himself had been appealed to. He intervened, but to little purpose indeed. The result was significant. An imperial officer had broken Valentinian's principle of non-interference. A rival power resting on popular choice had shown itself supreme in Rome. The prestige of the Christian pontiff seemed already to be a danger to the empire. A saying of Prætextatus, prefect of Rome, points to the growing sense of the episcopal power in that city: 'Make me Bishop of Rome,' he exclaimed, 'and I promise to become a Christian.'

Growth of the episcopal power in Rome

Another pagan, Ammianus Marcellinus, contrasts the dignity, the magnificence, and the luxury of the Bishop of Rome with the frugal, humble, and self-denying life of his provincial brethren. This glimpse at the history of the Roman Church will suffice at least to draw attention to one of the most intensely interesting lines of historical research—the growth and influence of the papal power.

Before we leave the history of Valentinian, an instance may be given of the tendency, the unconscious tendency of the Church to absorb within itself the powers of the world. A principal aim in Valentinian's government was to counteract ecclesiastical influence. Partly with this view he created a body of functionaries named *Defensores civitatum* (protectors of cities). These were placed in the several cities of the empire, charged with the duty of defending the popular rights and of redressing grievances. They were to be elected by the people, and confirmed in office by the emperor. The institution was intended to be a check on the popular authority of the Bishops. But before a generation had passed, the Bishop and clergy were associated in the election of this officer, who eventually became little else than the nominee and lieutenant of the Bishop.

There is little more in the reign of Valentinian that directly affects the Church. The ferocity of his character, which has been already mentioned, increased in intensity as he advanced in years. Instances are recorded, not only of cruelty, but of treacherous cruelty. The story is well known of the two pet bears which he kept in his own sleeping apartment, and to which he exposed condemned criminals to be torn in pieces under his own eyes.

The magistrates and officials in the provinces were ordered to carry out the same hard and cruel policy of suspicion and death. All this tended to augment the influence of the Church of Christ.

The Church a refuge from despotism

For everywhere men turned to the Church and to the episcopal rule, as the only refuge from the tyranny of the imperial government. In this way, without countenancing the thought of disloyalty, and without any consciously aggressive action, the Kingdom of God grew in power.

Some years before his death, Valentinian had nominated his son Gratian, then a boy eight years of age, to be his associate in empire with the title of Augustus. He expired in a fit of apoplexy, induced by a passionate interview with the ambassadors of the Quadi, a barbarous tribe with whom he was at war (375).

CHAPTER X.

VALENS—INVASION OF THE GOTHS.

THE East was regarded as the less arduous division of the world to govern; but Valens, brother and colleague of Valentinian, found himself entangled with difficulties from the first. While the threatening of a Persian war detained him in Syria, the news reached him of a formidable insurrection under Procopius in the western part of his dominions. Procopius, a kinsman of the emperor Julian, and at one time, it is said, designated as his successor, was considered too dangerous a subject to live. He escaped, however, the imperial officers who had been sent to arrest him, and found himself compelled to assume the purple rather than perish ignominiously as a rebel. He was soon surrounded by a considerable force. Perhaps we may trace in the first successes of Procopius renewed evidence of a pagan reaction.

Valens conquers Procopius

So formidable did the rising appear that Valens was eager to abdicate; but his officers disclaimed submission, and insisted on Valens giving battle to his rival. The field of Nacolia in Phrygia justified their resolution. Procopius was deserted by his officers, his troops listened to the persuasion of their old leaders, and the unfortunate Procopius, an emperor against his will, was captured and slain.

Valens had fallen under the influence of Eudoxius, the Arian Bishop of Constantinople. The religious interest of his reign lies, not in the struggle between

Christianity and paganism, but between Arianism and Catholic Christianity. The time had come when 'Chris-

An Arian persecution

tian love among the Churches looked the twin of heathen hate.' Everywhere pressure was laid on the orthodox Churches. Meletius, Bishop of Antioch, was driven into exile, and an Arian put in his place; in Alexandria the Arian Lucius was thrust into the see of Athanasius. An imperial order delivered over to pillage and the sword the monasteries of the Egyptian deserts. Many Christians who remained true to the Nicene faith were slain at Antioch and other cities of the East. A scene which took place at Edessa finely illustrates the Christian view of persecution. Valens had ordered a general massacre of the faithful assembled for worship in the 'martyry'[1] of St. Thomas in Edessa. A cordon of soldiers surrounded the church, when a poor woman bearing a little child tried to force her way into the congregation. Brought before the prefect and asked whither she was pressing, 'To the same place to which others are hastening,' she replied. 'Have you not heard that the prefect is about to put to death all who shall be found there?' 'Yes,' said the woman, 'and therefore I hasten that I may be present.' 'And whither are you dragging that little child?' said the prefect. 'That he also may be vouchsafed the honour of martyrdom,' was the mother's reply. Thus once more was the folly of persecution taught. It was vain to contend against a faith and against a community in which the women and little children were possessed of such calm courage.

The mind of Valens, too, was diverted from Christian

[1] Such was the name given to churches dedicated to martyrs.

persecution by a superstitious fear. It was a fashionable weakness of the day to dip into the secrets of the future by various devices. By one of these a revolving table and an alphabetical arrangement spelt out the names of destined dignitaries. Asked who should be the future emperor, the oracle gave forth the letters Th-e-o-d and then paused. By the voice of all the supreme power was promised to Theodorus, a person of some distinction. The designation was not only fatal to this Theodorus, but was a danger to all the unhappy persons who bore that name, or whose names began with the fatal letters.

Valens proceeded to put in force severe measures against all who professed or practised the arts of sorcery and magic. It is said that his zealous ministers contrived to include in this proscription sophists, neo-platonists and others whose sympathies were with the pagan system, and whose studious lives gave colour to the charge of divination. A story is told of St. Chrysostom in connexion with this imperial edict. Walking with a friend by the side of the Orontes he picked up a fragment of writing which to his horror he discovered to be part of a treatise on magic—a fatal possession. To fling it away or to keep it was equally dangerous. Fortunately he was not detected, but the incident made a deep impression on his mind.

An event now occurred which became a turning point in the history of the empire. For long different divisions of the Teutonic race had hung like a dark cloud on the borders of the Roman empire. Up to this time the Danube, strongly guarded by a succession of fortresses, had proved a sufficient

The Gothic invasion

barrier against the Gothic invasion. But now a new motive, rather a necessity for advance, pressed upon the Teutons. A fierce barbarian tribe of another race, the Turanian Huns, had swept down upon the Goths and forced them onwards. In countless hordes they stood on the northern banks of the Danube which flowed between them and the safe and fruitful plains of Mœsia, imploring permission to cross.

The Goths had in some measure come under the influence of Roman civilisation. Many of them had served in the imperial armies, and had carried home some lessons in the arts of peace and war. They must also have taken home the dangerous secret of the weakness of the empire and the declining valour and strength of Roman armies. In another respect they had grown akin to Rome. They had become Christians through the preaching of one of the greatest missionaries of our faith—Ulfilas, the latinised form of Wulfila or Wölfel. Ulfilas, a Goth, succeeded Theophilus, the first Bishop of the Goths, who had sat at the Nicene Council. His great work was the translation of the Scriptures into the language of the Goths. In order to accomplish this work it was necessary to compose an alphabet of twenty-four letters, four expressing sounds unknown to Greek or Latin. Fragments of this version are preserved, the most celebrated of which, the 'Codex Argenteus,' forms the most precious treasure of the University of Upsala. This 'superb codex' is written in gold and silver letters on a violet ground, it contains portions of the Gospels, and dates from the fifth or early in the sixth century. Ulfilas had subscribed the Creed

The conversion of the Goths

Gothic version of the Scriptures

of Ariminum, but his declared Arianism dates from a mission to Valens, from whom he petitioned assistance for the Christianised Goths in a feud against their still heathen brethren. Through the preaching of Ulfilas the Goths adopted an Arian type of Christianity, though it may be doubted whether the barbarian intellect grasped in any degree of accuracy the fine distinctions of the Arian teaching.

When the demand of the Goths to cross the Danube reached Valens, he hesitated for a while and then gave the permission. Their guide was Ulfilas. They claimed him as a second Moses to lead them across the stream to a land of promise.

The date of this important event is A.D. 376. Two conditions were exacted of the Goths: that they should deliver up their arms and their children. The latter were to be dispersed and brought up to civilisation among the cities of Asia. The terms were agreed to, but subsequent events soon rendered them inoperative. Their arms were for the most part retained by bribery, and victory restored the children to their parents. To permit the passage of the Goths was a fatal blunder on the part of Valens, but it tended to the strength and advance of the Christian cause. The officers of Valens added to the original blunder by their treatment of their Gothic allies. Markets were closed to them, food sold at an exorbitant price, and all the benefits of a fruitful land withheld. Meanwhile the Ostrogoths succeeded in crossing the Danube and joining their brethren the Visigoths.

The Goths cross the Danube

The seething discontent between the two nations broke out at Marcianopolis. A quarrel about rights of market ended in drawn swords and spilling of blood. A conflict followed in which the imperial forces were shamefully defeated by Fritigern and his victorious Goths. From that day the Goths were virtual rulers from the Danube to Constantinople. Their numbers were further augmented by a body of fellow-countrymen in the imperial service whom a studied insult turned against their masters.

The Goths occupy the imperial provinces

When intelligence of this threatening state of affairs reached Valens, he resolved to leave Antioch and meet the danger—for once unseasonably brave. Two incompetent generals, 'anhelantes quidem altius sed imbelles,' says Ammianus, were sent in advance.

The armies met near the southernmost mouth of the Danube. A fierce, sanguinary, and undecisive engagement damped the spirit of the barbarians. They were besieged in their camp and might have been reduced by famine, when an unlooked-for diversion occurred by a fresh incursion of Gothic tribes. The Roman general raised the siege, and the two branches of the Visigoths and Ostrogoths, uniting their forces, flooded the provinces south of the Danube with rapine and violence.

Valens had summoned to his aid his nephew Gratian, now covered with fresh glory from the defeat of the hosts of the Alemanni on the plains of Alsace. But his rash impatience, the scornful clamours of Constantinople, and some trifling successes of his generals urged Valens to instant action. He marched at the head of his army to Hadrianople, near which place the enemy were encamped. The long march of twelve miles was performed in the heat of the day. Fritigern increased his advantage by carrying on nego-

The battle of Hadrianople A.D. 378

tiations, while the men stood to their arms under the burning rays of the sun. The battle commenced with a rash attack made by Bacurius the Iberian, at the head of a body of archers. As they retreated, the Gothic horse swept like a thunder-bolt from the mountain, carrying all before them. The infantry alone stood their ground, but were surrounded and cut to pieces by the victorious Goths. 'In no battle since Cannæ,' says Ammianus Marcellinus, 'has such complete destruction befallen the Roman arms.'

There is some uncertainty about the fate of Valens; according to one account he was fatally wounded by an arrow while fighting in the ranks, and fell among the undistinguishable dead. Others state that he took refuge with a few attendants in a countryman's cottage, which was set on fire by a band of Goths who were ignorant of the prize which they might have secured. One only of the refugees escaped the flames to tell the tale.

Death of Valens

His pagan biographer gives Valens the praise of being a firm and faithful friend, stern in discipline, inflexibly just: on the other hand he accuses him of avarice, cruelty, and ignorance. He had the faults as well as some of the virtues of a tyrant. The Gothic war which withdrew him from the persecution of the Catholic Christians, seemingly the grave disaster of his reign, proved in the end to be the gain of the Church.

CHAPTER XI.

GRATIAN—ST. AMBROSE.

GRATIAN was sixteen years old when he succeeded his father. The army took the initiative in giving him as a colleague his younger brother Valentinian II.

The story of these ill-fated princes is closely connected with the name of the great Churchman who was at this time Bishop of Milan—St. Ambrose, who ranks with St. Jerome, St. Augustine, and Gregory the Great, as one of the four famous doctors of the Latin Church. His father was a Roman of distinguished position, who rose to high official rank as prefect of the Gauls, a term which includes Britain, Spain, France, and the Rhine countries. His birthplace is unknown. One or two stories of his boyhood have been remembered, of which the best known is one which is common to the childhood of Pindar and of Plato as well as of Ambrose. It narrates that a swarm of bees settled upon the head of the sleeping infant, some of them crawling over his parted lips. It was thought to be an omen of his future eloquence.

The childhood of Ambrose

When Ambrose grew up to manhood he took to the study and practice of law in Rome. There he attracted the notice of Anienus Petronius Probus, prefect of the city and a Christian, who introduced Ambrose into his court as secretary, and afterwards appointed him consular magistrate of Liguria and Aemilia, of which provinces Milan was the chief place, and therefore the official residence of Ambrose.

It is said that as Probus dismissed him to his post, he used the prophetic words: 'Vade, age non ut judex sed ut Episcopus' (Go, act not as judge but as bishop). If we remember the condition of the empire at this time, and the general character of the magistracy under Valentinian, this will be thought to be a significant direction. It points to a contrast between the acknowledged gentleness of the Christian and the harshness of the imperial rule; and it points to the fusion and mutual reaction on each other of the two kingdoms in the administration of justice.

<small>Ambrose goes to Milan</small>

The very remarkable scene which follows makes it clear that Ambrose had commended himself to the people of Milan as a just and clement magistrate.

On the death of Auxentius it became necessary to appoint a successor. The Bishops of the province were assembled for that purpose. The great basilica of Milan was crowded from end to end with an expectant throng. Ambrose was present in his capacity as magistrate to preserve order. The discussion of the electing Bishops was prolonged; when suddenly a voice from the assembly in the Church broke out, 'Ambrosius Episcopus' (Ambrose is Bishop). The cry was like the voice of a child, but it seemed to be inspired. The idea, strange and impossible as it might be thought, was taken up with acclamations. No one was more astonished and bewildered than Ambrose himself; as soon as the intention became evidently serious, he repudiated it by every means in his power. It was, indeed, a singular choice; Ambrose, though an earnest Christian and the son of Christian parents, was not even baptized. A statement of that fact might

<small>Ambrose elected Bishop</small>

have seemed a sufficient bar to his elevation, but it was impossible to resist the tide of popular feeling. Ambrose used every expedient to avert the act; he tried to make himself out to be cruel, to be unjust, to be licentious even. Then he fled from the city, and when he was discovered and brought back, for a time he concealed himself in the house of a friend. But the popular choice was approved by Valentinian, and at length Ambrose yielded. He was baptized and consecrated Bishop within ten days.

At every moment in the ecclesiastical history of this period interesting questions start up, which would take long to discuss fully. What are we to say for instance from the Church point of view of these two things,—of the deferred baptism of St. Ambrose, and of the irregular election? The first is an occurrence not only not rare, but even usual at this epoch. We find it in the case of St. Augustine and St. Chrysostom, as well as in the case of Constantine, of Constantius, and of Valentinian II. Here we only stop to remark that the practice seems to have arisen at least partly from an exaggerated feeling of the effect of post-baptismal sin, or perhaps we may say from a false practical inference from the effects of Holy Baptism.

As to the election of St. Ambrose, it was undoubtedly irregular, but it was not without parallel at this epoch. At Constantinople Nectarius, a layman, was hurriedly and against his wish pressed into the episcopate; and at Cæsarea in Cappadocia Eusebius, a layman of distinction, was elected to the Bishopric, much to the annoyance of Julian, who complained of having been deprived of the services of a capable magistrate.

In the case of Ambrose it was an instance either of quick-sighted popular intuition, or possibly of the intervention of some friends who knew him well and saw in him the solution of a pressing difficulty.

It is needless to say how completely the choice was justified. As a Bishop St. Ambrose was wise and tender and fearless. All these qualities were needed and exercised in turn.

One of the most touching episodes in his life is his intercourse with the young emperor Gratian. Between these two a great affection subsisted. Gratian writing to St. Ambrose with a request to be furnished with arguments in defence of the Catholic faith, addresses him as 'parens.' In answer Ambrose sent to Gratian two books 'De Fide' (concerning the faith) to which three others were added. This treatise is still extant, and is not the least valuable of the works of St. Ambrose.

St. Ambrose and Gratian

A quotation from Gratian's letter may be cited as a proof of this friendly, indeed loving, intercourse: 'I desire much,' he writes, 'to enjoy the bodily presence of him whose recollection I carry with me, and with whom I am present in spirit. Therefore, hasten to me, religious priest of God, to teach me the doctrine of the true faith.' .... Then at the end of the letter: 'May the Deity preserve you for many years, my father, worshipper of the eternal God, Jesus Christ whom we worship.'

The effect of this influence on Gratian may be traced in some of the laws passed by him, and in some of his public acts. He was the first of the Roman emperors to refuse the robe of office presented to the emperor as

Pontifex Maximus, or high priest of the pagan worship. He appears, however, to have retained the title on his coins. Among other acts which showed Gratian's zeal for the Christian faith was the removal of the altar of Victory from the senate house at Rome, and the confiscation of the endowments of the temple of Victory. His laws in respect to the stage, to apostasy from Christianity, and in favour of exemption of the poorer clergy from taxation, point in the same direction.

Gratian's policy in Church matters

The winning qualities of Gratian, his cultivated abilities, his graces of person and manner were unhappily associated with an indolence and a want of high capacity which rendered him unfit to govern in difficult times. In a rising under Maximus which spread from Britain to Gaul he was deserted by his troops and perished by a miserable and ignominious death.

The wisest, and in some respects the bravest, act of Gratian was the nomination of the great Theodosius as emperor of the East after the disastrous battle of Hadrianople (A.D. 378), in which, as narrated in the last chapter, Valens and two-thirds of his vast army were destroyed by the victorious Goths.

Theodosius was a Spaniard, the son of an illustrious general of the same name, who under Valentinian had suppressed a dangerous revolt in Africa. The elder Theodosius had subsequently been put to death, probably by the permission at least of Gratian. When, therefore, in the extremity of danger Gratian summoned to his aid the great capacity of Theodosius, he took a step which might have proved fatal to himself.

Theodosius

His confidence, however, was justified. Theodosius became the friend, and before long the brother-in-law, of Gratian by his marriage with his half-sister Galla. Afterwards he avenged his death by the defeat of the usurper Maximus.

For the ecclesiastical historian the election of Theodosius was in every way a memorable event. Under Gratian and Theodosius for the first time the civilised world was governed by orthodox Christian princes, and the relations between the great and powerful emperor Theodosius and the brave and pious Bishop of Milan exhibit in the most picturesque and instructive way the working out of some great problems in Church and State. The scenes in which these two great men took a leading part are among the most famous and the most familiar of historical events.

<small>St. Ambrose and Theodosius</small>

One of these was a tragedy of which the first act took place at Thessalonica. It was during the celebration of the games of the circus in that city. A favourite charioteer had been detained in prison on account of a shameful crime by Botheric, commander of the imperial troops. The pleasure-loving citizens, fired by resentment, made a furious attack upon Botheric, whom together with some of his principal officers they slew, and treated their bodies with inhuman indignities. It was a gross and open affront to the imperial honour, and Theodosius, whose gravest fault was a passionate disposition, determined on a speedy and bloody vengeance. He even sanctioned the use of treachery. The inhabitants were invited to an exhibition of games in the circus. The whole space was filled with eager spectators, when on a given signal

<small>The massacre at Thessalonica</small>

the soldiers of Theodosius rushed in and perpetrated an indiscriminate massacre.

This base and cruel action sent a thrill of horror through the Christian world. St. Ambrose was over- *Repentance of Theodosius* whelmed with indignant grief. He addressed a letter to Theodosius urging him to repent. He pointed out to the emperor that it was impossible for him to celebrate the Eucharist in the presence of one who was stained with recent and unrepented crime. Theodosius showed true greatness of soul in submitting to the rebuke of St. Ambrose. He openly did penance, appearing in the basilica of Milan stripped of his imperial robes, in the dress and posture of a suppliant. Theodoret, a later writer, makes a dramatic addition to the scene, which is set forth in a picture by Vandyke in the National Gallery, in which the emperor is represented as imploring admission into the Church on the Christmas festival, while St. Ambrose with his attendant priests and ministers, holding the Cross on high, refuses permission to enter.

The incident is, however, sufficiently marked and significant without any such doubtful additions. It was one which brought out the noblest traits in the characters both of the emperor and the bishop. It is no record of priestly pride or pomp, as Gibbon misrepresents it. Of that there is no trace in the letter or demeanour of St. Ambrose. Rather, it is a remarkable and striking proof of the advance of the power of Christ, both in its gentleness and in its strength. When a priest of His Church could be found fearless enough, and Christ-like enough to bear such testimony before great kings for the sake of Christ, and an emperor sufficiently obedient to the law of Christ, to acknowledge the guilt of a great political sin before his people, we have an acknowledgment of moral restraint, impossible in the days, we do not say of Nero or Caligula, but of Augustus or Diocletian. It was an act which marked an epoch in the history of the Church of Christ.

Other events in the life of Ambrose must be indicated rather than described. In those wild and turbulent times, there was frequent need of the exercise of Christian charity. When the barbarian Goths, after the defeat of Valens, carried off many Christian prisoners, St. Ambrose devoted all the resources of the Church to obtain their ransom. For that purpose he sold even the Eucharistic vessels. Deep as was his reverence for that Holy Sacrament, and for all connected with it, he held the lives and liberty of human beings to be more sacred still. 'If the Blood of Christ,' he said, 'redeemed their souls, should not the vessels which held that Blood be used to redeem their bodies? Again, we trace the same high courage which enabled him to brave the anger of the great Theodosius, when on two occasions he entered unprotected the camp of the usurper Maximus on an embassy of peace; or when he resisted with all his authority the Arianising policy of the empress Justina, mother of Valentinian II.

The history of that resistance is exciting and full of incident. Justina had demanded one of the Milan churches for the use of the Arians. St. Ambrose with a high sense of the sacredness of his trust refused his assent. The population of Milan

The empress Justina

was for the most part Catholic, and took the side of the Bishop. At Easter the quarrel came to a climax. Ambrose was ordered to appear before the council. He obeyed the summons, but the surging crowd of citizens who followed him to the palace made it dangerous to lay upon him any penalty, or to enforce any command. Eventually the ministers of Valentinian were compelled to appeal to Ambrose to guard the person of the emperor, and to calm the city. When the immediate danger was over, the imperial court returned to their rash and short-sighted policy of opposition to Ambrose. When the rumour spread that he was to be driven from the city, the people rose in defence of their beloved Bishop, who took refuge in the basilica, and there remained guarded by the devoted population until the court once more gave way. The weariness and suspense of this watch in the basilica were cheered by addresses from Ambrose, and by singing hymns—a practice said to have been then first introduced into the West from the Eastern Church.

It is also narrated that during this crisis the bodies of two martyrs, Gervasius and Protasius, were discovered beneath the pavement of the church, through a revelation to St. Ambrose; and St. Augustine, speaking of these days of excitement, confidently appeals to the people of Milan as witnesses of miracles wrought in confirmation of the Catholic faith.[1]

It was soon after these events that Justina, notwithstanding what had passed, implored the aid and

---

[1] *De Civitate Dei*, xxii. 8.

intercession of St. Ambrose against Maximus, who was rapidly marching upon Italy. This mission of Ambrose was ineffectual. But Maximus soon afterwards was defeated and slain by Theodosius.

Valentinian II. too came under the influence of St. Ambrose, who won him over to the orthodox faith. And when a cruel and treacherous death overtook the youthful emperor at Vienne in Gaul, Ambrose sincerely mourned him. He had died unbaptized, deferring the rite in accordance with a prevalent usage of the time. But St. Ambrose consoled his relatives with the thought that 'the desire for baptism was equivalent to the act, and that he had been baptized in his piety, as martyrs in their blood.'

<small>Ambrose and Valentinian II.</small>

St. Ambrose died as became the great and good bishop who had lived so nobly and so well. The statesman Count Stilicho said of him, that the death of such a man threatened death to Italy itself. The citizens of Milan implored him to pray for continued life. His answer was: 'I have not so lived amongst you that I should be ashamed to live; and I do not fear to die, because we have a good Lord.' He expired on the night of Good Friday, A.D. 397, and was buried in the basilica, which preserves his name, in the presence of an immense concourse of all ranks and classes of citizens, the pagan and Jewish population joining with the rest to do him honour.

<small>The death of Ambrose</small>

St. Ambrose had carried the authority of the Church in affairs of State to a higher pitch than any of his predecessors. His principles, indeed, on this point, if actually put in force, would destroy the just balance between civil and ecclesiastical government. But his practical assertion of the supreme authority of conscience and moral right in the government of the world, and the limitation thereby imposed on the imperial rule, gives a supreme importance to his episcopate. If on the one hand he put a strain upon the authoritative side of the Kingdom of God, on the other hand he was the first to place its legitimate influence in a conspicuous light before the eyes of rulers.

The work and policy of St. Ambrose

It was during the period sketched in this chapter that an event occurred which is noteworthy as the first instance when the penalty of death was inflicted by a Christian court for heretical opinions. This was the execution of Priscillian, Bishop of Avila in Spain, which took place at Trèves under the administration of the usurper Maximus. The doctrines professed by Priscillian and his followers may be described as a kind of Gnosticism. They were a strange medley of erroneous teaching. In accordance with the discipline of their sect, the Priscillianists practised the greatest austerities, and abstained from every kind of indulgence.

Heresy made a capital offence

This extreme act of persecution was condemned by the wisest of the Western Bishops, St. Ambrose of Milan, and St. Martin of Tours. The latter is said to have protested against the decision of an ecclesiastical cause by a secular tribunal (the appeal having been made to Maximus, at that time emperor of the West), and to have exacted a promise that the life of Priscillian should be spared. In this way the incident raised for solution the difficult question as to the duty of the State in point of orthodoxy, which remained unsettled, or was settled grievously in the wrong way, for many centuries of Christian life.

CHAPTER XII.

THEODOSIUS. A.D. 379—395.

WE have seen how the great Theodosius avenged the treacherous murder of Gratian, and sustained the cause of Valentinian II. by the defeat of Maximus in Pannonia. This was followed by his execution at Aquileia, A.D. 388, two years before the rising in Thessalonica, which was succeeded by the celebrated scene of the imperial penitence under the censure of St. Ambrose.

<small>Theodosius avenges the death of Valentinian II.</small>

Soon after this, Valentinian II. suffered the fate of his half-brother Gratian. He had ventured to resist the will of the most powerful of his generals, a Goth named Arbogastes, whom he attempted to dismiss from his command. Valentinian was found strangled in his bed. Arbogastes declined to assume the purple himself, but placed it on the shoulders of Eugenius, a rhetorician of some note.

After a slight hesitation, Theodosius determined on war. It is said that, before embarking on this enterprise, he took the precaution of consulting an Egyptian anchorite, John of Lycopolis, and was assured by him of victory, to be won, however, at the cost of much bloodshed. The story is interesting, as one instance among many of the dangerous vitality of pagan ideas, which in spite of higher and truer teaching continued to thrust themselves into Christian thought and practice. It is but a slight step from the priestess of Delphi to the hermit of Lycopolis.

Eugenius and Arbogastes had occupied Milan and the northern provinces of Italy. Ambrose had resolutely declined all the overtures of Eugenius and had left the capital. This conduct, worthy of the admirable and courageous Bishop, was appreciated by Theodosius when he returned in triumph to Milan after his hardly won victory.

The decisive contest took place under the walls of Aquileia, the scene of many momentous events in these critical times.

On the first day of battle the attack of Theodosius on the enemy's camp was repulsed with immense loss. For a moment his situation seemed to be desperate. But two things contributed to his success on the following day. In the morning a message came from the leaders of the enemy's troops, who had encircled his army, offering to desert Eugenius in the course of the engagement. Added to this, when the armies joined battle, a furious tempest poured down the passes of the Alps, and beat upon the faces of the troops of Arbogastes and Eugenius, blinding them with dust and hindering the use of their weapons. As of old 'the stars in their courses fought against' the enemies of the divine cause,—a thought which occurred to St. Ambrose, and which is nobly expressed in some magnificent verses by the poet Claudian :

The defeat of Eugenius

> Te propter gelidis Aquilo de monte procellis
> Obruit adversas acies ; revolutaque tela

> Vertit in auctores, et turbine reppulit hastas.
> O nimium dilecte Deo, cui fundit ab antris
> Æolus armatas hyemes, cui militat æther,
> Et conjurati veniunt ad classica venti.
> *In Ter. Cons. Honor.* 93-98.

The victory was complete and decisive. A different result would probably have been calamitous to the Church, because, though Eugenius professed Christianity, his strength probably lay in the heathen reaction, which would have inspired his policy if his enterprise had been successful.

Once more for a brief space the Roman world acknowledged a single master. But the death of Theodosius soon followed (395), and under his two sons Arcadius and Honorius the old divisions were resumed, Arcadius becoming emperor of the East at the age of eighteen years, Honorius a child of eleven nominally assuming the government of the West.

The death of Theodosius

The reigns of these weak emperors were marked by great and terrible events indicating the rapid decline of the empire. But while the empire was swiftly hurrying to its end, and the devastating hordes of barbarian invaders were pressing in on every side to the very heart of it, laying waste its fairest and most fruitful provinces, and storming and delivering over to pillage its wealthiest and most historic cities, the Church was gathering strength and laying up a rich store of guidance in the lives of some of her greatest and holiest sons.

The decline of the empire

The Church and the empire had been born together, but when the empire was rocking to its foundation, the Church was engaged in strengthening the outworks of that City of God which was de-

The Church rising on its ruins

stined to gather within its walls, and mould to its uses, the better elements of those barbaric forces which were breaking up the old and tottering society of the ancient world.

One great man, worthy to be placed in the catalogue of heroes for all ages, had for a while kept back the flood of invasion. This was the distinguished general, Stilicho, trained in the service of Theodosius and celebrated in the verse of Claudian. But in 408 Stilicho was slain.

<small>Stilicho</small>

In the same year Alaric king of the Goths laid siege to Rome. On this occasion his retreat was purchased by a vast and exhausting ransom. But twice again within the space of three years Alaric appeared before the unhappy city. Once the horrors of a sack were averted by a political arrangement, but in 410 Alaric, stung by the insults of the foolish Honorius, marched from Ravenna to Rome. The gates were opened by treachery, and Rome awoke to find itself at the mercy of its barbarian foe.

<small>The sieges of Rome by Alaric</small>

It is deeply interesting to find that even then and there the influence of Christianity was felt. Alaric himself gave orders that the Churches of the Apostles St. Peter and St. Paul should be spared, and that quarter should be given to unresisting citizens. Sacred vessels of gold and silver were rescued from pillage by an appeal to the conscience of the rude soldier to whom the treasure had been pointed out, and were even conveyed under an escort of Gothic troops to custody in the Vatican. There also many of the defenceless citizens were allowed to find a refuge.

Still, notwithstanding all gentler influences, the

proud capital of the world, unassailed for eight hundred years, suffered many of the worst horrors of a captured city, from slaughter, from fire, and from injuries more unbearable than these.[1]

CHAPTER XIII.

THE FALL OF PAGANISM.

BEFORE we leave the history of Theodosius some account should be given of the first Catholic emperor's direct dealing with paganism.

With Theodosius Christianity had become supreme. The question arose in a thousand breasts, how far it should permit the continued existence of paganism. Paganism had endeavoured to extirpate Christianity; should Christianity finally crush out paganism? Pagan persecution had failed, should Christian persecution be attempted? Or put in another form: was it right or allowable for a Christian prince to concede to his subjects freedom of religious thought and practice, even if freedom meant persistence in error?

Is toleration of paganism to be permitted in a Christian State?

The religious question in the ancient world started from premisses different from those which are recognised now. The conception of a religion in Rome, or at Athens, was intimately connected with the political constitution of the State. There was tolerance of all religions because each religion was national. The idea

---

[1] See ch. xviii. and xix., where these events are more fully narrated.

of an universal religion extending to all nations, or that of a religion which claimed to be the only true one, and whose truth proved all others false, or even the idea of a religion which demanded righteousness, and which professed to govern motives, was alien to the ancient spirit of statesmanship or religion. In the pagan system the connexion between the national religion and the State was intimate and close. With Christianity this connexion could not be continued or revived. For the first time religion claimed the position of an independent power. It became a possible rival of the State. It was the intuition of this which lay at the root of persecution and resistance to the growing power of Christianity.

All that was over now; but two questions of wide and deep importance rose for solution. One was the relation of the State to Christianity. The other was the relation of the Christian State or the Christian ruler to paganism.

Two great questions

We have seen the former working itself out in the reigns of Constantine, Valentinian, and Theodosius. One thing, at any rate, had become plain—that absolute neutrality in the ruler was impossible. One solution, which lay in the complete supremacy of the Church, had already been started and was destined to have great effects in the course of history. Another, the complete domination of the supreme State power over religion and the conscience, had been already condemned by the Christian history of the first three centuries. Christian resistance, even with death as a penalty, where obedience to Christ clashed with obedience to Cæsar, had once for all shown the impossibility of successful persecution. The failure of Constantine, Constantius and Valens indicated a like impossibility on the part of the civil ruler to impose a perverted view of Christianity on the Church.

The other question of the day was the relation of the Christian ruler to paganism.

The policy of Constantine the Great was to grant religious liberty to his subjects. In his letter to the eastern provinces, quoted by Eusebius, he says: 'Let no one molest another in this matter, but let everyone be free to follow his own inclination. But,' he adds, 'with regard to those who will hold themselves aloof from us, let them have, if they please, their temples of lies: we have the glorious edifice of the truth.'[1] Still, paganism continued to prosper, especially in Rome itself, where the chief families held to the ancient customs as much from family pride as from any other motive. In the year 331 the temple of Concordia was restored by the senate, and several altars were erected about the same time.

<small>Tolerance enjoined by Constantine</small>

A few instances only of disestablishment occurred. Temples were destroyed where immoral rites were carried on, and their revenues were devoted to Christian churches or to the building of Constantinople. Beyond this Constantine does not appear to have advanced. Many of the most distinguished persons about his court and in high military command were pagans; and even if severe edicts were enacted against heathenism—some Christian writers mention the penalty of death—they were probably inoperative.

[1] Euseb. *Vit. Const.* ii. 56.

Under the successors of Constantine the feeling against paganism grew in intensity. Lactantius writing under Constantine could say, 'religio cogi non potest: nihil est tam voluntarium quam religio' (Religion cannot be forced; nothing is so voluntary as religion). In the succeeding reigns a Christian writer refers the emperors to Deuteronomy xiii. 6–10, and urges upon them the duty of persecuting the 'crime of idolatry.' Constantius acted on the spirit of this advice, and expressly prohibited sacrifice—'volumus etiam cunctos sacrificiis abstinere' (It is our will that all men abstain from sacrifice). In these circumstances the name of pagan came into use, the followers of heathen rites and practices being compelled to take refuge in the country villages or *pagi*, while imperial officials, agents or spies (agentes in rebus, curiosi) were on the watch to detect any infraction of the edicts.

The policy of his successors

These measures of persecution did no good to the Christian cause. They were opposed to the higher and truer spirit expressed in the words of Lactantius—'religio cogi non potest'—and they could not fail to raise a prejudice against the Faith in the minds of the best and most religious pagan thinkers. On the other hand they compelled into a nominal profession of Christianity large numbers of the cowardly and worldly-minded who are always found on the winning side. Thoughtful and philosophic paganism gained somewhat of that unworldly and disinterested element which had been the essential characteristic of Christianity in the days of persecution.

The inutility of Christian persecution

This is an aspect of the gradual disendowment and disappearance of paganism on which the Church historian seldom dwells. And yet there were doubtless incidents of a touching and pathetic kind connected with that disappearance. It was among the dwellers in country villages that the old belief lingered the longest. With many it must have been hard indeed to relinquish the immemorial sacrifices or ancient custom hallowed through many generations—to do this, too, before the advancing tide of a Christianity which, in some cases, through the dangerous influence of power, had forgotten the spirit of gentleness and persuasion. Among the many lessons to be drawn from this epoch that is one which ought not to escape us.

The reaction under Julian has been already sketched. It probably made little impression on genuine Christianity, though the floating mass of time-servers again flowed into the stream of paganism.

The effects of Julian's policy

Jovian, Valentinian, and Valens pursued a policy of tolerance in respect to paganism. Gratian, however, took an important and decisive step in the movement towards the ascendency of the Church, when he refused or resigned the office of Pontifex Maximus. According to the account in Zosimus, when the pontifical robe was presented to Gratian as first Augustus, he declined it, though from the inscriptions of this date he appears to have borne the title of Pontifex for a while. In any case it was a step which severed the public connexion between the empire and paganism. Gratian proceeded to confiscate the revenues of heathen temples, and to deprive the priests and the vestal virgins of their immunities and State allowance (victum modicum justaque privilegia). Another blow created an even deeper impression and was struck at

Important action of Gratian

a higher power. A deeply venerated altar of Victory, and an historic statue of the goddess with flowing robes and outstretched wings, stood in the temple where the senate were accustomed to assemble. The presence of the goddess and the offerings made upon her altar had given a solemn sanction to the deliberations of the senate. Constantius had ordered their removal, but they were restored by Julian. By Gratian's order they were once more removed from the senate house, and the embassy which came to implore their restitution was refused audience, A.D. 382.

The significance of this transaction in the rivalry of the two *imperia* was so clearly seen by thoughtful pagans, that repeated attempts were made to reverse the imperial decision. A second embassy, again headed by Symmachus, the chief of the senate and pontifex maximus, approached Valentinian II. with a prayer for the restoration of the statue. He was confronted by St. Ambrose. It was a dramatic meeting between the power of the old world and of the new. All that was best in pagan morality or wisdom was to be found in Symmachus; he was an ardent advocate of the dying system, and all that could be said in its favour was urged by its representative pontifex with good taste and skill. He appealed to the generosity and high feeling of the young prince, not to crush out, by so mean a measure as confiscation, the religion which Rome had sanctioned for eleven centuries, nor to desert by his policy the gods under whose auspices the Roman legions had subdued the world. The answer of Ambrose was calm and assured. 'There was no need,' he said, 'to ascribe to imaginary gods

The meeting of St. Ambrose and Symmachus

what was due to the courage and discipline of Roman soldiers.' Then putting aside the arguments of sentiment, he contended for the absolute truth of Christianity. In part it was the argument of the 'City of God.' To Valentinian, in place of the appeal of Symmachus to personal pride or weakness, the argument was a threat of ecclesiastical censure.

If the mission to Valentinian II. was unsuccessful, it may be inferred that the repeated petition to Theodosius was condemned to failure A.D. 388. But Theodosius was resolved to push his victories further. It was a remarkable point in history when a Roman emperor proposed in formal language the question 'whether the worship of Jupiter or that of Christ should be the religion of the Romans.' This statement of Gibbon, resting on the authority of Prudentius, may be open to some doubt. But that some formal defence of Christianity was laid before the senate by the emperor, and found a majority in its favour, by whatever motives influenced, seems to be beyond question.

Theodosius brings the question of religion before the senate

The words of Prudentius are worth quoting:—

> Adspice quam pleno subsellia nostra senatu
> Decernant infame Jovis pulvinar, et omne
> Idolium longe purgata ex urbe fugandum.
> Qua vocat egregii sententia principis, illuc
> Libera cum pedibus, tum corde frequentia transit.[1]

But a still more decisive step of Theodosius was the absolute prohibition of sacrifice, and of all approach to pagan temples. Henceforth no victim was to fall before

[1] *In Symmachum*, i. 608 foll.

the images of the gods, no *lar* or household god was to be worshipped with fire, no *genius* appeased by offering of wine, no *penates* by the steam of sacrifice, no festive lamps, or fragrant incense, or garlands of flowers were to be used in honour of the gods.[1]

<small>Decisive measures of Theodosius</small>

In these circumstances the words of the Christian poet Prudentius exhibit an exultation which can be understood, though exception may be taken to the manner in which the final victory of the faith was won :—

> Et dubitamus adhuc Romam tibi, Christe, dicatam
> In leges transisse tuas ?

Though the poet may have anticipated the triumph of Christianity, his words are interesting, as the testimony of a contemporary who observed the signs of the times, and desired to lay his finger on the moment of this great crisis.

By the irony of fate the honours paid in past times to the memory of deceased pagan emperors were paid to the Christian Theodosius, whose death is represented by the poet Claudian as a reception among the gods in terms similar to those in which Virgil or Horace speak of the apotheosis of Julius or Augustus Cæsar.[2] But the instructed and philosophic pagans themselves felt that paganism was dead, as is shown by their vain attempts to reconcile paganism with Christianity. We now read apologies, not for Christianity and Christ, but for the heathen gods; and these apologies are penetrated with Christian ideas, the leaven was secretly at work even when the influence was most

<small>Pagan apologies</small>

---

[1] *Cod. Theodos.* xvi. 10, 12.
[2] iii. *Cons. Honorii*, 162 foll.

eagerly resisted. On the other hand the wisest of the Christian teachers claimed the harvest of the best thoughts of pagan philosophy. Jerome, for instance, enthusiastically praises the erudition of Christian writers, 'all of whom,' he says, 'in such wise fill their books with the teaching and thoughts of philosophers, that you know not what first to admire in them, the learning of the world, or the knowledge of the Scriptures' (Qui omnes in tantum philosophorum doctrinis atque sententiis suos referciunt libros, ut nescias quid in illis primum admirari debeas, eruditionem sæculi an scientiam Scripturarum).[1]

While the finer intellects were thus being influenced by argument, coarser and less excusable means sealed the fate of paganism in the populations of town and country. The pagan temples were closed. A few were afterwards converted into Christian churches, but before long by far the greater number were levelled to the ground by fanatical mobs of Christians, headed in many instances by the bishop and his clergy. In some districts a vigorous resistance was made by the pagan population, and anyone who has visited the ruined temples of Baalbec can understand how readily such buildings lent themselves to defence.

Pagan temples destroyed

A scene took place in the Lebanon, which illustrates the temper of the times, and the moderation of the government. The story is told by Sozomen. A Bishop named Marcellus commanded a party of soldiers in an attack on a large temple at Aulone in Apamea. He himself, being afflicted with the gout, remained behind while the fight proceeded. Here he was discovered by

[1] Jerome, Ep. 10, *ad Magnum oratorem*.

some of the pagans and slain. The council of the province, however, prevented his friends taking vengeance for his death, 'when they should rather return thanks to God for having accounted him worthy to die in such a cause.' For the same reason, Theodosius offered free pardon to those who had slain the Christians in the temple of Serapis at Alexandria, 'hoping thereby that they would be the more readily induced to embrace Christianity.'[1] Such instances indicate the need which was felt of moderation and clemency. There was still danger of a pagan reaction, and in face of such risings as those under Maximus or Procopius, it would be madness to exasperate too deeply pagan susceptibilities.

Theophilus, Bishop of Alexandria, was one of those who carried out the emperor's orders with inconsiderate violence. Determined to expose the whole system of idolatry, he caused the temple of Serapis to be ransacked, and the obscene figures of idolatrous worship to be paraded through the streets. This grave insult gave the signal for a massacre of the Christians. In the encounter the grammarians Helladius and Ammonius took a leading part. Helladius boasted that he had slain nine victims at the shrine of the insulted deities. It is a note of the complex relations of the time that Socrates, the ecclesiastical historian, was a pupil of these zealous champions of heathenism.

Theophilus of Alexandria

Theodosius, as we have seen, pardoned the rioters, but an imperial edict condemned the edifice. For a moment superstition stayed the destroyer's hand. A peculiar sanctity was attached to the statue of Serapis. It was believed that if a human

The destruction of the Serapeum

[1] Soz. vii. 15.

hand should touch the statue, the solid earth would open, and the heavens fall with a crash.[1] A brave soldier dispelled the superstition with a blow which cleft the head of the idol. The other fear that the enraged divinity would check the rising waters of the Nile was likewise belied by a flood which exceeded the usual height.

In this way the war against paganism was not without grievous excess and worldly motive on the Christian side, but on the other hand with an absence of heroism and faith on the side of paganism which marks a declining religion. St. Augustine contrasts the stedfastness of Christian martyrs with the cowardice of the pagan ministers: 'Which of them has been caught in the act of sacrifice which is against the laws, and did not deny it? Which of them has been caught worshipping idols, and did not in fear of the judgment exclaim, I did it not? Such are the devil's ministers' ('Quis eorum comprehensus est in sacrificio, cum his legibus ista prohiberentur, et non negavit? Quis eorum comprehensus est adorare idolum et non clamavit, non feci, et timuit ne convinceretur? Tales ministros Diabolus habebat').[2]

But if Christianity seemed to speed well externally, prosperity brought with it its accustomed evils. False and dishonest Christians brought on the faith the scorn of honest paganism. 'Why do you persuade me to be a Christian?' exclaims a heathen. 'I am innocent of false dealing, but have been cheated by a Christian. I who never swore a false oath have suffered from Christian perjury.'[3] 'If all Christians

Evils of prosperity

---

[1] Rufin. i. 23. [2] *Enar. in Psalm.* 141, § 20.
[3] Augustin. *Enar. in Psalm.* 25, § 14.

were as they ought to be,' says St. Chrysostom, 'there would be no unbeliever ("Ελλην) now.'

In the East there was less resistance to the imperial edicts than in the West. The Eastern provinces were traversed by monks commissioned to sweep away all traces of idolatry. In Alexandria, scenes of increased violence occurred in the episcopate of St. Cyril, and culminated in the cruel murder of the beautiful and gifted Hypatia.

Hypatia, daughter of the philosopher Theon, was not only so highly distinguished for her learning and eloquence as to draw crowds of eager listeners to her lectures, but even, pagan though she was, she won the admiration of Christian writers. 'Such was her self-possession,' says Socrates,[1] 'and ease of manner arising from the refinement and cultivation of her mind, that she not unfrequently appeared in public in presence of the magistrates without even losing, in an assembly of men, that dignified modesty for which she was conspicuous, and which gained for her universal respect and admiration.' But she fell a victim to the turbulent politics and evil surmisings of the time. She was supposed to use her influence over Orestes, the civil governor of Alexandria, to prevent his reconciliation with Cyril. A fanatical Christian reader, named Peter, with a band of followers, dragged Hypatia from her carriage, as she was driving home, carried her into the Church called the Cæsareum, and there stripped her of her clothes and murdered her, it is said, by tearing her flesh with oyster-shells.

'An act so inhuman,' says Socrates, 'could not fail

[1] vii. 15.

to bring the greatest opprobrium not only on Cyril, but also on the whole Alexandrian Church. And surely nothing can be farther from the spirit of Christianity than the allowance of massacres, fights, and transactions of that sort.'[1] 'Tantum religio potuit suadere malorum!' This was in the year 416.

In the West the severity of the movement against paganism relaxed under the weak Honorius. The laws remained unrepealed, but they were not enforced with the vigour of Theodosius. In some instances they were practically suspended. Honorius checked the destruction of temples, acknowledged the official position of heathen priests, and after having expressly stated that 'no one should be in any way connected with him who differed from him in faith and religion,' offered to nominate Generidus, a heathen, to command in Rhætia.

The weakness of Honorius

When Italy was invaded and Rome besieged by the Goths, a cry arose that the Christians were at the bottom of this humiliation and misery. It was this cry which gave occasion to St. Augustine's 'City of God.'

A widely prevalent belief amongst Christians assigned the second Advent of Christ to the three hundred and sixty-fifth year after His first appearance. This floating prophecy was interpreted by pagans to mean the limit of the Christian power, and both eagerly awaited the fulfilment of prophecy. But the year passed unmarked by either event, and when the Gothic invaders themselves embraced the Christian faith, the pagan argument was discredited. Later on even Valentinian III. could put forth edicts against paganism

The year 365

[1] vii. 16.

which a generation earlier would have required a strong ruler to enforce: 'All heresies, unbeliefs, schisms, and superstitions of the heathen, all errors opposed to the Catholic rule we visit with punishment.'

But here and there evidence appears of predominant paganism. In the year 443 the Council of Arles passes canons against Christians who have witnessed heathen rites without prohibiting them, against those who have denied the faith under persecution, or who have been forced by torture to do sacrifice. In Corsica sacrifices were still publicly offered, and a story is told of a Christian woman, named Julia, being crucified because she refused to take part in the pagan rites.[1]

Paganism still powerful in places

In Rome, too, some pagan observances were retained even in State affairs. Salvianus, a presbyter of Marseilles, about the year 440, declares that auguries were still taken from the flight or the feeding of birds for the election of consuls. He testifies to the continued passion for the circus in which the fights with wild beasts were still continued, and contrasts the emptiness of Christian churches with the crowded circus during the celebration of the games: 'not only do professing Christians (qui Christianos se esse dicunt) not come to church, but those who have come there in ignorance, if they hear that the games are going on, instantly quit the church.'

Evidence of Salvianus

All the great Christian writers of this period inveigh against the practice of taking part in the lascivious celebrations of heathen festivals; and Salvianus, speaking of the African Church, denounces those Christians who

[1] *Acta Sanctorum*, viii. 167, quoted by Gieseler.

enter Christian shrines when they are reeking with the steam of sacrifices offered to demons.

Such are some of the features of this great contention, of the relations of civil rulers to Christianity and to paganism, of the conditions under which the Kingdom of Christ was by slow and painful process moulding a new world.

CHAPTER XIV.

ST. JEROME. A.D. 346–420.

WE now turn to trace some of the directions in which the leaven of the Kingdom of God was transfusing itself into the mass of worldly opinion and motive, and was influencing human action.

The name of Jerome suggests an important movement and an important work—monasticism and the Vulgate.

The epoch which we are considering was a time when the conduct of life and the problems of society had *Theories of the Christian life* to be re-discussed. Christianity was still so new and undeveloped an element that its social relations were as yet undefined. How were Christian men and women to be in the world and yet not of it? The question was simple in the old days before the Church became a political force, and before Christians were exposed to the dangerous temptations of high position, of wealth, and of influence; but it was no longer simple; indeed it had become exceedingly intricate and complex. Accordingly the foremost theologians were putting forth thoughts, which were destined to take effect with more or less permanency.

One of these thoughts was monasticism. The monastic life is the expression of ideas which will always animate Christian society and Christian thought. It is a protest against the world. It is a refuge for disappointment, weariness, and hopeless sorrow, and a retreat for learning and piety of a special type. No system has been more abused or distorted in its application, or has more fully exposed itself at times to condemnation by the best and purest Christian judgment in particular epochs. But the system and life were infinitely varied, and in one place or another have given scope to the energy and intellect of such men as Jerome, Chrysostom, Anselm, St. Bernard, and Fra Angelico.

Egypt was the home of monasticism. Its influence in the West may be said to date from the visit of St. Athanasius to Rome, accompanied by two Egyptian monks. Athanasius had, himself, in early life been fascinated by the personal attraction of St. Anthony, whom he describes, in different terms from what we should have expected, as 'urbane and polished.' St. Anthony is regarded as the founder of Christian monasticism; and the life of this Saint, written by Athanasius, gave an impulse to the monastic tendency, which at one time strongly influenced St. Augustine also.

Monasticism in Egypt

Many causes increased the popularity of monasticism. The unsettled condition of society, the insecurity of possessions, the prevailing vice and iniquity of the age, the yearning in some minds for a life of quiet contemplation and the pursuit of learning; while others, guided by lower

Different phases of the monastic life

motives, may have seen in the solitary or cœnobitic life an avenue to spiritual influence or even high ecclesiastical position. Some who devoted themselves to the monastic life adopted rigid rules of abstinence and austerity. The more weird, desolate and lonely the spot, the harsher and more exacting the rule, the more sparing or even repulsive the diet, the greater was the attraction to many minds. Some voluntarily yielded themselves to what can only be described as a lifelong torture. Such were the pillar saints familiarised to English readers by Tennyson's 'St. Simeon Stylites.'

> Let this avail, just, dreadful, mighty God,
> This not be all in vain, that thrice ten years,
> Thrice multiplied by superhuman pangs,
> In hungers and in thirsts, fevers and cold,
> In coughs, aches, stitches, ulcerous throes and cramps,
> A sign betwixt the meadow and the cloud,
> Patient on this tall pillar I have borne
> Rain, wind, frost, heat, hail, damp, and sleet, and snow.

Simeon was a Syrian shepherd boy who left his flock on the mountains thirty miles east of Antioch for a monastic life, and not content with its austerities, raised a pillar within the enclosure of a sheep-fold or *mandra*, and with a ponderous chain attached to his body ascended the pillar and there remained for thirty years, not even descending to die.

But under all this crude fanaticism, there was a substratum of practical truth, and to the strange exaggerations of the principle there succeeded the sober and temperate discipline of life, which produced great scholars, great bishops, great thinkers. St. Basil of

Cæsarea, as we have seen, enjoyed the beauties of nature in the midst of which his monastery was placed, courted the society of his friend St. Gregory, and was delighted by the alternations of manual and mental exercise which he made the rule of his community.

In the West the history of monasticism connects itself with the name of St. Jerome, or Hieronymus. This great doctor of the Latin Church, whose character and example have left deep traces on the conception and discipline of the Christian life, was born at Stridon, near Aquileia, probably in the year 346.

After studying rhetoric in Rome, Jerome visited Spain, and then settled for a time at Aquileia, where his experience of the ascetic life began. He pursued this experience in the East, where he travelled for some while, visiting great cities—Jerusalem, Antioch, and Constantinople—and studying under distinguished teachers, one of whom was Gregory Nazianzen. During five years he lived in the Syrian desert, submitting himself to all the austerities of the solitary life. In 382 he was summoned to Rome by Pope Damasus. Here the whole weight of his great influence was directed to the advocacy of asceticism. He attracted a large and devoted following; but on the death of Damasus he resolved to quit Rome.

For his final retreat and monastic home he fixed upon the most interesting spot on earth, and was joined *St. Jerome at Bethlehem* at Bethlehem by his dearest friends and pupils, the lady Paula, and her daughter Eustochium. Nor was his life there one of idle contemplation and rest. On the contrary, it was filled with eager and arduous literary labours, with a wide correspondence, and often, it must be added, with hot and fierce controversy. Of these controversies the most important were those with Pelagius on the subject of original sin, of grace, and the human intellect; with Helvidius on the subject of the perpetual virginity of the Blessed Virgin Mary; and with Rufinus and others on the question of Origen's writings—a point of keen theological controversy at this period.

Into these subjects of dispute we do not propose to enter, but we cannot pass over without some description *The Vulgate* of the great literary achievement which has made the name of Jerome famous throughout all ages, which exercised a dominant influence over the whole Western Church, and which indirectly affects the life and thought of Englishmen at the present day, nay, even the very words which we use.

Jerome had been what we should now call a great classical scholar. He confesses that he had allowed himself to be carried away too far by his love for the famous writers of Greece and Rome, till the voice of a vision, telling him that he was not a Christian but a Ciceronian, made him turn to the almost exclusive study of the Bible. The scene and the country in which he wrote aided and stimulated him in his great work. In Palestine he was not only able to identify and visit Biblical scenes, but also to study with advantage the original language of the Old Testament. The result of these labours was the version of the Holy Scriptures from Hebrew and Greek into Latin, known to us as the *Vulgate* translation.

The English word Vulgate represents the Latin *Vulgata Editio*, 'the current edition' of the Bible, the edition to be understood of the people. This term was applied to versions of the Bible from Greek into Latin which had preceded Jerome's Vulgate. Jerome's first task was to correct these old, and in many cases corrupt, versions of the Greek Testament and of the Greek Old Testament or Septuagint. But the great and monumental work on which St. Jerome spent the immense energy and labour of the later years of his life was a translation of the Old Testament directly from the Hebrew. The books were published at intervals at the request of various friends from the year 389 to the year 404, the forty-fourth to the fifty-ninth of Jerome's life.

From this time the Vulgate took its place as the authorised Bible of the Western Church. With the exception of the Gothic Bible of Ulfilas, all the versions of the Bible into the languages of the West, our own included, are more or less directly founded on the Vulgate of Jerome. Wyclif's Bible (1324–1384) is a literal rendering of the current Vulgate text. The Bible of Tyndale and Coverdale rests chiefly on the Latin of Jerome and the German of Luther. Our own Authorised Version was accomplished by men to whom the Vulgate was the most familiar text. In this way the influence of St. Jerome has a close and interesting relation to modern life.

Jerome's literary labours

The Vulgate by no means exhausts the literary work of St. Jerome in Palestine. He wrote commentaries on portions of the prophetical books, on St. Matthew, and on several of the Epistles. He translated some of Origen's homilies. His book of Hebrew names and his questions on Genesis, written at this period, are of value to the present day.

St. Jerome. A.D. 346–420.

Besides these works biographies, controversial treatises, letters, and translations justified his retirement.

St. Jerome died in the year 420. His tomb is shown in the narrow cell, where he lived and wrote, near that rocky cavern to which a very ancient tradition points as the scene of the Saviour's birth.

CHAPTER XV.

St. Augustine. A.D. 354–430.

In turning from St. Jerome to St. Augustine we find ourselves in the presence of a gentler influence and assuredly of a greater name in the Church of Christ.

Perhaps it is the early life of St. Augustine, the child of many tears, which has most widely touched human hearts. His mother Monnica, her tender care, her loving anxiety, her prayers, her tears; then the dissolute youth of this great saint; then his conviction of sin, his inward struggles, his search after truth, his conversion and reconciliation with God—all these things told in the glowing and passionate language of the 'Confessions' have found a response in every generation: 'Mentem mortalia tangunt.'

St. Augustine's early life

But perhaps the light in which the name of St. Augustine is most justly honoured in the Church is that in which he is regarded as the founder of systematic theology. He was the first of great ecclesiastical teachers to touch with no uncertain hand those deep and mysterious questions which began to agitate the minds of men in respect of the relation of the soul to God, and the acts or thoughts or attitudes on which its eternal destinies depend—

Fixed fate, free will, foreknowledge absolute.

These were the high, and, we may add, the insoluble, themes which engaged the mind of Augustine.

The 'Confessions' of St. Augustine refer to the period of his life which preceded his baptism. This did not take place till the thirty-third year of his age. For at least nine years of his early manhood he had been led away by Manichæism, a system which recognises a dual government of the world by the equal and contending powers of good and evil, a kingdom of light and a kingdom of darkness.

<small>The 'Confessions' of St. Augustine</small>

The crisis came when he obtained an appointment as teacher of rhetoric at Milan. There he became known to St. Ambrose, by whose eloquence and goodness he was at once attracted; at first, however, in a critical spirit. 'I listened diligently,' he says in his 'Confessions,'[1] 'to him preaching to the people, not with that intent I ought, but as it were trying his eloquence, whether it answered the fame thereof, or flowed fuller or lower than was reported of the matter. I was as a careless and scornful looker-on . . . and yet,' he says, 'was I drawing nearer little by little and unconsciously.' Such was the beginning of that sweet and fruitful intercourse of these two great Saints.

<small>St. Augustine at Milan meets St. Ambrose</small>

Augustine returned to Africa after his conversion. Here he became associated with Valerius, Bishop of

[1] v. 13.

Hippo, who ordained him. On the death of Valerius St. Augustine succeeded to the comparatively unimportant bishopric. But his influence extended far and wide beyond the limits of his see; for no voice swayed men's minds more effectively than St. Augustine's, no one directed the current of thought on momentous questions with greater authority, or affected the course of the Church's history more profoundly than the Bishop of Hippo.

Is made Bishop of Hippo

The influence of St. Augustine

The most famous controversies in which he was engaged were, first, that in which he upheld the discipline and the doctrine of the Catholic Church on the one hand against the Donatists, who asserted the possibility of maintaining an ideally pure and holy Church on earth, and separated themselves from the Church of their brethren, in which they could trace laxity of discipline or the elements of sin; next, that against the Pelagians, who denied the need or efficacy of the grace of God, and attributed to the unassisted human will and intellect the capacity of attaining righteousness.

We cannot enter into these important subjects at length, nor can we here describe or estimate the wealth and value of St. Augustine's literary works. But something must be said of the 'De Civitate Dei' or the 'City of God,' or, more accurately, 'Concerning the Divine State, or the Kingdom of God' —a book which had immense weight in determining men's minds at the time, and has influenced the history of the world more perhaps than any other book.

The 'De Civitate Dei'

The 'De Civitate Dei' was written at a memorable epoch and with a memorable purpose. The epoch was the capture of Rome by Alaric in 410; the purpose was to confute the idea that the calamities of the time were due to Christianity. It is the wisest and most complete of Christian 'apologies,' a searching enquiry into the meaning of history, a vindication of the Kingdom of Heaven.

The sack of Rome produced an indescribable shock through the civilised world. Society seemed to be falling into ruin. Men looking about for a cause blamed Christianity. St. Augustine proves incontestably that it was by the vices and corruptions of the old pagan system that ruin had overtaken the empire. He shows the helplessness of paganism and of the philosophic systems which had succeeded it, and then exhibits the lofty aims, the mighty progress, the assured future, the blessed hopes and promise of the 'City of God.' It is at once a review of history and an exposition of the discipline and doctrine of the Catholic Church. There are few things finer in literature than the comprehensive sweep of St. Augustine's intellect in his criticism of the events and politics of the pagan past, of all philosophy and of all aspects of life, in his 'City of God.'

Nothing can be gentler or more generous than his attitude towards mistaken beliefs. Nothing can exceed his readiness to recognise what is beautiful and noble in character or in nationality, or his eagerness to claim it for Christianity. Nor is there any fear in the interests of Christianity for results of research or keenness of analysis. It is polemic theology at its best.[1]

---

[1] St. Augustine is chosen as the exemplar of polemic theology in the noble and impressive fresco by Simone Memmi in the Spanish Chapel of Santa Maria Novella in Florence.

So far as outward events were concerned the life of St. Augustine was quiet and uneventful till close upon its end. Then it was disturbed, as all north Africa was disturbed, by the cruel and desolating invasion of the Vandals under Genseric. The Count Boniface had thrown himself into the city of Hippo, which was at once closely invested. 'There,' writes Gibbon, ' in the third month of the siege, and in the seventy-sixth year of his age, St. Augustine, the light and pillar of the Catholic Church, was gently released from the actual and impending calamity of his country.'

Death of St. Augustine

CHAPTER XVI.

ST. CHRYSOSTOM. A.D. 347–407.

TURNING for a while from the West to the East, we will endeavour to trace at least in outline the life and work of the great Bishop and eloquent preacher John surnamed Chrysostom. In some respects his life is more modern in its characteristics and modes of influence than any of the others which have been described.

St. Chrysostom's life naturally divides itself into three parts—his rise into power and brilliance as a preacher at Antioch, his career at Constantinople, his sufferings in banishment at different places in Asia Minor.

John Chrysostom—we must remember that John was the only name by which he was known to his contemporaries, the title of Chrysostom, 'golden-mouthed,' being a later tribute to his eloquence—was born at Antioch in the year 347 and died in 407. He was gifted with great and brilliant ability, and seemed destined to be the foremost of rhetoricians in his native city. His mother Anthusa was a devout Christian; all that we know of her points to a sweet and loving nature, and to the utmost anxiety for her son's spiritual welfare. After some hesitation, and not until he had grown up to manhood, he was baptized, and renounced the world.

<small>Early life of St. Chrysostom</small>

The form of religion which suited his temperament was asceticism in its severest guise. But though he submitted to a rigid discipline, he yielded to his mother's tears and remained for a while under her roof. But he longed for a more rigorous self-denial, and for six years he exposed himself to privations among the Syrian mountains, which permanently injured his health. After this he returned to Antioch, was ordained, and began his course of Christian oratory which has left an imperishable fame. His promise had already been great. When Libanius, the most eminent sophist and rhetorician of his time, and the devoted friend of the emperor Julian, was asked on his deathbed who should take his place when he was gone, he answered: 'It would have been John, had not the Christians taken him from us.'[1]

<small>His asceticism</small>

Soon events took place in Antioch which gave occasion to the most brilliant and the most moving of Chrysostom's homilies.

The East was at this time—in the year 387—groaning under an oppressive taxation, which had become

[1] Socr. viii. 2.

necessary for the military operations in the West and for the approaching celebration of the *decennalia*, or festival on the tenth year of the emperor's reign. Seditious meetings were held at Alexandria, at Antioch, and at other chief towns in the Eastern empire. When the edict of taxation was proclaimed at Antioch a tumult broke out. The mob rushed into the governor's palace and overthrew the statues of the imperial family, which were placed in the hall of judgment. For three hours the madness raged through the city. The statues of Theodosius, his wife and family, in the city were hurled down and broken up or dragged along the streets. It was a deadly insult, and what made the sting more keenly felt by Theodosius was the recent death of his wife Flaccilla, to whom he was deeply attached.

<small>Seditious outbreak at Antioch</small>

In Antioch swift repentance and the gloomiest apprehensions followed the outbreak. The aged Bishop Flavian was sent with a deputation including, according to Zosimus, the pagan orator Libanius, to solicit the emperor's pardon. While the city waited in terrified suspense, the magistracy with miserable cowardice were sending victims to execution in order to shield themselves from blame of complicity. In this condition of things Chrysostom intervened. Every day in words of 'golden' eloquence he addressed the people who flocked to the basilica, exhorting them to calmness, to show what Christian courage meant in times of danger. He pointed to reasons for hopefulness from the ability of their advocates and the clemency of a Christian emperor. At the same time he took this opportunity to urge the need of repentance,

<small>Chrysostom calms the people</small>

and of trust in the Heavenly King. At length the imperial envoys came. As they moved through the streets they were met by the hermits from the mountains—strange figures—who for once had descended to the crowded city to intercede. The envoys, who were Christians, alighted and fell on their knees before the hermits, who with the utmost courage delivered their message of intercession.

A severe sentence had indeed already been issued. The city was degraded from its metropolitan position; the public baths, the circus and places of amusement were closed. But before severer measures were taken or sentences of death inflicted, a respite was granted and an appeal to the emperor allowed.

<small>The emperor's sentence</small>

Meanwhile Bishop Flavian returned bearing the joyous news that a pardon had been granted. He had pleaded in the emperor's presence in words which St. Chrysostom has preserved. The appeal to the Christianity of the emperor prevailed. 'If the Lord of the earth,' said Theodosius, 'who became a servant for our sakes, and was crucified by those whom He came to benefit, prayed for the pardon of His crucifiers, what wonder was it that man should forgive his fellow-servants?'

<small>Announcement of pardon</small>

It was an Easter of joyous thankfulness for Antioch. The whole scene was significant of the growing influence of Christianity. The historian has to take note of this new force in the world, this new possibility of clemency, this avenue to pity opened out by the Church. We read too without astonishment that 'one great and happy result of the recent trouble was a large accession of pagans to the ranks of the Church.' If the power that wins is the power that rules, the Kingdom of God had shown itself to be the stronger *imperium*.

The removal of Chrysostom from Antioch to Constantinople is another of those picturesque and dramatic incidents which fill the annals of this epoch. The episcopal throne of Constantinople was vacant. 'John,' says the historian Sozomen, 'was adjudged worthy in word and in deed, by all the subjects of the Roman empire, to preside over the Church of Constantinople. The clergy and people were unanimous in electing him; their choice was approved by the emperor; messengers were despatched for John; and, to confer greater solemnity on his ordination, a council was convened.' But the difficulty was to persuade St. Chrysostom to quit Antioch, or to steal their favourite preacher from the unwilling citizens. Both fraud and force were employed. He was tempted to go beyond the city walls, and there seized by imperial officers and carried a prisoner to the capital over which he had been elected to preside as Bishop.

Chrysostom becomes Bishop of Constantinople

At Constantinople Chrysostom found many evils to correct in the dissolute society of the capital. For himself he carried the simple and ascetic habit of his life at Antioch into the episcopal palace. It was his custom to eat alone and never to accept an invitation to a feast. Whatever his motive may have been, needed carefulness in diet, or a vow of abstinence, this seclusion made him unpopular. He endeavoured first of all to check the growing luxury of his clergy. Already the temptations of wealthy houses had sapped spiritual strength. Immorality too, or the danger of immorality, had produced scandals such as no true and pure Church could endure.

<small>Attacks abuses of the clergy</small> In sweeping away these evils, possibly with too harsh and unsparing a hand, St. Chrysostom raised enemies who combined against him when his time of trial came.

But St. Chrysostom was not content with restoring discipline to his clergy. He inveighed against the extravagance, the idleness, the finery of the fashionable world. The homilies and addresses of Chrysostom prove how uniform and monotonous are the lines on which human sin and folly proceed, and how alike the preacher's arguments must be in every age. 'As long as John attacked the clergy only,' says Socrates, ' the machinations of his enemies were utterly powerless; but when he proceeded to rebuke the nobles also with his characteristic vehemence, the tide of unpopularity began to set against him with far greater impetus, and the stories which were told to his disparagement found many attentive listeners.'

The eunuch Eutropius, who had been raised to the dignity of consul, and Gainas, the Gothic chieftain, and <small>He raises enemies by his faithfulness in rebuke</small> other persons of distinction assailed and upbraided by this courageous Bishop, became powerful adversaries. His most inveterate enemy however was Theophilus, Bishop of Alexandria, whose designs had been thwarted by the election of John to the see of Constantinople. But the gravest danger to St. Chrysostom lay in the hostility of the empress Eudoxia, who saw in him an obstacle to her complete ascendency over the emperor. At length through the joint practices of the empress and of Theophilus, by the vote of a packed synod composed of Bishops hostile to St. Chrysostom, meeting at a place called 'The Oak' near Chalcedon, he was condemned to exile. He fled from the city, but on the same night a violent storm excited the superstitious fears of Eudoxia, and Chrysostom was recalled. The population of the capital welcomed his return with demonstrations of delight.

<small>Antipathy of the empress</small>

However, the renewed friendship with Eudoxia was short-lived. On this occasion the fiery nature of St. Chrysostom seems to have carried him away. A silver statue of the empress had been placed on a porphyry pillar close to the Church of St. Sophia. At this pillar public games were performed which Chrysostom objected to as an insult to the sacredness of the place. The empress incensed at Chrysostom's protest endeavoured to convene another council against him. A synod of Bishops met, and though no formal decree was passed, the emperor Arcadius was persuaded to sign an order for the removal of Chrysostom.

Then took place in the Church of St. Sophia one of those wild and cruel scenes, to which this history has accustomed us. The sacrament of baptism was being administered; soldiers rushed in and interrupted the sacred rite. Chrysostom escaped from the church; but, as soon as the weak Arcadius could be persuaded to sign the decree of banishment, he was driven into exile. The place of exile was Cucûsus, a mountain village in the range of the Taurus to the north of Cilicia. After a journey hastened on with cruel expedition, he reached Cucûsus, where he was received with hospitality by many friends.

<small>Chrysostom driven into exile</small>

From that secluded village Chrysostom exercised an immense influence over the Church of the East, taking special thought of his own flock in Constantinople. Never was he more a Bishop than when he ruled from Cucûsus. But the end was near. His enemies were disappointed that the severities of exile had not slain Chrysostom. He was ordered to a spot still more bleak and dreary, Pityus in the Caucasian mountains. Thither he was hurried by guards, whose merciless haste proved fatal at Comana, a halting-place on the way. This was on September 14, A.D. 407. Thirty-one years afterwards, the remains of St. Chrysostom were translated with great pomp to his episcopal city, and placed in the Church of the Holy Apostles.

The times and scenes in which St. Chrysostom played no unimportant part exhibit some of the worst as well as some of the best and brightest features of ecclesiastical history. In his own early life we trace not only the coarse seductions of half-extinguished paganism, but the finer and more noble temptations of the trained intellect. When the change came, we see asceticism carried to an extreme and a narrowed conception of Christianity. On his own high and saintly character in its development it is a delight to dwell. It is as a beacon light thrown across the stormy sea of intrigue and sin. It is a delight also to trace the deep impress that his personality and his eloquent teaching made on society, especially on the masses of Antioch and Constantinople, who were enthusiastically attached to their eloquent guide.

Review of Chrysostom's life

Here is a beginning of that Christian influence on vast urban populations which it has always been the just ambition of the Church to secure. The new force has not only swayed the minds of emperors and claimed mercy as a right, but it has stirred multitudes of men by an appeal to the religious sense,—two modifications of imperialism, and mitigations of absolute power, undreamt of and impossible except in the light of Christianity.

We are, however, compelled to see darker lines in the picture. Christianity has not been able, as enthusiasts might have hoped, to sweep away the selfishness, the lust, the cruelty of the pagan world. Society was still unpurged; every page of Chrysostom's homilies teaches this. We note also an even darker stain, because seemingly more incurable, the beginning of ecclesiastical intrigue, the battle of pride and jealousy in the Church of Christ, the Church divided not by differences of religious thought or discipline, but, as in the contest between Theophilus of Alexandria and Chrysostom, by the base and mundane spirit of faction and that other dark spirit of rivalry and hate.

CHAPTER XVII.

HONORIUS. A.D. 395–423—RUFINUS, STILICHO.

A WEAK reign is the opportunity of powerful ministers; and in the eventful history of the falling empire it is not the names of Honorius and Arcadius that fill the pages of history. The whole of the administration of affairs was thrown into the hands of statesmen and generals who had thrust themselves into power, or of the more capable members of the imperial family.[1]

Accession of Honorius   Two men had gained surpassing influence in the closing years of Theodosius,—Rufinus and Stilicho, men of marked, but widely differing characters, one an extreme instance of corrupt and selfish ambition, the other not indeed a faultless character, yet a light in dark and evil days, and a support of falling Rome.

Rufinus, as we learn from the verses of Claudian, the chief authority for this period, was a native of Elusa, *Early life of Rufinus*   a small town of Aquitania. In the language of the poet he is summoned by Alecto from his mean penates by the temptations of wealth and power, to take his part in the movements of a larger world:—

> Otia te, Rufine, juvant ? frustraque juventæ
> Consumis florem patriis inglorius arvis ?
> Heu nescis quid fata tibi, quid sidera donent,
> Quid fortuna paret : toti dominabere mundo,
> Si parere velis.

Rufinus rose to eminence as a lawyer, and his eloquence and capacity for business attracted the attention *His rise*   of the emperor Theodosius, who advanced him from one post of dignity to another, until he became his leading minister and trusted adviser. The true character of Rufinus revealed itself by degrees. Only when the control of Theodosius was removed was the world to know the secret of his cruel and ruthless

---

[1] Zosimus, v. 1.

ambition. But we have authority for the belief that he stood by the emperor's side when he planned the massacre of Thessalonica, and that he resisted with all his force the humane and civilising influence of Ambrose. He would present at this crisis in the relations between Church and State the argument, which is true if not pressed to an extremity, that in civil administration and in great State questions the Church as such has no right to interfere. This point a minister may justly urge; but he may not forget that the principles of Christianity, of which the Church is the exponent, hold good in Church and State alike.

The crimes of Rufinus

The profound secresy with which the crime of Thessalonica was veiled until the moment of its perpetration is characteristic of the deep dissimulation attributed to Rufinus.[1] In his advance to supreme and undisputed influence two rivals stood in his way—Promotus, a soldier who had braved the dangers and hardships of campaigning by the side of Theodosius, and was now commander of the infantry; and Tatian, prefect of the palace. Promotus was the first victim. Stung by a scornful speech of Rufinus, he struck him on the cheek. The insult was avenged by an imperial order to Promotus to leave the capital for a fortress on the Danube. There, according to Zosimus,[2] he was slain in an ambuscade planned by Rufinus. Tatian was tried on the charge of maladministration. His son Proculus, who had been united with him in authority, had escaped, but the father was persuaded by the most perfidious promises to recall his

---

[1] βαθυγνώμων ἄνθρωπος καὶ κρυψίνοος, Suidas, quoted by Gibbon.
[2] iv. 5.

son. On his return Proculus was instantly slain before his father's eyes :—

> juvenum rorantia colla
> Ante patrum vultus strictâ cecidere securi,

writes Claudian in a passage in which he indignantly sums up the crimes of Rufinus.[1]

It is a significant mark of the influence of Christianity, and of the change which made an outward profession of it respectable, that an evil and unprincipled statesman should have deemed it expedient to include a church and monastery in the precincts of his palace near Chalcedon. The hypocrisy of false Christians, predicted by the Master,[2] which once seemed incredible, had come to pass. Christianity, instead of being perilous and scorned, had become safe and dignified.

With the accession of Arcadius, Rufinus enjoyed complete liberty of action. 'The whole power of sovereignty,' says Zosimus,[3] 'was with Rufinus in the East and with Stilicho in the West . . . all the edicts of the emperors were prescribed by Rufinus or by Stilicho.' In this position Rufinus acquired enormous wealth by the sale of prefectures and other high dignities. At length he aspired to imperial power. The first step was to be the marriage of his daughter to Arcadius.

Rufinus foiled in his ambition

This design was intercepted by a stratagem. Arcadius had been persuaded to discard the alliance with Rufinus, and to choose for his bride the beautiful Eudoxia. It is an interesting note

---

[1] *In Rufin.* i. 220-258.   [2] St. Luke xiii. 25, 26.   [3] v. 1.

of Byzantine art that the charms of Eudoxia were commended to Arcadius by means of a picture. This lady, the daughter of Bauto, a Frankish general, was residing in the house of one of the sons of Promotus, the rival of Rufinus. The scheme was arranged with the utmost secresy by Eutropius, a powerful eunuch of the palace. When the festive procession moved through the streets under the direction of Eutropius, a gorgeous robe and ornaments worthy of an emperor's bride being carried by attendants, instead of advancing to the palace of Rufinus, it turned aside and halted at the house where lived Eudoxia, who was clothed in the imperial robes and conveyed to the palace. This check to the ambition of Rufinus was followed after a short interval by his complete ruin.

Rufinus instinctively foresaw his doom in the march of Stilicho to the East, and he put forth every expedient *His fall and death* to hinder this dangerous advance. An order from Arcadius compelled Stilicho to stop at Thessalonica, but he was able to entrust the execution of his plans to the Gothic general Gainas.

To make the interest of this crisis intelligible it will be necessary to trace the earlier career of Stilicho.

If the glowing verse of Claudian may not be accepted as literally historical in every point, the greatness of Stilicho's career proves at least the substantial accuracy *The early life of Stilicho* of the poet. Claudian describes him as fired from boyhood with high and noble aspirations and as winning from his fellow-citizens a recognition of his youthful promise :—

taciti suffragia vulgi
Jam tibi detulerant quicquid mox debuit aula.

An embassy to Persia displayed his high capacity in another direction, and on his return he received a most distinguished mark of court favour in his marriage with Serena, the niece of Theodosius. This alliance brought with it a position of unrivalled power in the State. Stilicho received in succession the highest dignities which the empire could bestow, and eventually obtained the control of the whole military force of the West. On the death of Theodosius, Stilicho became the guardian of Honorius and Arcadius. In this office, according to some writers, Rufinus was associated with him; but in the West at least Stilicho was now supreme. His first act was to visit and reinstate the garrisons on the Rhine. He then proceeded to strike down the two great enemies of the empire — Gildo in Africa, and Rufinus at the court of Constantinople. The former, a tyrant of the most brutal and despotic character, had for twelve years oppressed Africa with a reign of terror:—

His rapid rise to power

Defeats Gildo

> Instat terribilis vivis, morientibus hæres,
> Virginibus raptor, thalamis obscœnus adulter.

The great danger to be apprehended from an interference with his rule was the stoppage of the corn supply from Africa, which had for centuries been the granary of Rome. Here Stilicho displayed his skill by arranging for a supply of corn from the province of Gaul, which was floated down the Rhone and so forwarded to the Roman market. The expedition against Gildo was entrusted to his brother Mascezel, who had taken refuge at Milan from the dangers which threatened him at home. For there had been a deadly feud between the two brothers; and Mascezel was now made desperate by a crowning act of atrocity—the murder of his children by Gildo.

The expedition was, in the language of later devotion, a crusade. The leader himself was a devout Christian; and on his way to Africa he landed at Capraria, in those days a settlement of monks, some of whom were persuaded to come on board his ships. The victory of Mascezel was complete, and even, as it appeared to some, miraculous. Gildo put himself to death; and Mascezel returned in triumph. But an accident in crossing over a bridge put an end to a life which might have been glorious. This was in the year 398. The attack upon Rufinus had taken place three years previously.

When Gainas approached Constantinople with his victorious troops, Arcadius and his minister, Rufinus, advanced to meet them. As Rufinus passed along the line, the wings of the army were observed to be closing in upon him. At length Gainas gave the signal, and a dagger was plunged into the breast of Rufinus, who instantly expired at the feet of Arcadius. It was an act which blackens the fair fame of Stilicho, a return to the tyrant's policy of government by assassination and fear. Nor did Stilicho gain the end at which he aimed, for the power of the Eastern court passed into the hands of the eunuch Eutropius, and of Gainas. The latter, no longer faithful to Stilicho, joined with Eutropius in resisting his influence at Constantinople. Stilicho consequently had the magnanimity to abandon the East, though the event of

Assassination of Rufinus

a civil war might have left him supreme at Constantinople as well as at Milan.

His prestige was enhanced by the betrothal of his daughter, Maria, to the emperor Honorius, who aban- *Marriage of Stilicho's daughter* doned the defence of the empire to his powerful minister, and gave himself up to such unexciting pursuits as feeding poultry. Stilicho was, in fact, virtually emperor, and that at a time of critical importance. In a fine passage Claudian describes the solitary greatness achieved by this distinguished soldier and statesman, his prescience of danger, and his fortitude in meeting it:—

> Solus erat Stilicho qui desperantibus augur
> Sponderet meliora manu ; dubiæque salutis
> Dux idem vatesque fuit.[1]

He praises the courage with which he raised the fainting hopes of Italy, until at length 'she dared to emerge from the darkness of despair and to rest assured with so mighty a hostage for her destiny.'

CHAPTER XVIII.

ALARIC AND THE GOTHS.

THE threatening cloud of danger to which Claudian alludes was the approach of the Goths. The death of *Invasion of Alaric* Theodosius had been the signal for their incursion; and they crossed the Danube under the leadership of Alaric. The position and strength

---

[1] *De Bello Getico*, 267.

of Constantinople—the first object of attack—determined Alaric to retreat in order to press his invasion on another quarter of the empire. In the year 396 he followed the historic footsteps of the Persian invader, passing through Macedonia and Thessaly to the narrow defile of Thermopylæ, where, as in the days of Leonidas, a handful of men might have opposed his advance. No resistance, however, was offered; but the defenders of the pass were treacherously withdrawn by the orders of their leader Gerontius. Alaric led his army past Thermopylæ, 'as though,' says a scornful writer, 'he were traversing a racecourse.' Thence he advanced to the sack of defenceless cities in the plains of Phocis and Bœotia, making a broad track of flame and ruin long afterwards discernible. 'Even now,' writes Zosimus,[1] 'all the Bœotians and other Grecian peoples point to a desolation which dates from this period.' All males capable of bearing arms were slain, the women and children were carried off with the rest of the spoil. Thebes was spared, partly owing to the strength of its fortifications, partly to Alaric's impatience to reach Athens. Here it is said that the goddess Pallas appeared to protect the sacred walls, and that Alaric consented to honourable terms of peace, and entered Athens rather as an invited and distinguished guest than as a dreaded conqueror. He next turned his arms against Megara, which fell at the first blow, crossed the Isthmus, again through the treacherous negligence of Gerontius, and finally secured entire mastery over the Peloponnesus.

Stilicho, the only Roman general capable of stem-

[1] v. 5.

ming the tide of ruin, hastened to Greece, and in a brief space of time compelled the Gothic army to take refuge in Mount Pholoe, where it was surrounded by his troops. From this desperate position Alaric only escaped by the negligence of his enemies, who allowed themselves to be enticed by the amusements of a pleasure-loving people, and relaxed the rigours of the siege. This was in the year 396. Alaric conducted his retreat with masterly skill, and then, without delay and with consummate policy, concluded with the court of Constantinople a treaty of peace which was no doubt facilitated by jealousy of Stilicho's success.

Stilicho repels the invasion

A still more surprising stroke of statesmanship followed. Alaric was proclaimed master-general of Eastern Illyricum. No government could inflict a more cruel insult on its subjects who had fought and suffered in the cause of their country. In a passage of generous indignation Claudian contrasts the times when the good old custom prevailed of rewarding high desert and crushing the rebel, with his own time, when 'he who breaks treaties grows rich, he who keeps them comes to want: the scourge of Greece, the devastator of Epirus is master of Illyricum, enters by right the cities which he besieged, and metes out justice to the men whose wives he ruined and whose sons he slew.' Alaric used his authority to furnish his troops with military supplies and equipment from the armouries of Greece. He turned the discord of the Eastern and Western empires to his own aggrandisement, and soon felt himself strong enough to attempt the cherished object of his ambition—the conquest of Italy and Rome.

Of Alaric's first campaign in Italy in the year 402 few particulars are known. Probably after occupying the northern provinces of Istria and Venetia he recrossed the Alps to draw reinforcements from the Danube.

Alaric's first invasion of Italy

Once more all hopes of resistance to the Gothic invasion were centred in Stilicho, who was worthy of the general trust. His first concern was to urge the timid Honorius to hold his ground in Milan, until an army should be collected to check the advance of Alaric; then in mid-winter he crossed the Alps to subdue a barbarian tribe which had invaded Rhætia. A rapid conquest gave him fresh recruits and released the troops engaged in tranquillising the district. He then issued orders to call in the Roman legionaries from the remotest regions of the empire. The Rhine frontier was denuded of troops; even our own island had to give up her protecting garrison in this dire necessity of Rome:

Confidence in Stilicho

His measures

> Venit et extremis legio prætenta Britannis,
> Quæ Scoto dat frena truci.[1]

The advance of Alaric, favoured by the unusual dryness of the spring, was swifter than Stilicho had calculated. Honorius fled before him and took refuge in Asta, a small Ligurian town, where he was besieged by Alaric and driven to the verge of a capitulation. At the moment of his extremity Stilicho appeared at the head of an advanced guard with which he cut his way through the investing lines. The rescue of Honorius was followed by a

Defeat of Alaric

---

[1] Claudian, *De Bello Getico*, 416.

general attack on the forces of Alaric at Pollentia, a few miles south of Asta and twenty-five miles southeast of Turin. The Goths were surprised during the celebration of the Easter festival. The battle raged all day with varying success, but ended in the utter defeat of the Goths. The spoils of the East fell into the hands of Western conquerors, and thousands of captives, 'released,' to use the poet's words, 'by the slaughter of their masters, impressed grateful kisses on the bloodstained hands of their deliverers.'[1]

In his retreat Alaric resolved to seize the important fortress of Verona; but his line of march and design were betrayed to Stilicho. His troops were caught in the mountain defiles, and attacked in front, flank, and rear. Another crushing defeat left him with a small body of survivors, who prepared for a desperate resistance on some mountain fastness. But, probably through the policy of Stilicho, Alaric was allowed to escape.

It was a great success, and one which might have awakened visionary hopes of a restored Rome, resting once more on the valour and wisdom of her citizens. But this was not the destined course of history, and a more exact judgment decides that the seeds of corruption were too widely sown in the declining empire to make it worth while or possible to rebuild the shattered edifice on the old lines.

The victory too late to save Rome from ruin

Behind the glitter of the procession, in which Honorius and Stilicho celebrated the victories over Alaric and the Goths, a keen eye might discern the

[1] Claudian, *De Bello Getico*, 618, 619.

real and enduring forces which were to mould the future empire. It is in vain that Claudian recalls the examples of ancient Rome, and speaks of this phantom triumph as if it meant the same thing as the triumph of Marius or of Scipio. The Church and Kingdom of Christ, which Claudian never names, and the Teutonic races, which a proud inscription and a train of captives The real forces in the world declared to have been vanquished utterly, were the realities which lay behind this glorious semblance of imperial power.

Two incidents occurring at this time respectively manifested the two forces which were beginning to rule the world and to determine the events of history.

1. One was the daring feat of the monk Telemachus during this visit of Honorius to Rome.

2. The other was the resolution of Honorius to abandon Milan for the secure retreat of Ravenna.

1. One of the most revolting features of Roman civilisation was the exhibition of gladiatorial shows, in Gladiatorial shows stopped by Christianity which slaves or captives taken in war were compelled to slay each other in cold blood, 'to make a Roman holiday.' Christianity had from the first raised a protest against this inhuman and degrading barbarity. The practice had even been formally condemned in the code of the first Christian emperor; but the cruel custom, to which thousands were sacrificed every year in the chief towns and cities of the empire, lived on.

At length the needed self-devotion came. When Honorius entered the ancient capital of the world to celebrate his triumph, the games were being celebrated on a magnificent scale. But when the time arrived for the gladiatorial combats, hardly had the fight begun when Telemachus, an Oriental monk, stepped down from the circle of spectators on to the arena, and parted the combatants. He was instantly stoned to death by the indignant populace, but his heroic act stopped once and for ever the barbarities of gladiatorial shows in Roman amphitheatres.[1]

2. We have seen how Honorius was stayed for a while in Milan by the imperious bidding of his minister, and how he had fled before the Goths to Asta. After this experience Milan ceased to be a possible capital for a monarch who had a 'pre-eminence of cowardice.' The chosen seat of imperial timidity was Ravenna. This transference of the capital was a well-marked step in the decadence of the empire. Milan had been chosen to be a frontier fortress against a Gothic invasion; Ravenna was chosen to be a secure retreat from Gothic attack.

The transference of the capital

Ravenna, like Venice, was built on piles at the edge of a vast lagune or swamp. The surrounding marshes were only passable by means of bridges. At one time it had been a naval station and port; but by degrees the harbour was filled with alluvial deposits from the Po, and the strip of land thus formed between the city and the sea was covered with a belt of pine wood. In this way nature continued to contribute to the defences of Ravenna.

Ravenna

The political history of Ravenna is the history of cowardice, of decline, and of shrinking from high responsibilities. But viewed from another side, it has

[1] Theodoret, v. 26.

associations and an interest of the most sacred and ennobling kind. In the storms and revolutions of this turbulent and changeful age, monuments of Christian art were growing into existence, with matchless and undying beauty of form and colour, under the care and direction of Galla Placidia. Five of the churches of Ravenna owe their origin to her, and are the enduring memorials of her reign. Externally plain and uninteresting, the churches of Ravenna still preserve on their walls and vaulted roofs, almost in original brightness and truth of colouring, the imperishable mosaics placed there by Byzantine artists of the fifth and sixth centuries. It is possible to see, in the long processions there depicted, the shape and colour of priestly vestments and imperial robes, and the features of men and women who made history at this epoch. Here are the earliest of Christian symbols of priceless interest and value: the Cross itself both in the ground-plan of the churches and represented on the monuments; the Lamb of God; the emblems of the Evangelists; the Christ Himself, always a youthful beardless figure, now as the Good Shepherd, now as the Conqueror bearing on high the flag of victory, now, it would seem, committing heretical works to the flames, now calmly enthroned. Another symbol has a peculiar importance in this age. More than once two stags are represented coming to a fountain of water, which is interpreted as an emblem of the heathen world being brought into the Church of Christ. One shrine in Ravenna, the Chapel in the Archbishop's palace, still used for daily service, stands without alteration, hallowed by uninterrupted rites since the days of St. Peter

The artistic and historical interest of Ravenna

Chrysologus, who founded it in this century. The body of Galla Placidia herself was placed in a chapel of surpassing beauty, beneath a vault of deep blue mosaic spangled with golden stars. For eleven centuries her form could be seen clothed as in life with imperial robes and seated on a throne of cypress wood. In 1577 by an unhappy accident this was destroyed by fire.

Such are the memorials which still lend an unfailing interest to Ravenna. By its very seclusion, rendered still more guarded by the gradual withdrawal of the sea, this sheltered city has preserved unimpaired the unique monuments of an age which has elsewhere left few memorials.

While Honorius sought protection in the security of his new capital, Stilicho was once more engaged in the defence of the empire. A fresh invasion of barbarian hordes poured down the passes of the Alps, this time under the guidance of Radagaisus, a type of barbarian very different from Alaric. Alaric was a Christian, and as a soldier and statesman understood the rules of civilised warfare, and acknowledged the obligation of treaties. Radagaisus was not only a barbarian and a pagan, but a fierce and merciless tyrant. Many cities had fallen before his arms, and the siege of Florence was being pressed with eager haste, when at the moment of direst extremity Stilicho came to the relief.

The invasion of Radagaisus

He declined a pitched battle with Radagaisus, preferring to reduce the enemy by the slower process of starvation. He drew lines around the barbarian forces and maintained the blockade with such strictness that the enemy were compelled to capitulate. Radagaisus was put to death—an act utterly unjustifiable—and his soldiers were sold into slavery.

St. Augustine has some remarks on this decisive Christian victory in the 'De Civitate Dei.'[1] In his view it was a direct conflict between paganism and Christianity; for Radagaisus openly appeased the gods and invited them to his aid by daily sacrifices, 'a thing,' says Augustine, finely indicating the religious revolution, 'which the Christian religion forbids Roman citizens to do.' It was the firm belief and the subject of boast in the pagan army, that the gods would never suffer a nation who neglected them to vanquish so devout a worshipper as Radagaisus. St. Augustine describes the victory as miraculous and swift, achieved without the cost of a single life, even without a wound, in the Christian army—an exaggeration, perhaps, but owing to the defensive tactics of Stilicho not impossible. St. Augustine goes on to point out the providence by which the capture of Rome was effected, not by an idolatrous pagan, who knew no mercy, but by a general who, if he was a barbarian, was yet a Christian, under whose auspices—for the first time in the history of the world—men and women were spared who fled for refuge to the sanctuary of Christian churches.

St. Augustine's view of the defeat of Radagaisus

Though Alaric took no part in this campaign, he, nevertheless, must have watched it with a keen interest. When it was over, he took an unexpected step in seeking an alliance with the court of Ravenna, and broke off his relations with the Eastern emperor. He even succeeded in gaining the

Alaric allies himself with the Western empire

[1] v. 23.

friendship of his great adversary Stilicho. In recognition of these advances, he was appointed master-general of the Roman armies in Illyricum, and, through the influence of Stilicho, obtained a subsidy from the Roman senate. The shame of this last concession was bitterly felt by the senators themselves, even when they supported Stilicho by a reluctant vote. 'This is not peace, but a contract of slavery,' exclaimed the senator Lampadius, in words so true to the crisis and so welcome to popular feeling, that the Greek historian Zosimus, wishing the *ipsissima verba* to be remembered, has preserved them in the Latin language in which they were pronounced.

Stilicho had taken an unpopular step. He was accused of undue favour to the barbarians, and of neglecting his Roman soldiers. Olympius, the new favourite of Honorius, destroyed the reputation of Stilicho, by accusing him of scheming to place his son Eucherius on the imperial throne. Honorius was persuaded to believe in Stilicho's ambition and treason, and gave his sanction to the intrigues which planned his downfall.

Stilicho's policy unpopular

At Pavia, where the troops were encamped on their way to a campaign in Gaul against the usurper Constantine,[1] a massacre of Stilicho's friends took place. Officers of the highest distinction were mercilessly cut down by the partisans of Olympius, and the emperor was forced to approve the deed, and pardon the assassins. Stilicho, who was at Bologna, consulted his friends, but hesitated to take up arms against the empire. Instead of choosing the only path of safety

Intrigues against Stilicho

[1] See p. 165.

open to him, and one which promised success, he threw himself into Ravenna, the stronghold of his enemies, and took refuge at the altar. He was induced to leave his sanctuary by a perfidious falsehood of Count Heraclian, who, the instant Stilicho left the church, produced the warrant for his execution. 'He fell,' says Gibbon, 'with a courage not unworthy of the last of the Roman generals.' Zosimus awards him the high praise of unselfish moderation. Notwithstanding his imperial condition, and the vast sums of money placed at his disposal, he took no occasion of enriching himself, and he conferred no higher dignity on his only son than the office of Præfectus Notariorum (Præfect of the Notaries or Clerks).

His death

Sozomen sums up contemporary opinion when he says of Stilicho: 'he had attained almost absolute power; and all men, so to speak, whether Romans or barbarians, were under his control.'[1] His death occurred in August 408.

A significant incident took place in the Italian garrison towns, which helps us to understand the policy and position of Stilicho. As soon as the news of his death reached the soldiers quartered in the various cities, they attacked the wives and children of the barbarians, massacred all whom they found, and carried off their goods.

Stilicho's wisdom proved by events

Nothing could indicate with greater clearness the wise and temperate policy of Stilicho. His death was the signal for an outbreak of the race hatred between the Romans, or subjects of the emperor, and the barbarians. Stilicho's later policy, on which he shipwrecked

[1] Book ix. c. 4.

his personal fortune and popularity, was to recognise the presence of the barbarian element in the empire. He alone had the statesman's prophetic insight to discern the rising and irresistible force—the force of the new world now working itself into existence—which lay in the Teutonic race. The true policy of Rome was, he saw, to win over, and to assimilate, if possible, this vigorous element with the imperial system. For this reason an alliance with Alaric, at first sight a startling departure, became indispensable, because Alaric alone could efficiently direct the new force. Events proved the soundness of this policy, but it was the cause of Stilicho's fall. The Romans, as the subjects of Honorius were still proud to call themselves, resented the idea of making terms with the barbarians.

The death of Stilicho gave the commanding voice in the court and empire to Olympius. His first measures were to pursue the relatives and friends of Stilicho with relentless cruelty. The empress Thermantia, daughter of Stilicho and sister of Maria, the first wife of Honorius, was divorced. Many of the fallen minister's partisans were tortured to obtain evidence of their master's treason, but no discovery was made. The innocence of Stilicho is established in history.

Olympius

Olympius then proceeded to disqualify from State service all pagans and all persons tainted with Arianism. This sweeping measure lost to the imperial armies numbers of the most skilful officers and some thirty thousand of the bravest soldiers. Passed at that critical epoch it was a measure fatal to Rome. Alaric himself could not have shaped a policy

Disqualification of pagans

more favourable to his cause than one which gave him thousands of recruits and a motive which fired their indignation.

It was a blunder in State policy, and it was a mistake in ecclesiastical discipline. It has taken many centuries to determine that the relations between the State and the Church do not prevent the State from employing the services of all its citizens. But in this instance the policy pursued sprang from no high principle; it was simply the result of rancorous hatred of Stilicho and his measures.

The natural result followed. Alaric instantly invaded Italy, and most of the towns in the north opened their gates to him. Leaving unapproachable Ravenna behind him, he marched swiftly against Rome itself and formed the siege (408). 'During a period of six hundred and nineteen years,' writes Gibbon, 'the seat of empire had never been violated by the presence of foreign enemies.' A siege of Rome therefore seemed to be like a violation of a fixed law of nature. The first feelings were those of shame and indignation, and then in an access of suspicion—a frequent phenomenon in such cases—a cruel deed was wrought.

Invasion of Italy by Alaric
The siege of Rome

Serena, widow of Stilicho and niece of Theodosius, was within the walls of the city. A rumour spread that she was in league with the Goths, and that her death would be the signal for their departure. The aunt and mother-in-law of the emperor was mercilessly slain; but still the siege went on with increasing severity.

The Romans sent an embassy to negotiate. When the legates spoke of the fierce resistance of a people maddened by despair, Alaric's scornful answer was: 'The thicker the hay, the easier it is mowed.' At length the terms of retreat were arranged on payment of an enormous fine.

The negotiations which followed were marked by the presumptuous folly of Olympius, who soon afterwards suffered the fate of favourites, and was supplanted by Jovius, the prætorian prefect.

The palace had learned by experience the evil results of the edict against pagans and Arians. The restriction was removed, and many Roman soldiers returned to their standard. Among these was Generidus, who presented an example of unselfishness and magnanimity, a type of character not seldom to be found in the history of a losing cause. Generidus, the heathen, displayed the qualities which a prosperous Christianity was in danger of losing. He refused to be restored to his rank in the army by a *privilegium*, preferring to wait until his brethren of the ancient faith could re-enter the imperial service with him. He afterwards served with distinction on the frontier of northern Italy. There the old Roman discipline seemed once more to revive, and Generidus was able to protect the Dalmatian frontier from the attacks of fresh barbarian foes.

Generidus

Some efforts were now made to bring about a reconciliation between Alaric and the emperor. Alaric met the imperial envoys at Ariminum; but Honorius was firm for once, when it was impolitic to be firm, and though he granted to Alaric as much corn and money as he might desire, he sternly refused to put him in command of the cavalry and infantry. Accordingly

Alaric was soon again at the gates of Rome. He seized on the port of Ostia and stopped the importation of supplies, so that the city was starved into submission. Alaric entered in triumph, and proclaimed Attalus, then prefect of Rome, emperor in place of Honorius. Once more a Roman emperor reigned in Rome. Alaric was placed at the head of the Roman armies, and his brother-in-law, Ataulf (Adolphus), was raised to the command of the domestic cavalry. So strong did the position of Attalus appear that Honorius offered to share the imperial dignity with him, when an unexpected intervention once more turned the scale in favour of Honorius. A body of four thousand men arrived unexpectedly at Ravenna, and by their aid the city was secured. Meantime Rome was again exposed to the horrors of famine, through the cessation of the accustomed supplies of food from Africa. Attalus, completely discredited, and now deserted by Alaric, had no course left but to submit to Honorius. He was stripped of his imperial robes, but by the favour of Honorius was allowed to live.

Second siege of Rome by Alaric

Attalus proclaimed emperor

Again there was a prospect of peace between Alaric and the emperor, but again the folly of Honorius turned the arms of the Goths against Rome. Sarus, a barbarian chieftain then at the court of Ravenna, dreading the influence of Alaric, attacked his forces with a body of three hundred men, and after inflicting much loss on the Gothic army, sheltered himself within the walls of Ravenna. Receiving no satisfaction for this insult and the damage which he sustained, Alaric for the third time marched upon Rome.

The gates were opened by treachery, and this time

the city was given over to be sacked and plundered by the barbarian soldiers. The scenes which followed are those with which military historians of all ages have made us familiar. But for the first time in the history of the world there was some mitigation of the horrors of a sack. The Christian historians record with pride the immunity from sacrilege granted to the sanctuary of the 'large and beautiful Church erected around the tomb of St. Peter.'[1] They relate instances where the chastity and the courage of Christian ladies commanded the respect and secured the protection of the barbarians. St. Augustine is careful to emphasise the details of this capture of Rome. 'All the desolation, the butchery, the plunderings and burnings, the misery wrought in this recent disaster, belong to the usages of war; but that which is new, the choice of spacious basilicas to serve as places of refuge where men and women can be safe from the sword, from slavery, from violence of every kind—all this is to be attributed to the Christian name and to a Christian epoch.'[2]

Rome occupied by the Goths A.D. 410.

The fall of Rome (410) sent a shock through the civilised world. Though long deserted by the sovereign power, and no longer the seat of empire, Rome, with her great and undying associations, still held men's minds in thrall. One of the chief and proudest of these associations was her freedom from conquest; and when at length the spell was broken, no fresh development of history could astonish mankind. This great disaster, as it seemed, marked the beginning of a new epoch. A new Rome, Christian instead of pagan, rose from the ashes of Alaric's conflagration.

Results for Christianity

[1] Sozomen, ix. 9.   [2] *De Civ.* i. 7.

The ancient capital of the world had been the stronghold of the old religion. The patrician families clung to their ancestral rites more from pride than from religious conviction. But the sword and flames of the Gothic conquerors wrecked the fortunes of the Roman patriciate, and involved their pagan clients and followers in the same ruin.

It would have been different if Radagaisus had triumphed. The sword of Stilicho saved Rome and the world at least from a temporary revival of paganism. Alaric swept away paganism, and left Rome, still crowned with its ancient prestige, to be the capital, no longer of Cæsarism, but of Christianity. 'The capture of Rome by Alaric,' writes Milman, 'was one of the great steps by which the Pope arose to his plenitude of power. There could be no question that from this time the greatest man in Rome was the Pope; he alone was invested with permanent and real power; he alone possessed all the attributes of supremacy, the reverence, it was his own fault, if not the love of the people.'[1] The removal of the seat of government from Milan to Ravenna contributed to the same result. The influence of St. Ambrose, centred at the court, and both supported and deferred to by the temporal power, dominated the Western Church. But at Ravenna no great churchman had appeared, and Ravenna was rather a refuge from the barbarians than the capital of an empire. Rome became once more the foremost city of the West, and the power which ruled there was not the empire but the Church.

Alaric withdrew his troops from Rome after an

[1] *Latin Christianity*, ii. 1.

occupation of six days, and proceeded to ravage the fruitful fields and prosperous cities of southern Italy.

<small>Death and burial of Alaric</small> His designs extended to a conquest of Sicily and Africa, but his career was closed by death in 412. If the story told by Jornandes, a writer who lived a century and a half after the event, is to be credited, Christianity had failed to quell the native savagery of the Goths. This author narrates that the waters of the little river Busentinus were diverted, and the tomb of Alaric placed in the vacant bed. The stream was then allowed to return to its natural channel; and in order that the place of the great conqueror's sepulchre might be concealed for ever, the captives who had been employed in its construction were inhumanly massacred.

CHAPTER XIX.

THE WEST UNDER HONORIUS.

THE feebleness of Honorius began to bear fruit in the distant parts of the empire. Both in regard to <small>The hold on the West by the two empires</small> Church and State the Western provinces had shown a tendency to independent government. But in all probability the Churches of Gaul were more subservient to the see of Rome than the civil and military administration to the central authority at Ravenna. Pope Innocent I. claimed for the Roman see obedience from the Churches of Britain, Gaul, Spain, and Africa, as well as from those of Italy, on the ground that St. Peter and his successors were the founders of each and all of these Churches. In great measure this wide and unhistorical claim was admitted. The juster claims of the imperial power had scant recognition in the West. The legionaries in Britain revolted, and after electing and deposing two emperors in swift succession, agreed in the choice of a common soldier named Constantine, whose sole merit seems to have consisted in his illustrious name. Notwithstanding his incapacity—such was the weakness of the imperial administration—this new Constantine was able to establish himself in Britain, and to overrun Gaul from Boulogne to the Cottian Alps. His son Constans was equally successful in Spain, where he made himself master of the province, the only serious opposition being offered by two brothers named Didymus and Verinian, who were related to the emperor Honorius. After a gallant resistance the rising was quelled and the brothers taken and slain. Constantine himself crossed the Alps and penetrated into Italy as far as to Verona. Here the rebellion collapsed. Alanicus, commanding the troops of Honorius, who was about to betray his master's cause, was assassinated in a procession, and Gerontius, one of the ablest of Constantine's generals, deserted him, setting up a rival emperor named Maximus.

The usurper Constantine

Constantine retreated from Italy and threw himself into Arles. Here he was besieged first by Gerontius, who, hearing of the approach of the imperial forces under Constantius, raised the siege. Gerontius was surrounded, and at length, driven to desperation, put himself to death. The Christian historian, Sozomen, names with commendation the conduct of his wife Nunechia, who was a Christian. It is interesting in this strange complexity of intricate rebellion to be brought in contact with the thought of Christian life and love going on bravely through the storm. Gerontius, we read, might easily have escaped with his life had not his affection for his wife detained him by her side. And when all hope was gone, Gerontius first, in compliance with his prayer, slew the one friend who had remained with him, and then his wife besought him to do the like to her, lest she should fall into the hands of her enemies. Accordingly, he complied with her request before falling on his own sword. Sozomen adds, without the hesitation which might occur to deeper Christian thought: 'Thus died one who manifested a degree of courage worthy of her religion; for she was a Christian.'

Meantime the siege of Arles was pressed, and Constantine, despairing of the succour for which he had hoped, had recourse to a strange and suggestive expedient. Casting aside his purple robe and imperial ornaments, he caused himself to be ordained a priest, and, trusting to the protection of the sacred office, surrendered himself to Constantius, who sent him under a guard to Ravenna together with his son Julian. Both, however, were slain before they reached that city, and the various leaders who had risen against Honorius suffered the same fate. It was indeed a remarkable fact, carefully noted by the Christian historians, that seven usurpers who had successively risen against this feeble and incompetent, though pious and orthodox, emperor, failed to make any effective head against his power, and fell almost without striking a blow. One alone of these threatened to be formidable; for a time Jovinus was aided by the alliance with

Constantine is slain

Ataulf, the king of the Visigoths in succession to Alaric. For some unexplained reason Constantius retreated before him, leaving the whole of Gaul open to the usurper. But before long Ataulf found cause to withdraw his alliance and turn his arms against Jovinus, who fell as swiftly as he had risen to power. Ataulf proved his loyalty to Honorius by sending to him the heads of Jovinus and his brother Sebastian.

<small>The end of Ataulf</small>
The disturbed and unsettled condition of Western Europe had opened the gates of Spain to the incursions of the Vandals, the Suevi, and the Alani. In the process of conquest the unhappy country endured untold miseries of war, rapine, and famine. Ataulf was directed to recover the possession of Spain for his imperial brother-in-law. He took Barcelona by surprise, but was assassinated within its walls by one of his slaves, who had been a follower of Sarus, one of his vanquished rivals.[1]

<small>Galla Placidia</small>
His widow was Galla Placidia (a name memorable in the history of Christian art), sister of the emperor Honorius, who had been captured in the sack of Rome. In spite of the protests of the Roman court, she was united in marriage with Ataulf, whose affection for his bride, and whose pride in the imperial alliance, gave the court of Ravenna the support of his services, with the brief exception of his transitory alliance with Jovinus. The death of Ataulf exposed Galla Placidia to the scornful cruelty of Singeric, his short-lived successor. Under Wallia, who after the death of Singeric was chosen king of the

---

[1] This invasion of Ataulf laid the foundation of the Gothic kingdom in Spain and south-western Gaul. See Freeman's *Historical Geography*, p. 89; Gibbon, iii. 455.

Visigoths, Galla Placidia was restored to her brother on the payment of a ransom.

It was at this period of confusion that the Roman legions left Britain and abandoned the Celtic inhabitants of our island to the attacks of the Teutonic invaders—the Saxons, Jutes, and English. This definite act on the part of the Roman armies gave a character to the settlement of Britain entirely different from that of Gaul and Spain. In the latter countries the settlement was gradual, and the barbarian invaders adopted in great measure the language, customs, and religion of the Roman population. In the case of Britain the invading force consisted of uncivilised and pagan strangers. The conflict was one of extermination. The victorious Saxons, Jutes, and English assimilated nothing. They swept away the race, the religion, and the stores of Roman civilisation.

Britain

This difference of settlement deeply affected the ecclesiastical history of Britain and south-western Europe. In Britain a fresh process of conversion had become necessary. In Gaul and Spain Christian teaching and influence were continuous and progressive. The Gothic kingdoms remained in some sense an integral part of the empire, long after Britain had become isolated and independent by the desertion of the Roman government.

The effects of the Saxon invasion

The express testimony of Zosimus places this important movement in the time of the usurper Constantine.[1] The events, therefore, which have just been narrated mark a crisis in British ecclesiastical history, which is,

---

[1] ἡ μὲν Βρεταννίας καὶ τῶν ἐν Κελτοῖς ἐθνῶν ἀπόστασις καθ' ὃν ἐτυράννει χρόνον ὁ Κωνσταντῖνος ἐγένετο.—*Lib.* vi. c. 6.

as it were, cleft in two at this point by the wedge of Saxon paganism. Politically, Britain was separated for ever from the empire; but its ecclesiastical relations with Rome were destined to be close and important, with varied results of good and evil.

Previous to this time, although the British Church was too far removed from the centre of imperial authority to be brought into close connexion with the higher civil administration, though it had sent forth no St. Ambrose or St. Jerome to sway the councils of emperors, or to decide the course of religious controversy, yet there is evidence of an important and flourishing Church in the British Isles, full of missionary zeal and saintly examples, which sent Bishops to the Councils of Arles, Ariminum and Sardica. The era of St. Patrick is placed in the year 433, and in Ireland there were probably more Bishops in the fifth century than at any subsequent period. The rise of Pelagianism is a stain on the annals of the British Church, but the existence of false teaching, cast in a thoughtful and philosophical mould, implies the presence of culture as well as of religion in these isles. The influence of Christian teaching was probably deep and wide-spread during the Roman occupation. It is possible to believe that the new version of the Scriptures by Jerome, and the hymns of St. Ambrose, found a welcome within the walls of Uriconium or Silchester, and that the penance of Theodosius, the conversion of St. Augustine, and the pious deeds of Honorius and Placidia were discussed in all their freshness of interest by Christian men and women in country villas and military stations, from York to London, and from

Christianity in Britain

Bangor to Lincoln, in the land which sent forth the first emperor who dared to give Christianity a place in the imperial system.

CHAPTER XX.

THE EAST.

WE have brought the affairs of the Western empire under survey, up to the important epoch marked by the fall of pagan Rome, and by the defeat of the usurper Constantine, and its consequences in the Western provinces.

Events in the Eastern division of the empire have hardly the same critical and momentous character in determining the course of history; but they bear testimony to the same marvellous ascendency of the Church in the affairs of men which we have traced in the West. This supreme influence is so familiar that it is needful to remind ourselves, more than once, how recent the revolution was, which conferred this great authority on the Christian religion.

The Church and the empire in East and West respectively differed considerably in character. The East adopted the symbols and the state in which Oriental despotism is wont to clothe itself. All traces of republican freedom had vanished. An absolute monarch demanded the servile submission of his subjects. The eunuchs of the palace became the ministers of State. The career of Rufinus was closed, and he was succeeded by the eunuch Eutropius, a man of infamous antecedents.

Characteristics of Church and State in East and West

Eutropius

The poet Claudian exhausts the resources of language in describing the scorn and shame with which the rule of this misshapen and wrinkled being was accepted by the Roman subjects of Arcadius, and the satisfaction which the appearance of such a general and statesman gives to the enemies of the nation.

The ruling passion of Eutropius was avarice, though he could have no children to inherit his wealth. The commands of provinces were put up for sale by this 'trafficker of empire and dishonest broker of dignities' (Institor imperii, caupo famosus honorum). Claudian [1] describes the process of sale:—

> Certantum sæpe duorum
> Diversum suspendit onus; cum pondere judex
> Vergit, et in geminas nutat provincia lances.

Another plan of amassing wealth—a favourite one with tyrants—was to confiscate the estates of wealthy men condemned in the servile courts of law on simulated charges.

At length the gathering storm of hatred broke. The fall of Eutropius came to pass partly by the petition of the empress Eudoxia, partly by the demand of the Gothic general Gainas, who bitterly resented his influence and position.

Gainas, who had been sent to put down a rising of the Ostrogoths on the Hellespont, secretly joined hands with the enemy, and under pretence of making terms of peace pressed his own wishes upon the emperor. He represented that Tribigild, the leader of the Ostrogoths, demanded the execution of

<small>Gainas and the Goths</small>

---
[1] *In Eutrop.* i. 207.

Eutropius as the condition of laying down his arms, a demand which it would be impolitic to refuse.

Eutropius took refuge in the basilica. Chrysostom, who was officiating at the time, defended the trembling fugitive with all his eloquence, and obtained for him a promise that his life should be spared; but the enemies of the disgraced statesman soon found a pretext for breaking the promise. After a summary trial Eutropius was put to death at Chalcedon, not on the ground of the many enormities which had stained a flagrantly wicked life, but on a charge of high treason for having driven a pair of horses of a particular breed and colour reserved for the imperial use.

Gainas now pressed the ascendency which he had obtained. He placed himself at the head of the Goths, and dictated terms to Arcadius, who permitted him to cross over into Europe, and to occupy Constantinople with his troops. He then proceeded to demand one of the churches of the capital for the use of his Arian followers. Against this proposal Chrysostom protested. He assembled the Bishops then resident in the city, sought an interview with the emperor, whom in the presence of Gainas he urged to put in force the laws against heretics; 'it would be better,' he said, 'to be deprived of the empire than to betray the House of God into the hands of the impious.' 'Thus did John boldly contend in defence of the church that was under his care.'[1] The answer of Arcadius is not recorded; but events decided in favour of Chrysostom. The city was greatly excited. It was suspected that Gainas with his Goths was about to make a raid on the shops of the

[1] Sozomen, lib. viii. c. 4.

silversmiths, who accordingly protected their stores. The Goths retaliated by an attempt to fire the palace. The next day the gates of the city were closed and a massacre ensued in which thousands of the barbarians were slain. Gainas thus lost the flower of his army; a vast number of the remainder perished in a desperate effort to cross the Hellespont. Eventually Gainas broke away from his main army and led a few faithful followers to the Danube, where he was encountered in Thrace by Uldin, king of the Huns, with superior forces, was defeated and slain.

The history of Chrysostom which belongs to this period has been already sketched.[1] No career illustrates more admirably or in a more picturesque way the variety of ecclesiastical life and the great religious conflicts of the fourth and fifth centuries; nor is there a more striking example of the influence, it may even be said of the ascendency, of the Church over the empire at this period.

CHAPTER XXI.

THEODOSIUS II. AND PULCHERIA.

IN the year 408 Arcadius died, and was succeeded by his son Thedosius II., then a child of eight. But besides Theodosius, Arcadius left three daughters, Pulcheria, Arcadia, and Marina. Pulcheria, the eldest, was only fifteen years of age, but from the first she showed a high intelligence and capacity for government, which sustained her brother's throne and

Pulcheria virtually regent

---

[1] See ch. xvi.

left a mark on history. Socrates[1] speaks of the government being entrusted to Anthemius, the Prætorian prefect, during the minority of Theodosius. Sozomen makes no mention of Anthemius, and certainly expresses himself as if the direction of affairs was controlled by Pulcheria, of whom he writes in terms of such unmeasured praise that he even checks himself, 'lest,' he says, 'I should be condemned as a mere panegyrist.'

Pulcheria took a step at the commencement of her reign, for such it proved to be, which was surely the strangest ever taken in the history of civil government, and which marks in a striking manner the revolution in thought which the last hundred years had witnessed. In the presence of priests and people she took a vow of perpetual virginity; in this vow her sisters associated themselves, and, as a memorial of this solemn act, the three imperial sisters dedicated an altar set with gold and precious stones in the Church of Constantinople.

Pulcheria's palace became a convent into which no male was permitted to enter, and so the empire of the East was administered from a cloister. The education of the young emperor was superintended by Pulcheria with the most exact and loving care. In the manly arts of horsemanship and war masters were provided; but Pulcheria herself undertook to teach him the graces of imperial manner, 'how to gather up his robes, and take his seat with dignity, how to assume a mild or formidable mien, as occasion might require.' Above all she taught him devotion to the Church and to its ministers, and the duty of regular attendance

The education of Arcadius

[1] Lib. vii. c. 13.

at its services. Pulcheria herself caused magnificent churches to be erected, and built hospitals, monasteries and other ecclesiastical houses. The private life of the sisters was in accordance with these outward acts of religion. Attendance in the house of prayer, charity to strangers and the poor, days and nights spent in singing the praises of God, together with such manual tasks as occupy the time of exemplary women, formed, as Sozomen tells us, the occupation of Pulcheria and her sisters.

The history of the young emperor's marriage is a romance. Athenais, the beautiful daughter of a Greek philosopher, learned in all the wisdom of her age, had been deprived by her brethren's fraud of the little legacy bequeathed her by her father. She came as a suppliant to Pulcheria, who listened to her prayer, and taking note of her intelligence and charm of manner, resolved that she should be empress. Her portrait was shown to Theodosius, who was further allowed to see the lady herself from a place of concealment. The emperor admired and loved. Athenais abandoned the pagan religion in which she had been brought up, and received the name of Eudocia at her baptism. The married life which followed was happy for Eudocia in its earlier part, but adventurous and melancholy at its close. Her scholarly tastes continued, but instead of the pagan classics, her former delight, she devoted herself to the study of the Holy Scriptures and Christian literature. She paraphrased in verse some of the books of the Old Testament, composed a Homeric poem on the life of Christ and the acts of St. Cyprian, and a panegyric on the Persian victories of Theodosius. When her daughter Eudoxia at the age

The empress Eudocia

of fifteen married Valentinian III., emperor of the West, Eudocia made a pilgrimage to Jerusalem. Her progress was magnificent and ostentatious; she showered gifts on Antioch and other cities through which she passed, and in Jerusalem itself rivalled the empress Helena by her alms and magnificence. On her return she vainly endeavoured to overthrow the ascendency of Pulcheria. The struggle ended in the disgrace of Eudocia and in the ruin of her most faithful friends. Unhappily, too, an estrangement arose between Eudocia and her husband. The empress was permitted to retire to Jerusalem, where, divested of all imperial state, she lived in exile, devoting herself to a religious life, and to the end protesting her innocence of the charges which her enemies had preferred against her.

The Persian war which broke out in 421 presents some points of interest to the ecclesiastical historian. *Persecution of Christians in Persia* The occasion of it as related by Theodoret [1] raises a question which reappears in every age. A certain pious Bishop named Abdas, carried away by zeal, caused a *pyræon* or fire temple to be destroyed. The Persian king, Isdegerdes, informed of this by the Magi, at first spoke kindly to Abdas, for he was a friend of the Romans, and had been in some sense regarded as protector of the young emperor. He ordered Abdas, however, to rebuild the temple. The Bishop refusing to do this was ordered to execution. A persecution followed which involved the demolition of the Christian churches. Theodoret's comment on the transaction is noteworthy. He cannot approve the act of destruction. 'For the Apostle Paul,' he says,

[1] *H. E.* v. 39.

'did not destroy any of the idolatrous altars which he saw in Athens, but preached truth to the citizens. At the same time,' adds Theodoret, 'I greatly admire the firmness of Abdas in consenting to die rather than re-erect the temple which he had destroyed, and I judge that he thereby merited a crown. Indeed to me it seems almost the same thing to erect a temple to fire, and to fall down and worship it as a deity.' A sounder Christianity will reject a logic which admits a wrong but holds it unrighteous to redress it. It will be remembered, however, that the same principle was pressed upon Theodosius by St. Ambrose in the case of the Jewish synagogue destroyed by Christian zeal at Fort Callinicus near Aquileia. It is at least evident from this incident that the spirit of martyrdom still animated the Christian Church.

Socrates, who gives the best account of this war, assigns as its immediate cause the refusal of the Romans to deliver up to the Persians some Christian fugitives who had fled from the persecution into Roman territory. The Romans refused to surrender these unhappy men, because 'they were ready to do anything for the sake of the Christian religion. They chose rather therefore to renew the war with the Persians than to suffer the Christians to be miserably destroyed.' In this answer we remark the decisive Christianity of the imperial councils at this period. The defence of the Faith is a *casus belli*, a noticeable step in Christian influence.

Christianity a casus belli

The war ended to the advantage of the Roman armies, though the fortress of Nisibis still refused to yield. The ecclesiastical historian turns aside from his narrative to record the incredible speed with which the Roman victories were announced by the messenger Palladius, who could cover the distance between Constantinople and the Persian frontier in the space of three days. It is instructive to read in these days with their modern application the shrewd words of one who said: 'This man by his speed seems to contract the vast expanse of the Roman territories.'[1]

Another story of Christian action deserves to be recorded. The Romans in the course of their successes had captured seven thousand Persian prisoners. A famine set in, to the great distress of the miserable captives. Acacius, Bishop of Amida, hearing of their sad case, called his clergy together and said: 'Our God, my brethren, needs neither dishes nor cups, for He neither eats nor drinks, nor is in want of anything. Since then, by the liberality of the faithful, the Church possesses many vessels both of gold and silver, it behoves us to sell them, that by the money thus raised we may be able to redeem the prisoners, and also supply them with food.' Accordingly the sacred vessels were melted down, and the captives were ransomed, furnished with all that was necessary for their journey, and so restored. This gracious act paved the way for an honourable peace.

<small>Christian charity</small>

Socrates, who is the professed advocate of Theodosius II., as Sozomen is of Pulcheria, breaks out into praise of his hero with amusing *naïveté*. 'Although I neither seek the notice of my sovereign, nor wish to make an exhibition of my oratorical powers, yet have I felt it my duty to record

<small>The character of Theodosius II.</small>

---

[1] Socrates, vii. 19.

without exaggeration the singular virtues with which the emperor Theodosius is endowed.'[1] He then proceeds to describe the courage and hardihood of one born to the purple, his wisdom and knowledge, his observance of Christian duties, his self-command, his humanity; never would he suffer capital punishment to be inflicted on any criminal. Theodoret adds a story which confirms this account of the religious feeling of Theodosius II. An ascetic had made a demand upon the emperor; when refused, he uttered a sentence of excommunication upon him. This had so deep an effect upon the emperor that he refused to sit down to table until the same monk who had pronounced the excommunication should come forward and remove it.

On the whole the reign of Theodosius II. deserves a special study in the particular point of view from which we are surveying history. Ecclesiastical discipline has laid its principles and rules on the highest executive power. A time when an empress studied the works of St. Cyprian, and the virtual sovereign lady of the land was as eager to keep the faith pure from heresy as the State free from attack, is surely too singular an epoch to be passed over or ignored.

Intimate union of Church and State

If it was a weak reign, it was not without its successes. The barbarians were still pressing on the frontiers of the empire, but as yet they had not threatened Constantinople. Again, if it was a weak reign, it was one in which the influence of the Church had become paramount, and the fair way to judge of Christian influence is to consider what a weak reign

[1] viii. 22.

would have been without the thought of the Cross or the discipline of the Church.

In one respect this age was greater than we shall probably ever be able to appreciate properly. It must have been pre-eminently an age of Christian art: the mosaics of Ravenna owe much to the study of Eastern designs and to the skill of Eastern artificers.

CHAPTER XXII.

THE WEST FROM THE DEATH OF HONORIUS.

WHILE rejoicings over the successes in the Persian war were proceeding at Constantinople, Placidia, sister of Honorius, arrived at that city. Already her strange and romantic history had seen her twice a captive. We have described her redemption from the hands of Wallia, king of the Visigoths. On her return to Ravenna, Honorius gave her in marriage, a reluctant bride, to Constantius, the general who had defeated the usurper Constantine. Her husband was associated in the empire, but only enjoyed the title of Augustus for some months. He left two children by Placidia, Honoria and Valentinian III. After the death of Constantius, Honorius and his sister lived together for a while on terms of the deepest affection, but by some evil intrigue hatred was sown between them, and Placidia left the court of Ravenna for Constantinople. Soon afterwards news came that Honorius was dead, A.D. 423.

The rightful successor, the infant Valentinian, was proclaimed and supported by Theodosius; but a high

[margin: Galla Placidia]

official at Ravenna named John seized the occasion
and assumed the imperial purple in the absence of
Valentinian and his mother. The struggle
for power ended in Valentinian's success, after
strange vicissitudes of fortune. John shut himself up
in inaccessible Ravenna. Ardaburius, a general of the
Western empire, embarked a large force to assert the
claims of Valentinian. But a storm dispersed his fleet,
and he was taken prisoner and carried to Ravenna.
Meanwhile the cavalry contingent under Aspar, son of
Ardaburius, marched successfully along the coast, and
surprised and took Aquileia, when the news of his
father's disaster reached him. All seemed to be lost;
but Ardaburius used his time so well at Ravenna that
the troops were persuaded to desert John and return to
their allegiance. Aspar was conducted across the difficult and treacherous morasses by a shepherd. After a
short struggle the gates of Ravenna were thrown open,
and the city taken. John was seized, carried to
Aquileia, and beheaded.

Theodosius II. by an express enactment acknowledged Valentinian III. as emperor of the West (425),
and though the two empires were associated
by the marriage of Valentinian with Eudoxia,
daughter of Theodosius II., the legal and final separation between East and West took place at this epoch. It
was a crisis in the history of the civilised world when
it was expressly declared that the laws of either
emperor should be valid only in his own dominions.

When this decisive act took place the world was
governed by two women. We have noted the ascendency of Pulcheria in the East. In the West Placidia,

daughter of the great Theodosius, was virtually supreme. Placidia, however, did not possess the governing capacity of Pulcheria, and the intrigues of her two great generals, Aetius and Boniface, resulted in the loss of Africa, and brought the empire to the verge of destruction.

Boniface had been true to the cause of Placidia; Aetius had supported John. When the rebellion collapsed, Aetius managed to regain the favour of the court, and abused his position by involving Boniface in war with the empire, first persuading Placidia to recall him from his command in Africa, and then persuading Boniface to refuse. This base intrigue was discovered too late. Boniface in despair allied himself with the Vandals, then the strongest power in Spain. The terrible Genseric had lately succeeded to the chief command, and the harbour of Cartagena was in his hands. At the instance of Boniface the hordes of the Vandals crossed the straits, and under the skilful guidance of Genseric and Boniface overran the fruitful province of Africa. The horrors of war were increased by the vengeance which the fanatical Donatists took on their Catholic oppressors. These fierce schismatics had been deprived of their churches, their revenues, and their civil rights. In the invasion of Genseric they saw their opportunity, and much of the barbarity of this invasion is to be ascribed to the unsparing vengeance of the Donatists, rather than to the ferocity of the Vandals.

Boniface and Aetius

The Vandals under Genseric invade Africa

Possidius, the biographer of St. Augustine, vividly describes the scenes of which St. Augustine was an eye-witness. 'They spared,' he writes, 'neither sex nor age, not even the priests and ministers of God, nor the very ornaments of churches, nor the sacred vessels, nor the buildings themselves. . . . That man of God witnessed states ruined, and the inhabitants of the country houses, some slain, some driven into exile and dispersed in many directions; in many places Christian worship had ceased, there was no one found to partake of the Holy Eucharist, or, if anyone came, there was no priest to minister. Thus the influence of the Catholic Church, as well as the authority of the imperial government, was extinguished in North Africa.'[1]

When the province was irretrievably lost to the empire, and when war, cruelty, and passion had wrought their accustomed horrors, Boniface discovered his fatal error. The intrigues of Aetius were unmasked; but it was too late to restore lost lives and ruined homes, as Genseric declined all overtures. All that Boniface could do was to turn his arms against his former ally. He was defeated, and then threw himself into Hippo, one of the few places which still held out against the Vandals. There, while the storm raged wildly round him, the aged Bishop Augustine was calmly ending his life. After a second defeat, Boniface sailed from Hippo for Ravenna, where Placidia received him with favour. Meanwhile Aetius, exasperated by the discovery of his treasonable practices, marched from Gaul into Italy at the head of an army. In the battle which ensued Boniface was victorious, but died of a wound which he had received at the hands of his great rival. Aetius took refuge among the Huns.

[1] Ch. xiii.

Meanwhile in Africa Genseric showed an unexpected moderation. Probably sedition in his own camp compelled him to negotiate. He made peace with the Romans, and relinquished a portion of his conquests. Then he proceeded to capture the one or two cities which remained unconquered. With treacherous professions of peace and friendship, he surprised Carthage, the capital of the African province. The wretched inhabitants of this wealthy and voluptuous city were exposed to the rapine and pillage of the barbarian soldiers. The noblest families and the most devoted Catholics were forced into slavery and exile. Europe was filled with fugitives from the sword of Genseric.

The capture of Carthage

A legend, which belongs to the age of the younger Theodosius, deserves notice as at least a picturesque and memorable illustration of the vast change which the two centuries, from the persecution of Decius to the time of Theodosius II., had brought upon the world.

The seven sleepers of Ephesus

The story runs that, in the days of the Decian persecution (A.D. 250), seven young men of Ephesus retired to a cave, in a mountain near the city, to take refuge from the danger to which the profession of their faith exposed them. The emperor gave orders that the mouth of the cave should be blocked with stones. Then the seven youths fell into a deep sleep, which was miraculously prolonged for two hundred years. When they woke up, unconscious of the lapse of time, one of them went to the city to buy bread. His strange speech, old-fashioned dress, and the ancient coins which he proffered in payment, discovered the miracle to the men of Ephesus. The young man (if, as Gibbon says, he can be termed young), in his turn was astonished at the changed world which he saw. The Cross—the symbol of Christianity—no longer proscribed, was displayed conspicuously over the principal gate of the city; everywhere Christ was acknowledged; everywhere there was an altered life; old Pagan abominations had been swept away; the world had become new. The story ends by narrating that the Bishop and clergy of Ephesus, even, it is said, the emperor Theodosius himself, hastened to the mouth of the cavern, where they received the benediction of the seven sleepers, who then peacefully sank to rest again.

CHAPTER XXIII.

THE HUNS AND ATTILA.

THE conquest of the empire by the Teutonic races had been a gradual process. The barriers of the Rhine, the Danube, and the Alps had sufficed to hold back the invasion while vigorous and martial emperors held sway. The temporary delay was an incalculable advantage to the provinces over which the flood of invasion was soon to sweep. The interchange of war and commerce had taught the barbarian to respect and imitate the arts of civilisation; and when the time came for the various barbarian tribes to settle in the vanquished territories, they were prepared to adopt the manners, the language, and the religion of the Roman provincials. In this way Christianity possessed herself of the new world which was growing out

The barbarians gradually civilised

of the changed, rather than the ruined, empire of Rome.

The Visigoths, converted to an Arian form of Christianity by the labours of Ulfilas, spread the same teaching among the Ostrogoths, the Vandals, and the Gepidæ. Even those tribes which, like the Burgundians and the Suevi, had received the purer doctrine of Catholicism, lapsed into the Arian error. The few Catholics who remained were exposed to bitter persecution in the new Teutonic kingdoms. This was especially the case in Africa, a province always characterised by the bitterness of religious conflict.

The interesting history of the recovery of the Gothic kingdoms to the Nicene faith belongs to a later period. The fact of historical importance at this epoch is that the Gothic invasion, while it seemed to shatter the empire, infused new force into the Christian Church, and carried within it the seeds of a stronger and purified order. The first signal service which the Teuton wrought for Christianity and civilisation in conjunction with the subjects of the empire, was the repulse of the Huns under the renowned and terrible Attila. We hear of this Turanian people about the year 372 in the region to the north of the Caspian Sea, whence they began to press westwards, driving before them in their march the Teutonic tribes, who were at length checked by the barrier of the Danube. We have narrated the circumstances of that famous passage of the Ostrogoths across the Danube in the reign of Valens.[1]

For a while the Turanian advance seemed to have

---
[1] Ch. ix.

spent its force. The restless and undisciplined warriors dissipated their strength in scattered expeditions, wherever hopes were held out of victory or spoil. There were Huns fighting side by side with Goths, when Stilicho hemmed in the troops of Radagaisus on the ridge of Fæsulæ; and in the formidable rebellion, after the death of Honorius, Aetius led sixty thousand Huns to the support of the usurper John.

Under Rugulas, the uncle of Attila, the Huns were united and threatened the existence of the Eastern empire. Theodosius II. staved off the danger by conferring on Rugulas the title of general and by the payment of three hundred and fifty pounds of gold, as an annual tribute.

On the death of Rugas or Rugulas, struck by a thunderbolt, as Socrates would have us believe, his nephews, Attila and Bleda, not only doubled the tribute, but imposed other ignominious conditions. Attila soon possessed himself of sovereign power by the murder of his brother Bleda, and gained an absolute ascendency over his countless followers, whom he now prepared to lead to victory. A vivid description of Attila's personal appearance has been preserved. 'The large head, swarthy complexion, deep-seated eyes, flat nose, sparse hairs, broad shoulders, short square body, of nervous strength though of disproportioned form,'[1] present a picture not to be forgotten. Under the guidance of this terrible hero began the incursion into Europe, which gave him the title of 'Scourge of God.'

Unlike the Teuton races, the Huns had never been

[1] Gibbon, ch. xxxiv.

won by Christianity, or assimilated the culture of the older civilisation. The savagery of the race gave no promise of yielding to the influences of Rome. Their victories were marked by a broad line of ruin, and by the destruction of all that was ancient, or revered, or beautiful. They left behind them burning towns and desolated plains. The founding of the Gothic kingdoms was the salvation of Europe and the starting-point of modern progress; the triumph of Attila would have rolled back the tide of civilisation and have changed the course of European history to an extent which it is impossible to estimate. This is the reason which makes the ultimate repulse of Attila a determining event in ecclesiastical history.

The sources for the history of Attila's campaign are scanty, but we learn that the spark which fired the train was the refusal of the Byzantine court to deliver up to the king of the Huns the Bishop of Margus and some fugitives from his justice. Instantly Attila's troops were in movement; the whole stretch of country from the Euxine to the Adriatic was swept by his armies. The Bishop of Margus, wise in his generation, made friends with the Huns by opening the gates of his city to the invaders. One after another, cities—some of which have grown familiar in the history of this century —fell before his ruthless sword, Sirmium, an imperial capital, Sardica, the scene of the famous Council (p. 50), and other places. The imperial troops which ventured to dispute the advance of Attila were defeated in three successive engagements, and were finally driven to bay in the Thracian Chersonese. When Attila appeared beneath the walls of Constantinople, he was absolute

The invasion begins

master from the Danube to the Hellespont. No mercy had been shown, and the land behind him was a waste. A concession of territory along the Danube, extending over a fifteen days' journey, a tribute thrice as large as before, now amounting to twenty-one thousand pounds of gold, release of all Huns who had been taken prisoners, a shameful surrender of refugees—such were the hard and ignominious conditions of peace with Attila.

The death of Theodosius II. brought a change (450). His successor Marcian declined to pay the exorbitant tribute, whereupon Attila instantly resolved to renew the war. But he hesitated whether he should carry his arms first into the West or East.

The West was virtually ruled by Aetius, the rival of Boniface. In his early days he had been a friend of Attila, and familiar with the camp of the barbarians. This had been his refuge, when the rebellion of John failed, and again, when he was defeated by Count Boniface. This friendship and alliance continued. A detachment of Huns was employed by Aetius in the defence of Gaul, but their march through the province is described by the poet as formidable alike to friend and foe :—

'Nam socium vix ferre queas qui durior hoste.'[1]

Theodoric, son of Alaric and king of the Visigoths, had established a powerful dominion in southern Gaul. Eager to extend his rule, he matched his forces against the Roman army. Aetius, however, was everywhere victorious, and at Narbonne, which lay

Theodoric

---

[1] Paulinus of Perigord. See Gibbon, ch. xxxv.

midway between Toulouse and Arles, the respective capitals of the Goths and Romans, Theodoric suffered a disastrous defeat. This he avenged, in the temporary absence of Aetius, by a complete victory over the Roman general, Litorius. Aetius hastened to retrieve the disaster. But, when the two armies were drawn up facing one another, and awaiting the signal for conflict, one of those unexpected incidents occurred which seem to be characteristic of this epoch. The two generals, each conscious of the other's strength, and each in turn victorious, came to terms of peace without the arbitrament of battle. This act, in the highest sense civilised and Christian, had momentous and salutary results for the future of Christianity and civilisation.

Circumstances soon brought Theodoric and Aetius into closer alliance. Theodoric had suffered a cruel wrong at the hands of Genseric, king of the Vandals; he took up arms against Genseric, who in turn sought the alliance of Attila. A dispute between two brothers for the kingdom of the Franks, who at that time occupied the lower Rhine and spread westward to the Somme, gave further occasion to Attila for interference in the West by force of arms. A strange and remarkable incident afforded a third pretext for the intended invasion. The princess, Honoria, sister of Valentinian III. and daughter of Placidia, weary of the enforced celibacy and conventual life which had been imposed upon her at Constantinople, formed the extraordinary resolution of offering herself in marriage to Attila. This proposal, at first treated with scorn, was conveniently revived by Attila when his designs were ripe for an invasion of Gaul. Before attacking the

<small>Attila's pretexts for war</small>

empire, he laid claim to the hand and dowry of the princess Honoria.

With such excuses for the war, Attila began his famous march across Europe. The friendship of the Franks who followed his banner facilitated the passage of the Rhine. One by one the cities of eastern Gaul yielded to the merciless invaders. Resistance was short and ineffectual, and no quarter was given. Cities and their inhabitants perished in indiscriminate massacre and ruin. The first check was received before the walls of Orleans, where the brave Bishop Anianus inspired the garrison with courage, and was the first to announce the approach of succour in the united armies of Theodoric and Aetius. A common danger induced the Goth and the Roman to join forces, and in the cause of Christianity to give battle to the barbarian Huns.

Attila marches across the Rhine

Attila raised the siege of Orleans, and awaited the enemy in the plain of Chalons. The site of the battlefield has not been identified. The level country spreads widely, and by some the scene of conflict is placed fifty miles to the south-east of Chalons, near Méry-sur-Seine.

The battle of Chalons

The tactics of this great and decisive battle were simple. By a furious charge the cavalry of the Huns pierced and rode through the centre of the Teuton army, and then, wheeling to the left, attacked the enemy's right, which was commanded by Theodoric in person. The javelin of an Ostrogothic chief reached Theodoric, who fell mortally wounded, and was trampled under foot by his own cavalry, thus fulfilling, it is said, a prediction of the aruspices consulted by Attila.

At this crisis in the fight Torismond, son of Theodoric, descended from the height which he had occupied at the commencement of the day, poured his forces into the flanks of the Huns, and threw them into confusion. The Visigoths recovered their order, and turned upon the enemy. Attila was defeated; but the approach of night covered his retreat to the entrenched camp. A few days afterwards he carried the remnant of his army across the Rhine, thus acknowledging the repulse.

The overthrow of Attila and the Huns was the redemption of Europe from a savage slavery. It was a decisive victory for Christianity, and for the refining culture, the love of freedom, and respect for law and order which are the charm and security of modern society, and which make progress safe and inevitable.

But Attila's spirit was far from being crushed. In the spring of the following year he repeated his demand for Honoria, and on being refused crossed the Alps. Aquileia was stormed, taken, and so dealt with that scarcely a vestige was left to show where the city of many memories once stood. Other places shared the same fate. The cities and homesteads of northern Italy so often exposed to the devastation of conquest were almost effaced by the havoc of Attila's advance. Milan and Pavia enjoyed a partial immunity. The buildings of these cities and the lives of the inhabitants were spared from the flame and the sword; but enormous contributions were exacted.

Attila invades the north of Italy

At this point an embassy from Valentinian reached Attila's camp. It was headed by Avienus, a senator of high distinction, and Leo, Bishop of Rome. The most effective arguments were the dowry of Honoria—a magnificent bribe—and, possibly, the demoralisation of the barbarian forces. The majestic looks and eloquence of Leo seem also to have had their influence on the rude conqueror. Attila retired, threatening, it is said, a speedy return.

Europe, however, was saved by the death of the tyrant. Attila died suddenly in Pannonia, by the bursting of an artery during the night, after having celebrated with great festivities his marriage with a beautiful maiden of the country named Ildico, A.D. 453.

CHAPTER XXIV.

LEO I. AND THE CHURCH OF ROME.

THE prominent position of Leo on the embassy to Attila marks the consideration which his great ability and vast organising power had acquired for the Bishop of Rome and the see which he ruled. The sources of this prestige have been already indicated. As the empire continued to decline, these elements of greatness in the Papacy increased to an enormous extent.

Prestige of the Roman see

Two lines of influence tended to this result: first the growth in power of the Roman see in regard to jurisdiction; secondly the separate advance of its authority and claims over other Churches. In the first of these two lines of influence the progress of Rome was at first parallel with that of other

This prestige due to growth of jurisdiction

Churches. The legal sanction which Constantine gave to episcopal decisions in ecclesiastical causes was continued and confirmed by his successors.

In a law of Honorius A.D. 399, it was laid down: 'In matters of religion it is fitting that Bishops should decide' (quotiens de religione agitur episcopis convenit judicare).[1] This sanction gave no authority to Bishops in civil cases. On the other hand, two rights which were acknowledged to rest with the clergy,—the right of moral supervision, and the right of intercession for prisoners,—were so used as to give great weight to the voice of the Church in judicial cases. It was in accordance with the first of these two rights that Ambrose excommunicated Theodosius the Great. As early as the year 314 A.D. at the Council of Arles it was ruled that Christian magistrates should, on their promotion to another sphere of duty, carry with them letters to the Church of the place to which they were appointed 'in order that the Bishop might exercise supervision and punish any infringement of discipline by excommunication' (Ut in quibuscunque locis gesserint ab episcopo ejusdem loci cura de illis agatur, et cum cœperint contra disciplinam agere tum demum a communione excludantur). This power of excommunication for the correction of morals was put in force in well-known instances by St. Athanasius, by Synesius, and by Cyril, whose encroachments on the civil administration of the city were violently resented by the prefect Orestes, and are condemned by the ecclesiastical historian, Socrates.[2]

The right and duty of intercession for condemned

---

[1] *Cod. Theod.* xvi. xi. 1.   [2] vii. 7, 13.

persons were grounded by St. Augustine on the impossibility of repentance after death; 'therefore,' he says, 'we are forced by charity to intercede for prisoners, lest their punishment end not with their life.' But there were wise Churchmen who saw the danger to public polity involved in the abuse of this right, and the emperors Theodosius I. and Arcadius found it necessary to restrain by law the interference of the clergy with the course of justice. But the very terms of the edicts show the extent to which this claim had been pushed, and the influence which it must have given to the clergy.

The growing wealth of the Church was another source of political power. Imperial liberality and gifts and legacies from private persons so enriched ecclesiastical treasuries that the clerical profession became attractive to worldly-minded people, and the pressure into its ranks became a danger to the State. Constantine prohibited rich men seeking holy orders. The sacred offices were to be filled by persons of slender means (fortuna tenuis), and those who had no State functions to discharge. Afterwards the resignation of worldly goods was a duty imposed on those who entered the ministry. On the other hand clerical avarice became a scandal and had to be checked by law. Of this Jerome writes to Nepotianus: 'It is not of the law that I complain, but I grieve that we have deserved the law. Cautery is good, but how comes the wound that needs cauterising?'[1]

The increase in wealth

The general result of this influx of wealth was to place lucrative offices and large estates at the dis-

[1] *Ep.* 34.

posal of Bishops. The clergy became in all respects, even for their maintenance, dependent on the Bishop. Another element of strength in the episcopal position was the popular consent and suffrage from which it proceeded, and on which it rested. In the words of a letter quoted by Theodoret, the election of a Bishop was made 'in a synod of Bishops, by the vote of the clergy, by the demand of the people,' who cried out ἄξιος, or *bene meritus* ('he is worthy'), if the choice were acceptable.

These advantages placed the Bishops in a position of high dignity and power. This was implied by the titles which began to be assigned to the office, such as, successors of the Apostles, most blessed, most reverend, or most sacred lords. Other titles, such as Vicar of Christ, Papa or Pope, Apostolicus, Summus Pontifex, afterwards associated with the see of Rome, were at first applied to Bishops in general, especially to those who presided over metropolitan sees. On the principle that the priesthood stands above royalty, marks of reverence were exacted from the emperors and their wives, who would descend from their thrones, bow their heads, and kiss the hands of Bishops. It is no wonder that episcopal pride was a term which found its way into the vocabulary of the time. 'They swell with the pride of episcopacy,' says Jerome; 'they imagine they have been entrusted not with the stewardship of Christ, but with sovereignty; let priest and Bishop know that the people are not their servants but their fellow-servants.'

<small>Growth of episcopal power</small>

Some checks, however, were placed on this growing political power of the Church. 'Ever since the emperors became Christian,' writes Socrates, 'ecclesiastical affairs depended on them, and the most important synods have met, and still do meet, by their will.' This statement was in large measure true, but the extent of its truth varied according to the character of the ruling emperor, and to the firmness of the Bishops; moreover, it expresses the condition of the Eastern more accurately than that of the Western Church.

<small>Checks on the power of the Church</small>

Ultimate appeals lay to the emperor, not only in respect of ecclesiastical property, but also in some cases of doctrine. When many sects claimed severally the title and right to term themselves Catholic, it became necessary for the emperors to decide the question. With this object they summoned councils, over which they sometimes presided themselves, and sometimes appointed commissioners to preside.

On the whole, the authority of the emperor in ecclesiastical causes was unhesitatingly allowed. But this was especially the case in the East, where the imperial influence was powerful in the choice of Bishops, particularly for the see of Constantinople. Flattery went so far as to attribute to the emperor a sacerdotal character; 'chief priest and emperor' ($ἀρχιερεὺς$ $βασιλεύς$) was a term used at a council at Constantinople, A.D. 448.

Such were the causes in general which tended to make the episcopate a strong political force. The powers and influence which we have indicated in some degree surrounded the throne of every Bishop. In a special degree they were centred in what were termed the patriarchal sees of Constantinople, Alexandria, Antioch, and Jerusalem[1] in the East (though it

[1] Raised to this position at the Council of Chalcedon A.D. 451.

must be observed that the title of Patriarch was originally common to all Bishops),[1] and, in the West, pre-eminently of Rome.

The reasons which gave Rome this singular and striking supremacy have been partly indicated. The fierce and intricate religious controversies, which troubled, divided, and consequently weakened the Eastern Church, left Rome practically unassailed. More than this, they had the effect of placing Rome in the position of arbiter and judge of the points in dispute, a position quickly seized and improved by the successive Bishops of Rome. Not only the ancient prestige, but the immobility of Rome helped to secure this authority. Other imperial capitals had shifted and changed more than once since the empire became Christian. Nicomedia, the capital of the last of the persecuting emperors, had given place to Constantinople; Sirmium had been all but submerged in the flood of barbarian invasion; the same terrible cause had driven the imperial court from Milan to Ravenna, and further west from Trèves to Arles. But Rome stood fixed and firm like the stedfast rock of its own Capitol (Capitoli immobile saxum) in the majesty of eternal empire.

Rome becomes the arbiter of disputes

Another cause of pre-eminence, which told far more effectively in the fifth century than can be adequately conceived now, was the undoubted Apostolical origin of the Church of Rome. The voice of the Bishop of Rome carried with it the transmitted authority of St. Peter. This deep and vivid impression of the ever present and authoritative direction of

The apostolical origin of the see

---

[1] See Suicer *sub voce*.

the chief of the Apostles, had much to do with the influence of Rome in centuries far beyond the times with which we are now dealing. It was the argument, for instance, which turned the decision so important for the history of the English Church at the Council of Whitby, A.D. 664.

The character, policy, and career of Leo the Great, Bishop of Rome from 440–461, sum up in a striking and instructive way the aims and position of the Roman see at this epoch. Leo included in his authority not only the various general elements of episcopal power which we have traced, but also those special sources of prestige which became attached to the throne of St. Peter. Moreover by the aid of his vigorous intellect Leo added considerably to the strength of his position, and gave evidence in his policy of a far-sighted intuition of the future.

<small>The authority of Leo</small>

The distinguished natural abilities of Leo placed him early in life in a prominent position. As Archdeacon of Rome, he stood next to the Bishop in rank; and letters addressed to Leo on important occasions at this period attest the estimation in which he was held. His high qualities were recognised by the State, and in the year 439 or 440 he was sent on a special mission to Gaul, to compose the difference between Aetius and a rival general, Albinus. During his absence Pope Sixtus died, and Leo was elected to fill his place. He accepted the immense responsibilities of this dignity without diffidence or false humility, only asking for the prayers of the people for success in his administration.

<small>His rise to the Papacy</small>

Leo took a magnificent and imperial view of the Roman pontificate, which has impressed itself upon history. In claiming for the see of Rome a supremacy at least over the Western Churches, Leo had some pre-cedents on which to rely. A custom had arisen of referring disputed questions to Rome as the apostolical mother-church of Western Christendom. Innocent I., the greatest of Leo's predecessors, had written to the effect that important cases should, even after a Bishop's decision, be referred to Rome for confirmation, and that nothing should be regarded as defined and settled until it should have come under the cognisance of the Apostolic see.[1]

His claims for the see of Rome

The great stress of Leo's policy was directed to establish this principle, which appeared necessary for the unity of Christendom. The experience of after ages has shown the need of limiting and guarding such a principle; but at this epoch the sentiment of unity was forced upon the Church by the imperial idea, while the sentiment of unity combined with autonomy of separate Churches had not presented itself as conceivable.

The idea of the unity of Christendom

In Italy itself the Roman supremacy was not completely acknowledged; the Bishops of Milan, of Aquileia, and Ravenna claimed independence. At the same time there was no open revolt against the authority of Rome.

Italy not wholly subservient to Rome

Eastern Illyricum, though politically assigned to the Eastern empire, continued to be subject to the Roman patriarchate.

Illyricum

In the southern part of Gaul, which was still subject to the empire, a dispute for precedence had arisen between the Bishops of Vienne and Arles. An appeal

---

[1] Gieseler, § 94, note 20.

was made to Rome. Zosimus, who was then Pope (A.D. 417), declared in favour of Arles, and appointed the Bishop Patroclus his vicar in Gallia Narbonensis. In the time of Leo, Hilary was Bishop of Arles, a man distinguished for eloquence and the vigorous administration of his office. Charges having been brought against Celidonius, one of the Bishops within his jurisdiction, Hilary summoned a council and deposed him. Celidonius appealed to Leo, whereupon Hilary instantly journeyed to Rome on foot, and protested against the appeal being made. Leo, however, reversed the judgment of Hilary, and removed the sentence of deposition from Celidonius. Other accusations of ecclesiastical tyranny and misrule were brought against Hilary; and Leo, insisting on his supremacy, withdrew the privileges which had been conferred on the see of Arles by his predecessor. In this assertion of prerogative, Leo obtained the support of an imperial decree. Valentinian III. was persuaded to issue a constitution affirming the primacy of the Roman pontiff. 'No one was to presume to attempt anything without the authority of the Roman see. The peace of the Churches all over the world will only be preserved if the whole of Christendom (universitas) acknowledges its ruler. Let no one be allowed, contrary to ancient use and custom, to take any measures without the sanction of the venerable Pope of the eternal city.' This decree bears evidence of Leo's influence over the feeble mind of Valentinian, and cannot be regarded as a spontaneous expression of imperial policy.

Disputes with Leo

Spain, which was no longer under the sway of the empire, felt the influence of the Papacy. The opinions of Priscillian, who was put to death by the usurper Maximus, had survived in Spain, and deeply affected the purity of religion in that country. Turibius, Bishop of Astorga, appealed to Leo for advice, and by his recommendation two councils were held, in which the pernicious and immoral doctrines of the Priscillianists were condemned.

<small>Spain</small>

The African Church which had been distinguished by some of the greatest names and most saintly memories in the early history of Christianity, had never surrendered her independence to Rome. The one or two occasions on which disputed questions were referred to the see of St. Peter, left the liberties of the Church of Tertullian and Cyprian intact.

<small>Africa</small>

More than once Rome was convicted of grievous misjudgment. In 419 Zosimus endeavoured to sustain an African presbyter deposed by his own Bishop. The Pope's legates boldly produced as their authority certain canons which they alleged to be decrees of the Nicene Council, establishing a right of appeal to Rome from the whole of Christendom. The members of the African synod, however, were able to show conclusively that the alleged canons issued from the Council of Sardica and not of Nicæa. The proceeding displayed incredible ignorance or incredible fraud on the part of the Roman legates. To add to their humiliation, the accused presbyter was proved by his own confession to have been guilty of the most heinous crimes. In the time of Leo, however, the misfortunes of the African Church drew it nearer to Rome. The persecution by Genseric grew fiercer and more vindictive towards the close of his reign. The Arians

<small>Mistakes of the Roman see</small>

were everywhere triumphant, and the persecuted Catholic Bishops even welcomed the intervention of the Bishop of Rome.

Thus the policy of Leo prevailed throughout the Western empire. In the East he was less successful. Notwithstanding the influence of Valentinian and Placidia, Leo was unable to persuade Theodosius to yield to his wish for a general council to be held in Italy. Nor did the Eastern Bishops acknowledge the authority of Rome, as their Western brethren were content to do. At the great Council of Chalcedon, A.D. 451, though the Roman legates were allowed to preside, and though Leo's famous letter to Flavian, defining the doctrine of the Incarnation, was received with respect and with the general assent of the assembly, a decree was passed which placed the see of Constantinople on an equality with that of Rome. Leo bitterly protested against the decree; and this twenty-eighth canon of the Council of Chalcedon has been justly regarded by historians as one of the causes which ultimately led to the separation between the Eastern and Western Churches.

The influence of Leo in the East

Nowhere was the strength of Leo's character more conspicuously shown than in his vigorous action against the various heresies which were distracting the Church; he seemed to make the extinction of heresy his special work in every quarter of Christendom. Here too, as in his assertion of supremacy, he called in the aid of the civil power. His counsel in the struggle of the Catholic Bishops in Spain against Priscillianism has been mentioned. With still greater vigour did he fling himself into the conflict with

Leo's attitude towards heresy

Manicheism. This sect was increased in Rome by fugitives from Genseric's cruelties in Africa. Theoretically, Manicheism was an attempt to infuse into Christianity the teaching of Zoroaster; but, actually, Manicheism had been given over to the practice of the grossest immorality. This Leo determined to suppress by means of the ecclesiastical and civil powers. A council was held, and revelation was made of shameful sensuality even in the religious ceremonial of this sect. Valentinian made the profession of Manicheism a penal offence, and Leo exposed its real character by sermons and letters addressed to different Bishops.

The relations of Leo with Eutyches and with Eutychianism, and the part which he took in regard to the councils of Ephesus and Chalcedon, belong to a different side of ecclesiastical history. The general result was to place his personal influence and the authority of his see in a commanding position throughout the civilised world.

The most picturesque and impressive scenes in the life of Leo were those in which he appeared as the champion of Rome against barbarian invasion. Twice it was his fortune to come forward in order to mitigate the horrors of war. We have seen how he confronted Attila on the shore of lake Benacus, and forced or persuaded him to retire. On a still more memorable occasion he advanced to meet Genseric before the gates of Rome.

Leo and the barbarian invasion

Valentinian III. deservedly met his death as a direct consequence of a cruel act of licentiousness. Petronius Maximus, the husband of the lady whom he had wronged, became emperor. He in turn misused his power by forcing the empress Eudoxia to take the place of his own wife, who had died since his accession. Eudoxia in her resentment invited Genseric to invade Italy.

Leo intercedes for Rome with Genseric

The Vandal conqueror landed at Ostia and was soon in the neighbourhood of Rome. Leo headed a procession of his clergy to intercede with Genseric for his unhappy countrymen. Though it was not given to Leo to turn the tide of conquest a second time, he procured some concessions. Those who made no resistance should be spared—the buildings of the city were to be protected against conflagration—the captives were not to be exposed to torture. If Leo's mediation gained little, it was an impressive lesson and full of promise for Christendom.

The sack of Rome by the Vandal army swept away the last relics of heathenism. The gilded roof of the Capitol, and the statues of the gods of Rome, were carried off by the same hands which pillaged the Christian churches. But for paganism the ruin was irreparable. No lingering enthusiasm cared to rebuild the fallen temples of the gods.

Leo's death in A.D. 461 coincided with the death of Majorian, who had made a gallant effort to stay the progress of calamity, but failed. After his death, the empire swiftly hastened to its end. The feeble rulers who close the line of the Western empire leave no mark in history. Leo not only stands out as the grandest figure among the Churchmen of his day, but he was the only great statesman of his time in Italy. The relations between Church and State, as he defined them, were

Leo the greatest statesman as well as the greatest Churchman of his day

recognised for centuries to be the only true relations. The position of the Roman see among the Churches of the West, as he left it, continued to be for centuries its acknowledged position. The contest which Leo sustained in defence of the Catholic faith against the heresies of East and West deservedly gave a prestige to the see of Rome, which in his time and afterwards was upheld by far more questionable means.

The pontificate of Leo sums up the general results of Christianity as a force in the affairs of the world, as a powerful factor in history. At the special epoch when it occurred, the strength and unity which his powerful intellect achieved for the Church were undoubtedly needed in view of the coming disruption. But the insignificance to which the imperial power had been reduced in the feeble hands of Valentinian III., and in the seclusion of Ravenna, gave a dangerously large share of influence to the rival power of the Church, wielded by a masterful genius in the city with which twelve hundred years of empire had irreversibly associated the idea of supremacy.

Nearly an equal term of years was granted to the new empire to complete and develop the statesmanship of Leo; and when the break in the unity occurred, it was the Roman see, and not the Church of Christ, which was impaired.

INDEX.

ABDAS, Bishop, 176
Acacius, Bishop, 178
Aetius, 182, 189-191, 199
African Church, the, 33
Alaric, 106, 146-164
Alban, St., 18
Albinus, 199
Alemanni, 60
Alexandria, 44
Ambrose, St., 92-103, 194
Ammianus Marcellinus, 64, 79, 90
Anianus, Bishop, 191
Anthony, St., 49, 122
Anthusa, 132
Antioch, 26, 57, 69, 131, 133
Apollinarii, the two, 67
Apostate, meaning of, 58
— Julian the, *see* Julian
Aptunga, Bishop of, 33
Aquileia, 48, 104, 181, 192
Arbogastes, 103
Arcadius, the emperor, 105, 137
Ardaburius, 181
Arianism, 41, 158
Arles, 165, 190, 198, 200
— council at, 34
Ariminum, council of, 54
—, creed of, 81, 83, 88
Arius, 40, 46
Asceticism, 49, 132
Aspar, 181
Asta, 149

Ataulf, 161, 167
Athanasius, St., 43, 45, 48, 49, 53, 55, 78, 194
Athenais, *see* Eudocia
Athens, 58, 72, 147
Attalus, 161
Attila, 185-193
Augustine, St., 127-131
Auxentius, 81, 93
Avienus, 192

Baptism, deferred, 94
Basil, St., of Cæsarea, 56, 59, 71-76
Basileia (βασιλεία) the, 1
Bethlehem, 124
Bologna, 156
Boniface, 131, 182
Botheric, 97
Britain, 149, 168, 169
Busentinus, the river, 164

Cæcilian, 33
Carus, the emperor, 6
Celibacy, 36
Chalcedon, council of, 203
Chalons, battle of, 191
Charito, 79
Chrysostom, St., 131-139
Church and State, 53, 78, 81, 82, 101, 108

Circumcellions, 34
'City of God,' the, 79, 119, 129, 155
Claudian, 104, 143, 146, 150
Classics, the study of, questioned, 66
'Confessions,' the, of St. Augustine, 127
Constans, 47, 50, 51
Constantine the Great, 21, 27–40, 46
Constantine II., 47
Constantine the Usurper, 165, 168
Constantinople, 39, 188
Constantius Chlorus, 10
Constantius, son of Constantine I., 47, 50, 51, 62
Constantius, general under Honorius, 165, 180
Crispus, 38
Cross, the, abolished as a legal penalty, 35
Cucûsus, 137
Cyril, Bishop of Alexandria, 194

Dadastana, 79
Damasus, Pope, 80, 124
Danube, passage of, by the Goths, 89
Defensores Civitatum, 83
Diocletian, 6–20, 25, 26
Donatism and Donatists, 33, 34, 129, 182

Edessa, scene at, 85
Education, Christian, 66
Ephesus, the seven sleepers of, 184
Eudocia, 175
Eudoxia, wife of Arcadius, 136
Eudoxia, wife of Valentinian III., 175, 181
Eudoxius, 85

Eugenius, 103
Eusebia, 57
Eusebius of Cæsarea, 42, 43
Eusebius of Nicomedia, 45, 58
Eustochium, 124
Eutropius, 136, 145, 170

Fausta, 23
Felix of Aptunga, 33
Flaccilla, 133
Flavian, Bishop of Antioch, 133
Fritigern, 90

Gainas, 136, 143, 171–173
Galerius, 10, 13, 22, 23
Galla Placidia, 153, 167, 180, 182, 203
Gallus, 48, 56
Generidus, 119, 160
Genseric, 131, 182–184, 190, 205
George of Cappadocia, 53
Gerontius, 147
Gildo, 144
Gladiatorial shows, 151
Goths, the, 87–91, 146–164
Gratian, the emperor, 81, 92–96, 111
Gregory Nazianzen, 56–59, 71–76
Gregory, usurping Bishop of Alexandria, 50

Hadrianople, 32, 38, 90
Helena, the empress, 21
Helvidius, 125
Heraclian, 157
Hilary of Poitiers, 81
Hilary, Bishop of Arles, 201
Hippo, 129, 131, 183
Honoria, 190, 192
Honorius, the emperor, 105, 139–146
Huns, the, 88, 185–193
Hypatia, 108

ILDICO

Ildico, 193
Innocent I., Pope, 164
Intercession, right of, 194
Isdegerdes, 176

Jerome, St., 121-127
Jerusalem, Temple of, 64
Jews favoured by Julian, 64
John, *see* Chrysostom
— of Ravenna, 181
— of Lycopolis, 103
Jovian, the emperor, 76-79
Jovius, 160
Julian, the emperor, 48, 56-70
Julius, Pope, 48
Justina, 99

Kingdom of God, 1, 29

Labarum, the, 28, 77
Laws, influence of Christianity on, 35
Leo the Great, 199-206
Libanius, 132, 133
Liberius, Bishop of Rome, 82
Licinius, the emperor, 23, 37
Lucifer, Bishop of Cagliari, 52

Macrina, 72
Magnentius, 51
Manicheism, 204
Marcella, 49
Mardia, battle of, 37
Margus, 8, 188
Maria, 146
Martin, St., of Tours, 60, 102
Mascezel, 144
Maxentius, 22, 28, 30
Maximian, the emperor, 10-22
Maximin, 20, 22, 32
Maximus, 99, 101, 102, 103
Meletius, Bishop of Antioch, 86

PULCHERIA

Milan, edict of, 31
— council at, 51
— 92, 128, 192
Monasticism, 49, 73, 122
Monnica, 127
Mosaics at Ravenna, 153
Mursa, battle of, 51

Narbonne, 189
Nicæa, council of, 43
Nicene Creed, 44
Nicomedia, 9, 15, 21, 198
Nisibis, 77, 177

Olympus, 156
Ordination, forced, 74, 93
Orleans, 156

Pagan reaction, 62, 63, 85
Paganism, derivation of the word, 110
—, revival of, by Julian, 63
—, persecution of, 110
Patrick, St., 169
Patroclus, Bishop, 201
Paula, 124
Pavia, 192
Pelagianism, 129, 169
Pityus, 138
Placidia, *see* Galla Placidia
Pola, 57
Pollentia, 150
Pompeianus, 29
Ponte Molle, battle of, 30
Possidius, 182
Prætextatus, saying of, 83
Prisca, 16, 25, 32
Priscillian, 102, 202
Prisons affected by Christianity, 36
Procopius, 85
Prudentius, 113
Pulcheria, 173-180

RADAGAISUS, 154
Ravenna, 19, 152-154, 157, 161, 163, 181, 198
Rome, deserted as a seat of empire, 9, 30
—, sieges of, 159, 161, 162
—, See of, 48, 193, 198, 206
Rufinus, 139-143, 145
Rugulas, 187

SALONA, 25
Salvianus, 120
Sapor, 77
Sardica, 188
—, council of, 50
Sarus, 161
Sasima, 74
Serena, 144, 159
Severus, 20
Simeon Stylites, 123
Singeric, 167
Sirmium, 62, 188, 198
Slavery, 36
Spain, 201
Stilicho, 101, 139, 143-146, 149, 154, 156, 157
Supervision, moral, of Bishops, 194
Symmachus, 112
Synesius, Bishop, 194

TARSUS, 32
Telemachus, the monk, 151
Tennyson quoted, 123
Theodoric, 189-191
Theodosius I., 96-107, 113, 134

Theodosius II., 173-180, 189
Theophilus, Bishop of Alexandria, 116, 136
Thermantia, 158
Thessalonica, 97, 143
Toleration, religious, 107
Torismond, 192
Trèves, 9, 47, 198
Triumph, last at Rome, 11
Turin, 29

ULFILAS, 88
Upsala, 88

VALENS, the emperor, 80, 85-91
Valentinian I., 79-84
Valentinian II., 92, 101-103
Valentinian III., 201, 204
Valeria, 16, 25, 32
Vandals, 131, 167, 182
Verona, 29, 150, 165
Victory, altar of, 96
Vienne, 101, 200
Vulgate, the, 125

WALLIA, 167
Wealth, growth of, in the Church, 195

YORK, city of, 20

ZOSIMUS, Pope, 201, 202

EPOCHS OF CHURCH HISTORY.

Edited by the Rev. M. CREIGHTON, M.A.
Professor of Ecclesiastical History in the University of Cambridge.

Fcp. 8vo. price 2s. 6d. each.

THE REFORMATION IN ENGLAND. By the Rev Canon PERRY. [*Ready.*

THE ENGLISH CHURCH IN OTHER LANDS; or, THE SPIRITUAL EXPANSION OF ENGLAND. By Rev. H. W. TUCKER, M.A. Secretary to the Society for the Propagation of the Gospel. [*Ready.*

THE EVANGELICAL REVIVAL IN THE EIGHTEENTH CENTURY. By the Rev. Canon OVERTON, M.A. [*Ready.*

THE HISTORY OF THE UNIVERSITY OF OXFORD. By the Hon. G. C. BRODRICK, D.C.L. Warden of Merton College. [*Ready.*

THE CHURCH OF THE EARLY FATHERS. By Rev. A. PLUMMER, D.D. Master of University College, Durham. [*Ready.*

THE CHURCH AND THE ROMAN EMPIRE. By Rev. A. CARR, M.A. late Fellow of Oriel College, Oxford. [*Ready.*

The following is a List of the Volumes at present proposed:

THE UNIVERSITY OF CAMBRIDGE. By J. BASS MULLINGER, M.A. Lecturer of St. John's College, Cambridge.

THE GERMAN REFORMATION. By Rev. M. CREIGHTON, M.A. D.C.L. Professor of Ecclesiastical History in the University of Cambridge.

ENGLAND AND THE PAPACY. By Rev. W. HUNT, M.A. Trinity College, Oxford.

WYCLIF AND THE BEGINNINGS OF THE REFORMATION. By REGINALD LANE POOLE, M.A. Balliol College, Oxford.

THE ARIAN CONTROVERSY. By H. M. GWATKIN, M.A. Lecturer and late Fellow of St. John's College, Cambridge.

THE CHURCH AND THE EASTERN EMPIRE. By Rev. H. F. TOZER, M.A. Lecturer and late Fellow of Exeter College, Oxford.

CHURCH AND STATE IN MODERN TIMES.

THE WARS OF RELIGION.

THE COUNTER-REFORMATION.

ECCLESIASTICAL PROBLEMS IN ENGLAND, 1570-1660.

THE CHURCH AND THE TEUTONS.

CHRISTIANITY AND ISLAM.

HILDEBRAND AND HIS TIMES.

THE POPES AND THE HOHENSTAUFEN.

MONKS AND FRIARS.

London: LONGMANS, GREEN, & CO.

Epochs of Modern History.

Edited by C. COLBECK, M.A.

18 vols. fcp. 8vo. with Maps, price 2s. 6d. each volume:—

CHURCH'S BEGINNING OF THE MIDDLE AGES.
COX'S CRUSADES.
CREIGHTON'S AGE OF ELIZABETH.
GAIRDNER'S HOUSES OF LANCASTER AND YORK.
GARDINER'S THIRTY YEARS' WAR, 1618-1648.
GARDINER'S FIRST TWO STUARTS AND THE PURITAN REVOLUTION, 1603-1660.
GARDINER'S (Mrs.) THE FRENCH REVOLUTION, 1789-1795.
HALE'S FALL OF THE STUARTS, AND WESTERN EUROPE FROM 1678-1697.
JOHNSON'S NORMANS IN EUROPE.
LONGMAN'S FREDERICK THE GREAT AND THE SEVEN YEARS' WAR.
LUDLOW'S WAR OF AMERICAN INDEPENDENCE, 1775-1783.
McCARTHY'S EPOCH OF REFORM, 1830-1850.
MOBERLY'S THE EARLY TUDORS.
MORRIS'S AGE OF ANNE.
MORRIS'S THE EARLY HANOVERIANS.
SEEBOHM'S PROTESTANT REVOLUTION.
STUBBS'S THE EARLY PLANTAGENETS.
WARBURTON'S EDWARD THE THIRD.

Epochs of Ancient History.

Edited by the Rev. Sir G. W. COX, Bart. M.A. and by

C. SANKEY, M.A.

10 vols. fcp. 8vo. with Maps, price 2s. 6d. each volume:—

BEESLY'S GRACCHI, MARIUS, AND SULLA.
CAPES'S EARLY ROMAN EMPIRE, from the Assassination of Julius Cæsar to the Assassination of Domitian.
CAPES'S ROMAN EMPIRE OF THE SECOND CENTURY, or the Age of the Antonines.
COX'S ATHENIAN EMPIRE, from the Flight of Xerxes to the Fall of Athens.
COX'S GREEKS AND PERSIANS.
CURTEIS'S RISE OF THE MACEDONIAN EMPIRE.
IHNE'S ROME TO ITS CAPTURE BY THE GAULS.
MERIVALE'S ROMAN TRIUMVIRATES.
SANKEY'S SPARTAN AND THEBAN SUPREMACIES.
SMITH'S ROME AND CARTHAGE.

London: LONGMANS, GREEN, & CO.

MARCH 1887.
GENERAL LISTS OF WORKS
PUBLISHED BY
Messrs. LONGMANS, GREEN, & CO.
39 PATERNOSTER ROW, LONDON, E.C.

HISTORY, POLITICS, HISTORICAL MEMOIRS, &c.

Abbey's The English Church and its Bishops, 1700-1800. 2 vols. 8vo. 24s.
Abbey and Overton's English Church in the Eighteenth Century. Cr. 8vo. 7s. 6d.
Arnold's Lectures on Modern History. 8vo. 7s. 6d.
Bagwell's Ireland under the Tudors. Vols. 1 and 2. 2 vols. 8vo. 32s.
Ball's The Reformed Church of Ireland, 1537-1886. 8vo. 7s. 6d.
Boultbee's History of the Church of England, Pre-Reformation Period. 8vo. 15s.
Buckle's History of Civilisation. 3 vols. crown 8vo. 24s.
Cox's (Sir G. W.) General History of Greece. Crown 8vo. Maps, 7s. 6d.
Creighton's History of the Papacy during the Reformation. 8vo. Vols. 1 and 2, 32s. Vols. 3 and 4, 24s.
De Tocqueville's Democracy in America. 2 vols. crown 8vo. 16s.
Doyle's English in America : Virginia, Maryland, and the Carolinas, 8vo. 18s.
— — — The Puritan Colonies, 2 vols. 8vo. 36s.

Epochs of Ancient History. Edited by the Rev. Sir G. W. Cox, Bart. and C. Sankey, M.A. With Maps. Fcp. 8vo. price 2s. 6d. each.

Beesly's Gracchi, Marius, and Sulla.
Capes's Age of the Antonines.
— Early Roman Empire.
Cox's Athenian Empire.
— Greeks and Persians.
Curteis's Rise of the Macedonian Empire.

Ihne's Rome to its Capture by the Gauls.
Merivale's Roman Triumvirates.
Sankey's Spartan and Theban Supremacies.
Smith's Rome and Carthage, the Punic Wars.

Epochs of Modern History. Edited by C. Colbeck, M.A. With Maps. Fcp. 8vo. price 2s. 6d. each.

Church's Beginning of the Middle Ages.
Cox's Crusades.
Creighton's Age of Elizabeth.
Gairdner's Houses of Lancaster and York.
Gardiner's Puritan Revolution.
— Thirty Years' War.
— (Mrs.) French Revolution, 1789-1795.
Hale's Fall of the Stuarts.
Johnson's Normans in Europe.

Longman's Frederick the Great and the Seven Years' War.
Ludlow's War of American Independence.
M'Carthy's Epoch of Reform, 1830-1850.
Moberly's The Early Tudors.
Morris's Age of Queen Anne.
— The Early Hanoverians.
Seebohm's Protestant Revolution.
Stubbs's The Early Plantagenets.
Warburton's Edward III.

Epochs of Church History. Edited by the Rev. Mandell Creighton, M.A. Fcp. 8vo. price 2s. 6d. each.

Brodrick's A History of the University of Oxford.
Overton's The Evangelical Revival in the Eighteenth Century.

Perry's The Reformation in England.
Plummer's The Church of the Early Fathers.
Tucker's The English Church in other Lands.

*** *Other Volumes in preparation.*

London : LONGMANS, GREEN, & CO.

Freeman's Historical Geography of Europe. 2 vols. 8vo. 31s. 6d.
Froude's English in Ireland in the 18th Century. 3 vols. crown 8vo. 18s.
— History of England. Popular Edition. 12 vols. crown 8vo. 3s. 6d. each.
Gardiner's History of England from the Accession of James I. to the Outbreak of the Civil War. 10 vols. crown 8vo. 60s.
— History of the Great Civil War, 1642–1649 (3 vols.) Vol. 1, 1642–1644, 8vo. 21s.
Greville's Journal of the Reign of Queen Victoria, 1837–1852. 3 vols. 8vo. 36s. 1852–1860, 2 vols. 8vo. 24s.
Historic Towns. Edited by E. A. Freeman, D.C.L. and Rev. William Hunt, M.A. With Maps and Plans. Crown 8vo. 3s. 6d. each.
London. By W. E. Loftie.   Bristol. By Rev. W. Hunt.
Exeter. By E. A. Freeman.
*** *Other volumes in preparation.*

Lecky's History of England in the Eighteenth Century. Vols. 1 & 2, 1700–1760, 8vo. 36s. Vols. 3 & 4, 1760–1784, 8vo. 36s.
— History of European Morals. 2 vols. crown 8vo. 16s.
— — — Rationalism in Europe. 2 vols. crown 8vo. 16s.
Longman's Life and Times of Edward III. 2 vols. 8vo. 28s.
Macaulay's Complete Works. Library Edition. 8 vols. 8vo. £5. 5s.
— — — Cabinet Edition. 16 vols. crown 8vo. £4. 16s.
— History of England :—
Student's Edition. 2 vols. cr. 8vo. 12s. | Cabinet Edition. 8 vols. post 8vo. 48s.
People's Edition. 4 vols. cr. 8vo. 16s. | Library Edition. 5 vols. 8vo. £4.

Macaulay's Critical and Historical Essays, with Lays of Ancient Rome In One Volume :—
Authorised Edition. Cr. 8vo. 2s. 6d. | Popular Edition. Cr. 8vo. 2s. 6d.
or 3s. 6d. gilt edges.

Macaulay's Critical and Historical Essays :—
Student's Edition. 1 vol. cr. 8vo. 6s. | Cabinet Edition. 4 vols. post 8vo. 24s.
People's Edition. 2 vols. cr. 8vo. 8s. | Library Edition. 3 vols. 8vo. 36s.

Macaulay's Speeches corrected by Himself. Crown 8vo. 3s. 6d.
Malmesbury's (Earl of) Memoirs of an Ex-Minister. Crown 8vo. 7s. 6d.
Maxwell's (Sir W. S.) Don John of Austria. Library Edition, with numerous Illustrations. 2 vols. royal 8vo. 42s.
May's Constitutional History of England, 1760–1870. 3 vols. crown 8vo. 18s.
— Democracy in Europe. 2 vols. 8vo. 32s.
Merivale's Fall of the Roman Republic. 12mo. 7s. 6d.
— General History of Rome, B.C. 753–A.D. 476. Crown 8vo. 7s. 6d.
— History of the Romans under the Empire. 8 vols. post 8vo. 48s.
Nelson's (Lord) Letters and Despatches. Edited by J. K. Laughton. 8vo. 16s.
Outlines of Jewish History from B.C. 586 to C.E. 1885. By the author of 'About the Jews since Bible Times.' Fcp. 8vo. 3s. 6d.
Pears' The Fall of Constantinople. 8vo. 16s.
Seebohm's Oxford Reformers—Colet, Erasmus, & More. 8vo. 14s.
Short's History of the Church of England. Crown 8vo. 7s. 6d.
Smith's Carthage and the Carthaginians. Crown 8vo. 10s. 6d.
Taylor's Manual of the History of India. Crown 8vo. 7s. 6d.

Walpole's History of England, from 1815. 5 vols. 8vo. Vols. 1 & 2, 1815-1832, 36s.
Vol. 3, 1832-1841, 18s. Vols. 4 & 5, 1841-1858, 36s.
Wylie's History of England under Henry IV. Vol. 1, crown 8vo. 10s. 6d.

BIOGRAPHICAL WORKS.

Armstrong's (E. J.) Life and Letters. Edited by G. F. Armstrong. Fcp. 8vo. 7s.6d.
Bacon's Life and Letters, by Spedding. 7 vols. 8vo. £4. 4s.
Bagehot's Biographical Studies. 1 vol. 8vo. 12s.
Carlyle's Life, by J. A. Froude. Vols. 1 & 2, 1795-1835, 8vo. 32s. Vols. 3 & 4, 1834-1881, 8vo. 32s.
— (Mrs.) Letters and Memorials. 3 vols. 8vo. 36s.
Doyle (Sir F. H.) Reminiscences and Opinions. 8vo. 16s.
English Worthies. Edited by Andrew Lang. Crown 8vo. 2s. 6d. each.
    Charles Darwin. By Grant Allen. | Marlborough. By George Saintsbury.
    Shaftesbury (The First Earl). By H. D. Traill. | Steele. By Austin Dobson.
     | Ben Jonson. By J. A. Symonds.
    Admiral Blake. By David Hannay. | George Canning. By Frank H. Hill.
    . *Other Volumes in preparation.*
Fox (Charles James) The Early History of. By Sir G. O. Trevelyan, Bart. Crown 8vo. 6s.
Froude's Cæsar: a Sketch. Crown 8vo. 6s.
Hamilton's (Sir W. R.) Life, by Graves. Vols. 1 and 2, 8vo. 15s. each.
Havelock's Life, by Marshman. Crown 8vo. 3s. 6d.
Hobart Pacha's Sketches from my Life. Crown 8vo. 7s. 6d.
Macaulay's (Lord) Life and Letters. By his Nephew, Sir G. O. Trevelyan, Bart. Popular Edition, 1 vol. crown 8vo. 6s. Cabinet Edition, 2 vols. post 8vo. 12s. Library Edition, 2 vols. 8vo. 36s.
Mendelssohn's Letters. Translated by Lady Wallace. 2 vols. cr. 8vo. 5s. each.
Mill (James) Biography of, by Prof. Bain. Crown 8vo. 5s.
— (John Stuart) Recollections of, by Prof. Bain. Crown 8vo. 2s. 6d.
— — Autobiography. 8vo. 7s. 6d.
Müller's (Max) Biographical Essays. Crown 8vo. 7s. 6d.
Newman's Apologia pro Vitâ Suâ. Crown 8vo. 6s.
Pasteur (Louis) His Life and Labours. Crown 8vo. 7s. 6d.
Shakespeare's Life (Outlines of), by Halliwell-Phillipps. 2 vols. royal 8vo. 10s. 6d.
Southey's Correspondence with Caroline Bowles. 8vo. 14s.
Stephen's Essays in Ecclesiastical Biography. Crown 8vo. 7s. 6d.
Wellington's Life, by Gleig. Crown 8vo. 6s.

MENTAL AND POLITICAL PHILOSOPHY, FINANCE, &c.

Amos's View of the Science of Jurisprudence. 8vo. 18s.
— Primer of the English Constitution. Crown 8vo. 6s.
Bacon's Essays, with Annotations by Whately. 8vo. 10s. 6d.
— Works, edited by Spedding. 7 vols. 8vo. 73s. 6d.
Bagehot's Economic Studies, edited by Hutton. 8vo. 10s. 6d.
— The Postulates of English Political Economy. Crown 8vo. 2s. 6d.
Bain's Logic, Deductive and Inductive. Crown 8vo. 10s. 6d.
    PART I. Deduction, 4s. | PART II. Induction, 6s. 6d.
— Mental and Moral Science. Crown 8vo. 10s. 6d.
— The Senses and the Intellect. 8vo. 15s.
— The Emotions and the Will. 8vo. 15s.
— Practical Essays. Crown 8vo. 4s. 6d.

London: LONGMANS, GREEN, & CO.

Buckle's (H. T.) Miscellaneous and Posthumous Works. 2 vols. crown 8vo. 21s.
Crozier's Civilization and Progress. 8vo. 14s.
Crump's A Short Enquiry into the Formation of English Political Opinion. 8vo. 7s. 6d.
Dowell's A History of Taxation and Taxes in England. 4 vols. 8vo. 48s.
Green's (Thomas Hill) Works. (3 vols.) Vols. 1 & 2, Philosophical Works. 8vo. 16s. each.
Hume's Essays, edited by Green & Grose. 2 vols. 8vo. 28s.
— Treatise of Human Nature, edited by Green & Grose. 2 vols. 8vo. 28s.
Lang's Custom and Myth: Studies of Early Usage and Belief. Crown 8vo. 7s. 6d.
Leslie's Essays in Political and Moral Philosophy. 8vo. 10s. 6d.
Lewes's History of Philosophy. 2 vols. 8vo. 32s.
Lubbock's Origin of Civilisation. 8vo. 18s.
Macleod's Principles of Economical Philosophy. In 2 vols. Vol. 1, 8vo. 15s. Vol. 2, Part I. 12s.
— The Elements of Economics. (2 vols.) Vol. 1, cr. 8vo. 7s. 6d. Vol. 2, Part I. cr. 8vo. 7s. 6d.
— The Elements of Banking. Crown 8vo. 5s.
— The Theory and Practice of Banking. Vol. 1, 8vo. 12s. Vol. 2, 14s.
— Economics for Beginners. 8vo. 2s. 6d.
— Lectures on Credit and Banking. 8vo. 5s.
Mill's (James) Analysis of the Phenomena of the Human Mind. 2 vols. 8vo. 28s.
Mill (John Stuart) on Representative Government. Crown 8vo. 2s.
— — on Liberty. Crown 8vo. 1s. 4d.
— — Examination of Hamilton's Philosophy. 8vo. 16s.
— — Logic. Crown 8vo. 5s.
— — Principles of Political Economy. 2 vols. 8vo. 30s. People's Edition, 1 vol. crown 8vo. 5s.
— — Subjection of Women. Crown 8vo. 6s.
— — Utilitarianism. 8vo. 5s.
— — Three Essays on Religion, &c. 8vo. 5s.
Mulhall's History of Prices since 1850. Crown 8vo. 6s.
Sandars's Institutes of Justinian, with English Notes. 8vo. 18s.
Seebohm's English Village Community. 8vo. 16s.
Sully's Outlines of Psychology. 8vo. 12s. 6d.
— Teacher's Handbook of Psychology. Crown 8vo. 6s. 6d.
Swinburne's Picture Logic. Post 8vo. 5s.
Thompson's A System of Psychology. 2 vols. 8vo. 36s.
Thomson's Outline of Necessary Laws of Thought. Crown 8vo. 6s.
Twiss's Law of Nations in Time of War. 8vo. 21s.
— — in Time of Peace. 8vo. 15s.
Webb's The Veil of Isis. 8vo. 10s. 6d.
Whately's Elements of Logic. Crown 8vo. 4s. 6d.
— — — Rhetoric. Crown 8vo. 4s. 6d.
Wylie's Labour, Leisure, and Luxury. Crown 8vo. 6s.
Zeller's History of Eclecticism in Greek Philosophy. Crown 8vo. 10s. 6d.
— Plato and the Older Academy. Crown 8vo. 18s.
— Pre-Socratic Schools. 2 vols. crown 8vo. 30s.
— Socrates and the Socratic Schools. Crown 8vo. 10s. 6d.
— Stoics, Epicureans, and Sceptics. Crown 8vo. 15s.
— Outlines of the History of Greek Philosophy. Crown 8vo. 10s. 6d.

London: LONGMANS, GREEN, & CO.

General Lists of Works. 5

MISCELLANEOUS WORKS.

A. K. H. B., The Essays and Contributions of. Crown 8vo.
    Autumn Holidays of a Country Parson. 3s. 6d.
    Changed Aspects of Unchanged Truths. 3s. 6d.
    Common-Place Philosopher in Town and Country. 3s. 6d.
    Critical Essays of a Country Parson. 3s. 6d.
    Counsel and Comfort spoken from a City Pulpit. 3s. 6d.
    Graver Thoughts of a Country Parson. Three Series. 3s. 6d. each.
    Landscapes, Churches, and Moralities. 3s. 6d.
    Leisure Hours in Town. 3s. 6d. Lessons of Middle Age. 3s. 6d.
    Our Homely Comedy; and Tragedy. 3s. 6d.
    Our Little Life. Essays Consolatory and Domestic. Two Series. 3s. 6d.
    Present-day Thoughts. 3s. 6d.   [each.
    Recreations of a Country Parson. Three Series. 3s. 6d. each.
    Seaside Musings on Sundays and Week-Days. 3s. 6d.
    Sunday Afternoons in the Parish Church of a University City. 3s. 6d.
Armstrong's (Ed. J.) Essays and Sketches. Fcp. 8vo. 5s.
Arnold's (Dr. Thomas) Miscellaneous Works. 8vo. 7s. 6d.
Bagehot's Literary Studies, edited by Hutton. 2 vols. 8vo. 28s.
Beaconsfield (Lord), The Wit and Wisdom of. Crown 8vo. 1s. boards; 1s. 6d. cl.
Evans's Bronze Implements of Great Britain. 8vo. 25s.
Farrar's Language and Languages. Crown 8vo. 6s.
Froude's Short Studies on Great Subjects. 4 vols. crown 8vo. 24s.
Lang's Letters to Dead Authors. Fcp. 8vo. 6s. 6d.
  —   Books and Bookmen. Crown 8vo. 6s. 6d.
Macaulay's Miscellaneous Writings. 2 vols. 8vo. 21s. 1 vol. crown 8vo. 4s. 6d.
  —   Miscellaneous Writings and Speeches. Crown 8vo. 6s.
  —   Miscellaneous Writings, Speeches, Lays of Ancient Rome, &c. Cabinet Edition. 4 vols. crown 8vo. 24s.
  —   Writings, Selections from. Crown 8vo. 6s.
Müller's (Max) Lectures on the Science of Language. 2 vols. crown 8vo. 16s.
  —   Lectures on India. 8vo. 12s. 6d.
Proctor's Chance and Luck. Crown 8vo. 5s.
Smith (Sydney) The Wit and Wisdom of. Crown 8vo. 1s. boards; 1s. 6d. cloth.

ASTRONOMY.

Herschel's Outlines of Astronomy. Square crown 8vo. 12s.
Proctor's Larger Star Atlas. Folio, 15s. or Maps only, 12s. 6d.
  —   New Star Atlas. Crown 8vo. 5s.
  —   Light Science for Leisure Hours. 3 Series. Crown 8vo. 5s. each.
  —   The Moon. Crown 8vo. 6s.
  —   Other Worlds than Ours. Crown 8vo. 5s.
  —   The Sun. Crown 8vo. 14s.
  —   Studies of Venus-Transits. 8vo. 5s.
  —   Orbs Around Us. Crown 8vo. 5s.
  —   Universe of Stars. 8vo. 10s. 6d.
Webb's Celestial Objects for Common Telescopes. Crown 8vo. 9s.

THE 'KNOWLEDGE' LIBRARY.
Edited by RICHARD A. PROCTOR.

How to Play Whist. Crown 8vo. 5s. | Pleasant Ways in Science. Cr. 8vo. 6s.
Home Whist. 16mo. 1s. | Star Primer. Crown 4to. 2s. 6d.
The Borderland of Science. Cr. 8vo. 6s. | The Seasons Pictured. Demy 4to. 5s.
Nature Studies. Crown 8vo. 6s. | Strength and Happiness. Cr. 8vo. 5s.
Leisure Readings. Crown 8vo. 6s. | Rough Ways made Smooth. Cr. 8vo. 6s.
The Stars in their Seasons. Imp. 8vo. 5s. | The Expanse of Heaven. Cr. 8vo. 5s.
Myths and Marvels of Astronomy. | Our Place among Infinities. Cr. 8vo. 5s.
    Crown 8vo. 6s.

London: LONGMANS, GREEN, & CO.

CLASSICAL LANGUAGES AND LITERATURE.

Æschylus, The Eumenides of. Text, with Metrical English Translation, by J. F. Davies. 8vo. 7s.
Aristophanes' The Acharnians, translated by R. Y. Tyrrell. Crown 8vo. 2s. 6d.
Aristotle's The Ethics, Text and Notes, by Sir Alex. Grant, Bart. 2 vols. 8vo. 32s.
— The Nicomachean Ethics, translated by Williams, crown 8vo. 7s. 6d.
— The Politics, Books I. III. IV. (VII.) with Translation, &c. by Bolland and Lang. Crown 8vo. 7s. 6d.
Becker's *Charicles* and *Gallus*, by Metcalfe. Post 8vo. 7s. 6d. each.
Cicero's Correspondence, Text and Notes, by R. Y. Tyrrell. Vols. 1 & 2, 8vo. 12s. each.
Homer's Iliad, Homometrically translated by Cayley. 8vo. 12s. 6d.
— — Greek Text, with Verse Translation, by W. C. Green. Vol. 1, Books I.–XII. Crown 8vo. 6s.
Mahaffy's Classical Greek Literature. Crown 8vo. Vol. 1, The Poets, 7s. 6d. Vol. 2, The Prose Writers, 7s. 6d.
Plato's Parmenides, with Notes, &c. by J. Maguire. 8vo. 7s. 6d.
Virgil's Works, Latin Text, with Commentary, by Kennedy. Crown 8vo. 10s. 6d.
— Æneid, translated into English Verse, by Conington. Crown 8vo. 9s.
— — — — — — by W. J. Thornhill. Cr. 8vo. 7s. 6d.
— Poems, — — — Prose, by Conington. Crown 8vo. 9s.
Witt's Myths of Hellas, translated by F. M. Younghusband. Crown 8vo. 3s. 6d.
— The Trojan War, — — Fcp. 8vo. 2s.
— The Wanderings of Ulysses, — Crown 8vo. 3s. 6d.

NATURAL HISTORY, BOTANY, & GARDENING.

Allen's Flowers and their Pedigrees. Crown 8vo. Woodcuts, 5s.
Decaisne and Le Maout's General System of Botany. Imperial 8vo. 31s. 6d.
Dixon's Rural Bird Life. Crown 8vo. Illustrations, 5s.
Hartwig's Aerial World, 8vo. 10s. 6d.
— Polar World, 8vo. 10s. 6d.
— Sea and its Living Wonders. 8vo. 10s. 6d.
— Subterranean World, 8vo. 10s. 6d.
— Tropical World, 8vo. 10s. 6d.
Lindley's Treasury of Botany. 2 vols. fcp. 8vo. 12s.
Loudon's Encyclopædia of Gardening. 8vo. 21s.
— — Plants. 8vo. 42s.
Rivers's Orchard House. Crown 8vo. 5s.
— Miniature Fruit Garden. Fcp. 8vo. 4s.
Stanley's Familiar History of British Birds. Crown 8vo. 6s.
Wood's Bible Animals. With 112 Vignettes. 8vo. 10s. 6d.
— Common British Insects. Crown 8vo. 3s. 6d.
— Homes Without Hands, 8vo. 10s. 6d.
— Insects Abroad, 8vo. 10s. 6d.
— Horse and Man. 8vo. 14s.
— Insects at Home. With 700 Illustrations. 8vo. 10s. 6d.
— Out of Doors. Crown 8vo. 5s.
— Petland Revisited. Crown 8vo. 7s. 6d.
— Strange Dwellings. Crown 8vo. 5s. Popular Edition, 4to. 6d.

London: LONGMANS, GREEN, & CO.

THE FINE ARTS AND ILLUSTRATED EDITIONS.

Eastlake's Household Taste in Furniture, &c. Square crown 8vo. 14s.
Jameson's Sacred and Legendary Art. 6 vols. square 8vo.
    Legends of the Madonna. 1 vol. 21s.
    — — — Monastic Orders 1 vol. 21s.
    — — — Saints and Martyrs. 2 vols. 31s. 6d.
    — — — Saviour. Completed by Lady Eastlake. 2 vols. 42s.
Macaulay's Lays of Ancient Rome, illustrated by Scharf. Fcp. 4to. 10s. 6d.
The same, with *Ivry* and the *Armada*, illustrated by Weguelin. Crown 8vo. 2s. 6d.
New Testament (The) illustrated with Woodcuts after Paintings by the Early Masters. 4to. 21s.

CHEMISTRY ENGINEERING, & GENERAL SCIENCE.

Arnott's Elements of Physics or Natural Philosophy. Crown 8vo. 12s. 6d.
Barrett's English Glees and Part-Songs: their Historical Development. Crown 8vo. 7s. 6d.
Bourne's Catechism of the Steam Engine. Crown 8vo. 7s. 6d.
    — Examples of Steam, Air, and Gas Engines. 4to. 70s.
    — Handbook of the Steam Engine. Fcp. 8vo. 9s.
    — Recent Improvements in the Steam Engine. Fcp. 8vo. 6s.
    — Treatise on the Steam Engine. 4to. 42s.
Buckton's Our Dwellings, Healthy and Unhealthy. Crown 8vo. 3s. 6d.
Clerk's The Gas Engine. With Illustrations. Crown 8vo. 7s. 6d.
Crookes's Select Methods in Chemical Analysis. 8vo. 24s.
Culley's Handbook of Practical Telegraphy. 8vo. 16s.
Fairbairn's Useful Information for Engineers. 3 vols. crown 8vo. 31s. 6d.
    — Mills and Millwork. 1 vol. 8vo. 25s.
Ganot's Elementary Treatise on Physics, by Atkinson. Large crown 8vo. 15s.
    — Natural Philosophy, by Atkinson. Crown 8vo. 7s. 6d.
Grove's Correlation of Physical Forces. 8vo. 15s.
Haughton's Six Lectures on Physical Geography. 8vo. 15s.
Helmholtz on the Sensations of Tone. Royal 8vo. 28s.
Helmholtz's Lectures on Scientific Subjects. 2 vols. crown 8vo. 7s. 6d. each.
Hudson and Gosse's The Rotifera or 'Wheel Animalcules.' With 30 Coloured Plates. 6 parts. 4to. 10s. 6d. each. Complete, 2 vols. 4to. £3. 10s.
Hullah's Lectures on the History of Modern Music. 8vo. 8s. 6d.
    — Transition Period of Musical History. 8vo. 10s. 6d.
Jackson's Aid to Engineering Solution. Royal 8vo. 21s.
Jago's Inorganic Chemistry, Theoretical and Practical. Fcp. 8vo. 2s.
Jeans' Railway Problems. 8vo. 12s. 6d.
Kolbe's Short Text-Book of Inorganic Chemistry. Crown 8vo. 7s. 6d.
Lloyd's Treatise on Magnetism. 8vo. 10s. 6d.
Macalister's Zoology and Morphology of Vertebrate Animals. 8vo. 10s. 6d.
Macfarren's Lectures on Harmony. 8vo. 12s.
Miller's Elements of Chemistry, Theoretical and Practical. 3 vols. 8vo. Part I. Chemical Physics, 16s. Part II. Inorganic Chemistry, 24s. Part III. Organic Chemistry, price 31s. 6d.
Mitchell's Manual of Practical Assaying. 8vo. 31s. 6d.

London: LONGMANS, GREEN, & CO.

Noble's Hours with a Three-inch Telescope. Crown 8vo. 4s. 6d.
Northcott's Lathes and Turning. 8vo. 18s.
Owen's Comparative Anatomy and Physiology of the Vertebrate Animals. 3 vols. 8vo. 73s. 6d.
Piesse's Art of Perfumery. Square crown 8vo. 21s.
Reynolds's Experimental Chemistry. Fcp. 8vo. Part I. 1s. 6d. Part II. 2s. 6d. Part III. 3s. 6d.
Schellen's Spectrum Analysis. 8vo. 31s. 6d.
Sennett's Treatise on the Marine Steam Engine. 8vo. 21s.
Smith's Air and Rain. 8vo. 24s.
Stoney's The Theory of the Stresses on Girders, &c. Royal 8vo. 36s.
Tilden's Practical Chemistry. Fcp. 8vo. 1s. 6d.
Tyndall's Faraday as a Discoverer. Crown 8vo. 3s. 6d.
— Floating Matter of the Air. Crown 8vo. 7s. 6d.
— Fragments of Science. 2 vols. post 8vo. 16s.
— Heat a Mode of Motion. Crown 8vo. 12s.
— Lectures on Light delivered in America. Crown 8vo. 5s.
— Lessons on Electricity. Crown 8vo. 2s. 6d.
— Notes on Electrical Phenomena. Crown 8vo. 1s. sewed, 1s. 6d. cloth.
— Notes of Lectures on Light. Crown 8vo. 1s. sewed, 1s. 6d. cloth.
— Sound, with Frontispiece and 203 Woodcuts. Crown 8vo. 10s. 6d.
Watts's Dictionary of Chemistry. 9 vols. medium 8vo. £15. 2s. 6d.
Wilson's Manual of Health-Science. Crown 8vo. 2s. 6d.

THEOLOGICAL AND RELIGIOUS WORKS.

Arnold's (Rev. Dr. Thomas) Sermons. 6 vols. crown 8vo. 5s. each.
Boultbee's Commentary on the 39 Articles. Crown 8vo. 6s.
Browne's (Bishop) Exposition of the 39 Articles. 8vo. 16s.
Bullinger's Critical Lexicon and Concordance to the English and Greek New Testament. Royal 8vo. 15s.
Colenso on the Pentateuch and Book of Joshua. Crown 8vo. 6s.
Conder's Handbook of the Bible. Post 8vo. 7s. 6d.
Conybeare & Howson's Life and Letters of St. Paul:—
  Library Edition, with Maps, Plates, and Woodcuts. 2 vols. square crown 8vo. 21s.
  Student's Edition, revised and condensed, with 46 Illustrations and Maps. 1 vol. crown 8vo. 7s. 6d.
Cox's (Homersham) The First Century of Christianity. 8vo. 12s.
Davidson's Introduction to the Study of the New Testament. 2 vols. 8vo. 30s.
Edersheim's Life and Times of Jesus the Messiah. 2 vols. 8vo. 24s.
— Prophecy and History in relation to the Messiah. 8vo. 12s.
Ellicott's (Bishop) Commentary on St. Paul's Epistles. 8vo. Galatians, 8s. 6d. Ephesians, 8s. 6d. Pastoral Epistles, 10s. 6d. Philippians, Colossians and Philemon, 10s. 6d. Thessalonians, 7s. 6d.
— Lectures on the Life of our Lord. 8vo. 12s.
Ewald's Antiquities of Israel, translated by Solly. 8vo. 12s. 6d.
— History of Israel, translated by Carpenter & Smith. 8 vols. 8vo. Vols. 1 & 2, 24s. Vols. 3 & 4, 21s. Vol. 5, 18s. Vol. 6, 16s. Vol. 7, 21s. Vol. 8, 18s.
Hobart's Medical Language of St. Luke. 8vo. 16s.
Hopkins's Christ the Consoler. Fcp. 8vo. 2s. 6d.

London: LONGMANS, GREEN, & CO.

Jukes's New Man and the Eternal Life. Crown 8vo. 6s.
— Second Death and the Restitution of all Things. Crown 8vo. 3s. 6d.
— Types of Genesis. Crown 8vo. 7s. 6d.
— The Mystery of the Kingdom. Crown 8vo. 3s. 6d.
Lenormant's New Translation of the Book of Genesis. Translated into English. 8vo. 10s. 6d.
Lyra Germanica: Hymns translated by Miss Winkworth. Fcp. 8vo. 5s.
Macdonald's (G.) Unspoken Sermons. Two Series, Crown 8vo. 3s. 6d. each.
— The Miracles of our Lord. Crown 8vo. 3s. 6d.
Manning's Temporal Mission of the Holy Ghost. Crown 8vo. 8s. 6d.
Martineau's Endeavours after the Christian Life. Crown 8vo. 7s. 6d.
— Hymns of Praise and Prayer. Crown 8vo. 4s. 6d. 32mo. 1s. 6d.
— Sermons, Hours of Thought on Sacred Things. 2 vols. 7s. 6d. each.
Monsell's Spiritual Songs for Sundays and Holidays. Fcp. 8vo. 5s. 18mo. 2s.
Müller's (Max) Origin and Growth of Religion. Crown 8vo. 7s. 6d.
— — Science of Religion. Crown 8vo. 7s. 6d.
Newman's Apologia pro Vita Suâ. Crown 8vo. 6s.
— The Idea of a University Defined and Illustrated. Crown 8vo. 7s.
— Historical Sketches. 3 vols. crown 8vo. 6s. each.
— Discussions and Arguments on Various Subjects. Crown 8vo. 6s.
— An Essay on the Development of Christian Doctrine. Crown 8vo. 6s.
— Certain Difficulties Felt by Anglicans in Catholic Teaching Considered. Vol. 1, crown 8vo. 7s. 6d. Vol. 2, crown 8vo. 5s. 6d.
— The Via Media of the Anglican Church, Illustrated in Lectures, &c. 2 vols. crown 8vo. 6s. each
— Essays, Critical and Historical. 2 vols. crown 8vo. 12s.
— Essays on Biblical and on Ecclesiastical Miracles. Crown 8vo. 6s.
— An Essay in Aid of a Grammar of Assent. 7s. 6d.
Overton's Life in the English Church (1660-1714). 8vo. 14s.
Supernatural Religion. Complete Edition. 3 vols. 8vo. 36s.
Younghusband's The Story of Our Lord told in Simple Language for Children. Illustrated. Crown 8vo. 2s. 6d. cloth plain; 3s. 6d. cloth extra, gilt edges.

TRAVELS, ADVENTURES, &c.

Alpine Club (The) Map of Switzerland. In Four Sheets. 42s.
Baker's Eight Years in Ceylon. Crown 8vo. 5s.
— Rifle and Hound in Ceylon. Crown 8vo. 5s.
Ball's Alpine Guide. 3 vols. post 8vo. with Maps and Illustrations:—I. Western Alps, 6s. 6d. II. Central Alps, 7s. 6d. III. Eastern Alps, 10s. 6d.
Ball on Alpine Travelling, and on the Geology of the Alps, 1s.
Brassey's Sunshine and Storm in the East. Library Edition, 8vo. 21s. Cabinet Edition, crown 8vo. 7s. 6d. Popular Edition, 4to. 6d.
— Voyage in the Yacht 'Sunbeam.' Library Edition, 8vo. 21s. Cabinet Edition, crown 8vo. 7s. 6d. School Edition, fcp. 8vo. 2s. Popular Edition, 4to. 6d.
— In the Trades, the Tropics, and the 'Roaring Forties.' Library Edition, 8vo. 21s. Cabinet Edition, crown 8vo. 17s. 6d. Popular Edition, 4to. 6d.
Froude's Oceana; or, England and her Colonies. Crown 8vo. 2s. boards; 2s. 6d. cloth.
Howitt's Visits to Remarkable Places. Crown 8vo. 7s. 6d.
Three in Norway. By Two of Them. Crown 8vo. Illustrations, 6s.

WORKS OF FICTION.

Beaconsfield's (The Earl of) Novels and Tales. Hughenden Edition, with 2 Portraits on Steel and 11 Vignettes on Wood. 11 vols. crown 8vo. £2. 2s.
Cheap Edition, 11 vols. crown 8vo. 1s. each, boards; 1s. 6d. each, cloth.

Lothair.	Contarini Fleming.
Sybil.	Alroy, Ixion, &c.
Coningsby.	The Young Duke, &c.
Tancred.	Vivian Grey.
Venetia.	Endymion.
Henrietta Temple.	

Black Poodle (The) and other Tales. By the Author of 'Vice Versâ.' Cr. 8vo. 6s.
Brabourne's (Lord) Friends and Foes from Fairyland. Crown 8vo. 6s.
Caddy's (Mrs.) Through the Fields with Linnæus: a Chapter in Swedish History. 2 vols. crown 8vo. 16s.
Haggard's (H. Rider) She: a History of Adventure. Crown 8vo. 6s.
Harte (Bret) On the Frontier. Three Stories. 16mo. 1s.
— — By Shore and Sedge. Three Stories. 16mo. 1s.
— — In the Carquinez Woods. Crown 8vo. 2s. boards; 2s. 6d. cloth.
Melville's (Whyte) Novels. 8 vols. fcp. 8vo. 1s. each, boards; 1s. 6d. each, cloth.

Digby Grand.	Good for Nothing.
General Bounce.	Holmby House.
Kate Coventry.	The Interpreter.
The Gladiators.	The Queen's Maries.

Molesworth's (Mrs.) Marrying and Giving in Marriage. Crown 8vo. 7s. 6d.
Novels by the Author of 'The Atelier du Lys':
The Atelier du Lys; or, An Art Student in the Reign of Terror. Crown 8vo. 2s. 6d.
Mademoiselle Mori: a Tale of Modern Rome. Crown 8vo. 2s. 6d.
In the Olden Time: a Tale of the Peasant War in Germany. Crown 8vo. 2s. 6d.
Hester's Venture. Crown 8vo. 6s.
Oliphant's (Mrs.) Madam. Crown 8vo. 3s. 6d.
— — In Trust: the Story of a Lady and her Lover. Crown 8vo. 2s. boards; 2s. 6d. cloth.
Payn's (James) The Luck of the Darrells. Crown 8vo. 3s. 6d.
— — Thicker than Water. Crown 8vo. 2s. boards; 2s. 6d. cloth.
Reader's Fairy Prince Follow-my-Lead. Crown 8vo. 5s.
— The Ghost of Brankinshaw; and other Tales. Fcp. 8vo. 2s. 6d.
Ross's (Percy) A Comedy without Laughter. Crown 8vo. 6s.
Sewell's (Miss) Stories and Tales. Crown 8vo. 1s. each, boards; 1s. 6d. cloth; 2s. 6d. cloth extra, gilt edges.

Amy Herbert. Cleve Hall.	A Glimpse of the World.
The Earl's Daughter.	Katharine Ashton.
Experience of Life.	Laneton Parsonage.
Gertrude. Ivors.	Margaret Percival. Ursula.

Stevenson's (R. L.) The Dynamiter. Fcp. 8vo. 1s. sewed; 1s. 6d. cloth.
— — Strange Case of Dr. Jekyll and Mr. Hyde. Fcp. 8vo. 1s. sewed; 1s. 6d. cloth.
Trollope's (Anthony) Novels. Fcp. 8vo. 1s. each, boards; 1s. 6d. cloth.

| The Warden | Barchester Towers. |

London: LONGMANS, GREEN, & CO.

POETRY AND THE DRAMA.

Armstrong's (Ed. J.) Poetical Works. Fcp. 8vo. 5s.
— (G. F.) Poetical Works:—
    Poems, Lyrical and Dramatic. Fcp. 8vo. 6s.
    Ugone: a Tragedy. Fcp. 8vo. 6s.
    A Garland from Greece. Fcp. 8vo. 9s.
    King Saul. Fcp. 8vo. 5s.
    King David. Fcp. 8vo. 6s.
    King Solomon. Fcp. 8vo. 6s.
    Stories of Wicklow. Fcp. 8vo. 9s.

Bowen's Harrow Songs and other Verses. Fcp. 8vo. 2s. 6d.; or printed on hand-made paper, 5s.
Bowdler's Family Shakespeare. Medium 8vo. 14s. 6 vols. fcp. 8vo. 21s.
Dante's Divine Comedy, translated by James Innes Minchin. Crown 8vo. 15s.
Goethe's Faust, translated by Birds. Large crown 8vo. 12s. 6d.
   — — translated by Webb. 8vo. 12s. 6d.
   — — edited by Selss. Crown 8vo. 5s.
Ingelow's Poems. Vols. 1 and 2, fcp. 8vo. 12s. Vol. 3 fcp. 8vo. 5s.
   — Lyrical and other Poems. Fcp. 8vo. 2s. 6d. cloth, plain; 3s. cloth, gilt edges.
Macaulay's Lays of Ancient Rome, with Ivry and the Armada. Illustrated by Weguelin. Crown 8vo. 3s. 6d. gilt edges.
The same, Popular Edition. Illustrated by Scharf. Fcp. 4to. 6d. swd., 1s. cloth.
Nesbit's Lays and Legends. Crown 8vo. 5s.
Reader's Voices from Flowerland, a Birthday Book, 2s. 6d. cloth, 3s. 6d. roan.
Southey's Poetical Works. Medium 8vo. 14s.
Stevenson's A Child's Garden of Verses. Fcp. 8vo. 5s.
Virgil's Æneid, translated by Conington. Crown 8vo. 9s.
   — Poems, translated into English Prose. Crown 8vo. 9s.

AGRICULTURE, HORSES, DOGS, AND CATTLE.

Dunster's How to Make the Land Pay. Crown 8vo. 5s.
Fitzwygram's Horses and Stables. 8vo. 5s.
Lloyd's The Science of Agriculture. 8vo. 12s.
Loudon's Encyclopædia of Agriculture. 21s.
Miles's Horse's Foot, and How to Keep it Sound. Imperial 8vo. 12s. 6d.
   — Plain Treatise on Horse-Shoeing. Post 8vo. 2s. 6d.
   — Remarks on Horses' Teeth. Post 8vo. 1s. 6d.
   — Stables and Stable-Fittings. Imperial 8vo. 15s.
Nevile's Farms and Farming. Crown 8vo. 6s.
   — Horses and Riding. Crown 8vo. 6s.
Steel's Diseases of the Ox, a Manual of Bovine Pathology. 8vo. 15s.
Stonehenge's Dog in Health and Disease. Square crown 8vo. 7s. 6d.
   — Greyhound. Square crown 8vo. 15s.
Taylor's Agricultural Note Book. Fcp. 8vo. 2s. 6d.
Ville on Artificial Manures, by Crookes. 8vo. 21s.
Youatt's Work on the Dog. 8vo. 6s.
   — — — — Horse. 8vo. 7s. 6d.

London: LONGMANS, GREEN, & CO.

SPORTS AND PASTIMES.

The Badminton Library of Sports and Pastimes. Edited by the Duke of Beaufort and A. E. T. Watson. With numerous Illustrations. Crown 8vo. 10s. 6d. each.

    Hunting, by the Duke of Beaufort, &c.
    Fishing, by H. Cholmondeley-Pennell, &c. 2 vols.
    Racing, by the Earl of Suffolk, &c.
    Shooting, by Lord Walsingham, &c. 2 vols.
    Cycling. By Viscount Bury.

⁎ *Other Volumes in preparation.*

Campbell-Walker's Correct Card, or How to Play at Whist. Fcp. 8vo. 2s. 6d.
Dead Shot (The) by Marksman. Crown 8vo. 10s. 6d.
Francis's Treatise on Fishing in all its Branches. Post 8vo. 15s.
Longman's Chess Openings. Fcp. 8vo. 2s. 6d.
Pease's The Cleveland Hounds as a Trencher-Fed Pack. Royal 8vo. 18s.
Pole's Theory of the Modern Scientific Game of Whist. Fcp. 8vo. 2s. 6d.
Proctor's How to Play Whist. Crown 8vo. 5s.
Ronalds's Fly-Fisher's Entomology. 8vo. 14s.
Verney's Chess Eccentricities. Crown 8vo. 10s. 6d.
Wilcocks's Sea-Fisherman. Post 8vo. 6s.

ENCYCLOPÆDIAS, DICTIONARIES, AND BOOKS OF REFERENCE.

Acton's Modern Cookery for Private Families. Fcp. 8vo. 4s. 6d.
Ayre's Treasury of Bible Knowledge. Fcp. 8vo. 6s.
Brande's Dictionary of Science, Literature, and Art. 3 vols. medium 8vo. 63s.
Cabinet Lawyer (The), a Popular Digest of the Laws of England. Fcp. 8vo. 9s.
Cates's Dictionary of General Biography. Medium 8vo. 28s.
Doyle's The Official Baronage of England. Vols. I.–III. 3 vols. 4to. £5. 5s.
Gwilt's Encyclopædia of Architecture. 8vo. 52s. 6d.
Keith Johnston's Dictionary of Geography, or General Gazetteer. 8vo. 42s.
M'Culloch's Dictionary of Commerce and Commercial Navigation. 8vo. 63s.
Maunder's Biographical Treasury. Fcp. 8vo. 6s.
    — Historical Treasury. Fcp. 8vo. 6s.
    — Scientific and Literary Treasury. Fcp. 8vo. 6s.
    — Treasury of Bible Knowledge, edited by Ayre. Fcp. 8vo. 6s.
    — Treasury of Botany, edited by Lindley & Moore. Two Parts, 12s.
    — Treasury of Geography. Fcp. 8vo. 6s.
    — Treasury of Knowledge and Library of Reference. Fcp. 8vo. 6s.
    — Treasury of Natural History. Fcp. 8vo. 6s.
Quain's Dictionary of Medicine. Medium 8vo. 31s. 6d., or in 2 vols. 34s.
Reeve's Cookery and Housekeeping. Crown 8vo. 7s. 6d.
Rich's Dictionary of Roman and Greek Antiquities. Crown 8vo. 7s. 6d.
Roget's Thesaurus of English Words and Phrases. Crown 8vo. 10s. 6d.
Ure's Dictionary of Arts, Manufactures, and Mines. 4 vols. medium 8vo. £7. 7s.
Willich's Popular Tables, by Marriott. Crown 8vo. 10s. 6d.

London: LONGMANS, GREEN, & CO.

A SELECTION
OF
EDUCATIONAL WORKS.

TEXT-BOOKS OF SCIENCE
FULLY ILLUSTRATED.

Abney's Treatise on Photography. Fcp. 8vo. 3s. 6d.
Anderson's Strength of Materials. 3s. 6d.
Armstrong's Organic Chemistry. 3s. 6d.
Ball's Elements of Astronomy. 6s.
Barry's Railway Appliances. 3s. 6d.
Bauerman's Systematic Mineralogy. 6s.
— Descriptive Mineralogy. 6s.
Bloxam and Huntington's Metals. 5s.
Glazebrook's Physical Optics. 6s.
Glazebrook and Shaw's Practical Physics. 6s.
Gore's Art of Electro-Metallurgy. 6s.
Griffin's Algebra and Trigonometry. 3s. 6d. Notes and Solutions, 3s. 6d.
Holmes's The Steam Engine. 6s.
Jenkin's Electricity and Magnetism. 3s. 6d.
Maxwell's Theory of Heat. 3s. 6d.
Merrifield's Technical Arithmetic and Mensuration. 3s. 6d. Key, 3s. 6d.
Miller's Inorganic Chemistry. 3s. 6d.
Preece and Sivewright's Telegraphy. 5s.
Rutley's Study of Rocks, a Text-Book of Petrology. 4s. 6d.
Shelley's Workshop Appliances. 4s. 6d.
Thomé's Structural and Physiological Botany. 6s.
Thorpe's Quantitative Chemical Analysis. 4s. 6d.
Thorpe and Muir's Qualitative Analysis. 3s. 6d.
Tilden's Chemical Philosophy. 3s. 6d. With Answers to Problems. 4s. 6d.
Unwin's Elements of Machine Design. 6s.
Watson's Plane and Solid Geometry. 3s. 6d.

THE GREEK LANGUAGE.

Bloomfield's College and School Greek Testament. Fcp. 8vo. 5s.
Bolland & Lang's Politics of Aristotle. Post 8vo. 7s. 6d.
Collis's Chief Tenses of the Greek Irregular Verbs. 8vo. 1s.
— Pontes Græci, Stepping-Stone to Greek Grammar. 12mo. 3s. 6d.
— Praxis Græca, Etymology. 12mo. 2s. 6d.
— Greek Verse-Book, Praxis Iambica. 12mo. 4s. 6d.
Farrar's Brief Greek Syntax and Accidence. 12mo. 4s. 6d.
— Greek Grammar Rules for Harrow School. 12mo. 1s. 6d.
Geare's Notes on Thucydides. Book I. Fcp. 8vo. 2s. 6d.
Hewitt's Greek Examination-Papers. 12mo. 1s. 6d.
Isbister's Xenophon's Anabasis, Books I. to III. with Notes. 12mo. 3s. 6d.
Jerram's Graecè Reddenda. Crown 8vo. 1s. 6d.

London: LONGMANS, GREEN, & CO.

Kennedy's Greek Grammar. 12mo. 4s. 6d.
Liddell & Scott's English-Greek Lexicon. 4to. 36s.; Square 12mo. 7s. 6d.
Mahaffy's Classical Greek Literature. Crown 8vo. Poets, 7s. 6d. Prose Writers, 7s. 6d.
Morris's Greek Lessons. Square 18mo. Part I. 2s. 6d.; Part II. 1s.
Parry's Elementary Greek Grammar. 12mo. 3s. 6d.
Plato's Republic, Book I. Greek Text, English Notes by Hardy. Crown 8vo. 3s.
Sheppard and Evans's Notes on Thucydides. Crown 8vo. 7s. 6d.
Thucydides, Book IV. with Notes by Barton and Chavasse. Crown 8vo. 5s.
Valpy's Greek Delectus, improved by White. 12mo. 2s. 6d. Key, 2s. 6d.
White's Xenophon's Expedition of Cyrus, with English Notes. 12mo. 7s. 6d.
Wilkins's Manual of Greek Prose Composition. Crown 8vo. 5s. Key, 5s.
— Exercises in Greek Prose Composition. Crown 8vo. 4s. 6d. Key, 2s. 6d.
— New Greek Delectus. Crown 8vo. 3s. 6d. Key, 2s. 6d.
— Progressive Greek Delectus. 12mo. 4s. Key, 2s. 6d.
— Progressive Greek Anthology. 12mo. 5s.
— Scriptores Attici, Excerpts with English Notes. Crown 8vo. 7s. 6d.
— Speeches from Thucydides translated. Post 8vo. 6s.
Yonge's English-Greek Lexicon. 4to. 21s.; Square 12mo. 8s. 6d.

THE LATIN LANGUAGE.

Bradley's Latin Prose Exercises. 12mo. 3s. 6d. Key, 5s.
— Continuous Lessons in Latin Prose. 12mo. 5s. Key, 5s. 6d.
— Cornelius Nepos, improved by White. 12mo. 3s. 6d.
— Eutropius, improved by White. 12mo. 2s. 6d.
— Ovid's Metamorphoses, improved by White. 12mo. 4s. 6d.
— Select Fables of Phædrus, improved by White. 12mo. 2s. 6d.
Collis's Chief Tenses of Latin Irregular Verbs. 8vo. 1s.
— Pontes Latini, Stepping-Stone to Latin Grammar. 12mo. 3s. 6d.
Hewitt's Latin Examination-Papers. 12mo. 1s. 6d.
Isbister's Cæsar, Books I.-VII. 12mo. 4s.; or with Reading Lessons, 4s. 6d.
— Cæsar's Commentaries, Books I.-V. 12mo. 3s. 6d.
— First Book of Cæsar's Gallic War. 12mo. 1s. 6d.
Jerram's Latiné Reddenda. Crown 8vo. 1s. 6d.
Kennedy's Child's Latin Primer, or First Latin Lessons. 12mo. 2s.
— Child's Latin Accidence. 12mo. 1s.
— Elementary Latin Grammar. 12mo. 3s. 6d.
— Elementary Latin Reading Book, or Tirocinium Latinum. 12mo. 2s.
— Latin Prose, Palæstra Stili Latini. 12mo. 6s.
— Latin Vocabulary. 12mo. 2s. 6d.
— Subsidia Primaria, Exercise Books to the Public School Latin Primer. I. Accidence and Simple Construction, 2s. 6d. II. Syntax, 3s. 6d.
— Key to the Exercises in Subsidia Primaria, Parts I. and II. price 5s.
— Subsidia Primaria, III. the Latin Compound Sentence. 12mo. 1s.
— Curriculum Stili Latini. 12mo. 4s. 6d. Key, 7s. 6d.
— Palæstra Latina, or Second Latin Reading Book. 12mo. 5s.

London: LONGMANS, GREEN, & CO.

A Selection of Educational Works. 15

Millington's Latin Prose Composition. Crown 8vo. 3s. 6d.
— Selections from Latin Prose. Crown 8vo. 2s. 6d.
Moody's Eton Latin Grammar. 12mo. 2s. 6d. The Accidence separately, 1s.
Morris's Elementa Latina. Fcp. 8vo. 1s. 6d. Key, 2s. 6d.
Parry's Origines Romanæ, from Livy, with English Notes. Crown 8vo. 4s.
The Public School Latin Primer. 12mo. 2s. 6d.
— — — — Grammar, by Rev. Dr. Kennedy. Post 8vo. 7s. 6d.
Prendergast's Mastery Series, Manual of Latin. 12mo. 2s. 6d.
Rapier's Introduction to Composition of Latin Verse. 12mo. 3s. 6d. Key, 2s. 6d.
Sheppard and Turner's Aids to Classical Study. 12mo. 5s. Key, 6s.
Valpy's Latin Delectus, improved by White. 12mo. 2s. 6d. Key, 3s. 6d.
Virgil's Æneid, translated into English Verse by Conington. Crown 8vo. 9s.
— Works, edited by Kennedy. Crown 8vo. 10s. 6d.
— — translated into English Prose by Conington. Crown 8vo. 9s.
Walford's Progressive Exercises in Latin Elegiac Verse. 12mo. 2s. 6d. Key, 5s.
White and Riddle's Large Latin-English Dictionary. 1 vol. 4to. 21s.
White's Concise Latin-Eng. Dictionary for University Students. Royal 8vo. 12s.
— Junior Students' Eng.-Lat. & Lat.-Eng. Dictionary. Square 12mo. 5s.
Separately { The Latin-English Dictionary, price 3s.
{ The English-Latin Dictionary, price 3s.
Yonge's Latin Gradus. Post 8vo. 9s.; or with Appendix, 12s.

WHITE'S GRAMMAR-SCHOOL GREEK TEXTS.

Æsop (Fables) & Palæphatus (Myths). 32mo. 1s.
Euripides, Hecuba. 2s.
Homer, Iliad, Book I. 1s.
— Odyssey, Book I. 1s.
Lucian, Select Dialogues. 1s.
Xenophon, Anabasis, Books I. III. IV. V. & VI. 1s. 6d. each; Book II. 1s.; Book VII. 2s.

Xenophon, Book I. without Vocabulary. 3d.
St. Matthew's and St. Luke's Gospels. 2s. 6d. each.
St. Mark's and St. John's Gospels. 1s. 6d. each.
The Acts of the Apostles. 2s. 6d.
St. Paul's Epistle to the Romans. 1s. 6d.

The Four Gospels in Greek, with Greek-English Lexicon. Edited by John T. White, D.D. Oxon. Square 32mo. price 5s.

WHITE'S GRAMMAR-SCHOOL LATIN TEXTS.

Cæsar, Gallic War, Books I. & II. V. & VI. 1s. each. Book I. without Vocabulary, 3d.
Cæsar, Gallic War, Books III. & IV. 9d. each.
Cæsar, Gallic War, Book VII. 1s. 6d.
Cicero, Cato Major (Old Age). 1s. 6d.
Cicero, Lælius (Friendship). 1s. 6d.
Eutropius, Roman History, Books I. & II. 1s. Books III. & IV. 1s.
Horace, Odes, Books I. II. & IV. 1s. each.
Horace, Odes, Book III. 1s. 6d.
Horace, Epodes and Carmen Seculare. 1s.

Nepos, Miltiades, Simon, Pausanias, Aristides. 9d.
Ovid. Selections from Epistles and Fasti. 1s.
Ovid, Select Myths from Metamorphoses. 9d.
Phædrus, Select Easy Fables,
Phædrus, Fables, Books I. & II. 1s.
Sallust, Bellum Catilinarium. 1s. 6d.
Virgil, Georgics, Book IV. 1s.
Virgil, Æneid, Books I. to VI. 1s. each. Book I. without Vocabulary, 3d.
Virgil, Æneid, Books VII. VIII. X. XI. XII. 1s. 6d. each.

London: LONGMANS, GREEN, & CO.

THE FRENCH LANGUAGE.

Albités's How to Speak French. Fcp. 8vo. 5s. 6d.
— Instantaneous French Exercises. Fcp. 2s. Key, 2s.
Cassal's French Genders. Crown 8vo. 3s. 6d.
Cassal & Karcher's Graduated French Translation Book. Part I. 3s. 6d. Part II. 5s. Key to Part I. by Professor Cassal, price 5s.
Contanseau's Practical French and English Dictionary. Post 8vo. 3s. 6d.
— Pocket French and English Dictionary. Square 18mo. 1s. 6d.
— Premières Lectures. 12mo. 2s. 6d.
— First Step in French. 12mo. 2s. 6d. Key, 3s.
— French Accidence. 12mo. 2s. 6d.
— — Grammar. 12mo. 4s. Key, 3s.
Contanseau's Middle-Class French Course. Fcp. 8vo. :—

Accidence, 8d.	French Translation-Book, 8d.
Syntax, 8d.	Easy French Delectus, 8d.
French Conversation-Book, 8d.	First French Reader, 8d.
First French Exercise-Book, 8d.	Second French Reader, 8d.
Second French Exercise-Book, 8d.	French and English Dialogues, 8d.

Contanseau's Guide to French Translation. 12mo. 3s. 6d. Key 3s. 6d.
— Prosateurs et Poètes Français. 12mo. 5s.
— Précis de la Littérature Française. 12mo. 3s. 6d.
— Abrégé de l'Histoire de France. 12mo. 2s. 6d.
Féval's Chouans et Bleus, with Notes by C. Sankey, M.A. Fcp. 8vo. 2s. 6d.
Jerram's Sentences for Translation into French. Cr. 8vo. 1s. Key, 2s. 6d.
Prendergast's Mastery Series, French. 12mo. 2s. 6d.
Souvestre's Philosophe sous les Toits, by Stiévenard. Square 18mo. 1s. 6d.
Stepping-Stone to French Pronunciation. 18mo. 1s.
Stiévenard's Lectures Françaises from Modern Authors. 12mo. 4s. 6d.
— Rules and Exercises on the French Language. 12mo. 3s. 6d.
Tarver's Eton French Grammar. 12mo. 6s. 6d.

THE GERMAN LANGUAGE.

Blackley's Practical German and English Dictionary. Post 8vo. 3s. 6d.
Buchheim's German Poetry, for Repetition. 18mo. 1s. 6d.
Collis's Card of German Irregular Verbs. 8vo. 2s.
Fischer-Fischart's Elementary German Grammar. Fcp. 8vo. 2s. 6d.
Just's German Grammar. 12mo. 1s. 6d.
— German Reading Book. 12mo. 3s. 6d.
Longman's Pocket German and English Dictionary. Square 18mo. 2s. 6d.
Naftel's Elementary German Course for Public Schools. Fcp. 8vo.

German Accidence. 9d.	German Prose Composition Book. 9d.
German Syntax. 9d.	First German Reader. 9d.
First German Exercise-Book. 9d.	Second German Reader. 9d.
Second German Exercise-Book. 9d.	

Prendergast's Mastery Series, German. 12mo. 2s. 6d.
Quick's Essentials of German. Crown 8vo. 3s. 6d.
Selss's School Edition of Goethe's Faust. Crown 8vo. 5s.
— Outline of German Literature. Crown 8vo. 4s. 6d.
Wirth's German Chit-Chat. Crown 8vo. 2s. 6d.

London: LONGMANS, GREEN, & CO.

Spottiswoode & Co. Printers, New-street Square, London.